Connected

Connected

*How a Mexican Village Built Its
Own Cell Phone Network*

Roberto J. González

UNIVERSITY OF CALIFORNIA PRESS

Oakland, California

© 2020 by Roberto J. González

Library of Congress Cataloging-in-Publication Data

Names: González, Roberto J. (Roberto Jesús), 1969- author.
Title: Connected : how a Mexican village built its own
  cell phone network Roberto J. González.
Description: Oakland, California : University of
  California Press, [2020] | Includes bibliographical
  references and index.
Identifiers: LCCN 2019058005 (print) | LCCN 2019058006
  (ebook) | ISBN 9780520344204 (cloth) |
  ISBN 9780520344211 (paperback) |
  ISBN 9780520975408 (ebook)
Subjects: LCSH: Cell phone systems—Mexico—Oaxaca
  (State) | Cell phone systems—Social aspects—
  Mexico—Oaxaca (State)
Classification: LCC HE 9715.M6 G66 2020 (print) |
  LCC HE 9715.M6 (ebook) | DDC 384.5/34097274—dc23
LC record available at https://lccn.loc.gov/2019058005
LC ebook record available at https://lccn.loc
  .gov/2019058006

ClassifNumber   PubDate
DeweyNumber'—dc23   CatalogNumber

Manufactured in the United States of America

29 28 27 26 25 24 23 22 21 20
10 9 8 7 6 5 4 3 2 1

For Mateo and Diego

CONTENTS

List of Illustrations ix

Acknowledgments xi

1. Connected
1

2. Innovation
28

3. Enchanted
55

4. Networks
85

5. Backlash
110

6. Posts
136

7. Aftereffects
169

8. Outro (Reconnected)
193

Notes 201

Glossary 223

References 231

Index 249

ILLUSTRATIONS

MAPS

1. Ethnolinguistic map of north central Oaxaca *33*

FIGURES

1. Talea de Castro and its surrounding lands *6*

2. Campesino using a cell phone, with Talea visible in the background *10*

3. Talea's *presidente municipal*, circa 2014 *20*

4. The village church, built in the late nineteenth and early twentieth centuries *48*

5. Talean women selling produce at the weekly market *52*

6. Banda Unión y Progreso in 1998 *64*

7. Villager carrying a pyrotechnic *torito* during a fiesta *70*

8. Talean family members spending time with deceased relatives during *Todos Santos* *77*

9. Scene from a village fiesta, with large puppets (*marmotas*) dancing in front of the municipal palace *83*

10. Talean men conversing at a social event *88*

11. Rhizomatica's coordinator speaks to Taleans about cell phone networks *101*

12. Talean children on their cell phones *107*

13. *Dizha Kieru* community radio, Talea GSM's headquarters *115*

14. Movistar's shop in Talea, which sells cell phones, data plans, selfie sticks, and other accessories *126*

15. The cast of *Danza de los Aztecas* includes Spanish conquistadors, Napoleonic soldiers, American GIs, and Aztecs *141*

16. Facebook photo of Talean women preparing *yht gu* (bean tamales) *153*

17. Talea's basketball team posing for a photo, circa 1993 *156*

18. Scene from *Linda Taleanita* video, featuring Banda Alma Taleana *166*

19. Workers assembling a mobile antenna in a Cajonos Zapotec village *173*

20. High-tech lynching in Puebla state: Acatlán de Osirio, August 2018 *186*

21. Field work, July 2007 *199*

ACKNOWLEDGMENTS

This book began as a short article for the journal *Anthropology Today*. Its editor, Gustaaf Houtman, provided keen advice as I developed the piece, and I am grateful for his enthusiasm and generosity. An early version of the epilogue appeared in *Anthropology Now*, and journal editor Rylan Higgins made helpful comments.

Many people offered encouragement, suggestions, and ideas for improving the book. These friends and colleagues include Salvador Aquino Centeno, Kike Arnal, Anna Basallaje, Peter Bloom, Heidi Kao, Richard and Christina Koci Hernández, Ramón Lozano, Claudia Magallanes-Blanco, Jay Ou, Daniela Parra Hinojosa, Laura Nader, David Price, Yanna Yannakakis, and Gabriela Zamorano Villarreal. Jeffrey Cohen and Erica Wortham critically reviewed the manuscript. So too did Stanley Brandes, whose work on ritual and fiestas has influenced my thinking. Over the years, Alejandro de Ávila has been a generous and hospitable friend. His vast knowledge of Oaxaca's biological and cultural heritage is inspiring and has informed parts of this book.

I am fortunate to have family members who read portions of the manuscript, including my parents, wife, and siblings. My wife and children deserve credit for introducing me to the striking work of Duncan Tonatiuh, who created this book's cover art.

Hundreds of Taleans have shared their ideas, knowledge, homes, and much more with me over the years. Most of the photos in this book were taken by villagers, and I sincerely appreciate the cooperation of Daniel Bautista Martínez, Ulises Canseco Peña, Teresa García Bautista, Israel Hernández García, Andrés Pérez Jerónimo, Dahir Teáhulos, and Charly Vásquez Chon. Others, including Wilfrido Martínez Velasco, Jaime Bautista Hernández, Willebaldo Heredia, Zoila Alonso, Mario Bautista, and the entire Chávez Labastida family (Juventino, Concepción, Rita, Elvira, Alfonso, Abigail, and Leonel), have been extraordinarily generous and welcoming. Special thanks also to Agustine Sacha and Peter Bloom for allowing me to use several photo images as illustrations.

San José State University (SJSU) supported this project by granting a semester-long sabbatical in Fall 2018. In the College of Social Sciences, Walt Jacobs, Ron Rogers, and Shishir Mathur implemented an innovative program (cryptically known in the college as "nine-three-three") that allowed me to complete the manuscript. Colleagues in the SJSU Anthropology Department supported this book in various ways. Jan English-Lueck agreed to serve as department chair during my sabbatical semester, and William Reckmeyer encouraged me to pursue the project. My department's wonderful administrative staff—Agnes Borja, Shannon Gallagher, and Kristen Constanza—helped by holding down the fort when I was writing and researching off campus. The SJSU Office of Research granted release time for preliminary and final portions of this project.

It has been a pleasure to work with Kate Marshall of the University of California Press. She expressed enthusiasm for the book from the moment I contacted her, and she expertly provided guidance at every subsequent stage. Enrique Ochoa-Kaup answered many questions regarding photo permissions and preparation of the final manuscript, for which I am grateful. I appreciate the efforts of production editors Cindy Fulton and Nicholle Robertson, and of copy editor Gabriel Bartlett for his careful attention to the text.

Nearly thirty years ago, Martha Menchaca introduced me to anthropology in a course at the University of Texas at Austin. She agreed to serve as an advisor for my undergraduate honors thesis, which was an analysis of the Bracero Program. I am thankful to her for helping me launch an academic career in the social sciences.

No one deserves more credit for encouraging me to write this book than Laura Nader. She convinced me to travel to Talea for the first time in 1994, and has generously shared her time and ideas ever since. As I was finalizing this project, she allowed me to review her field notes from the Rincón, neatly typed in triplicate form during the late 1950s and early 1960s. Her intellect, warmth, compassion, and sense of humor left a lasting impression on the people of Talea and surrounding pueblos, and she will always be a legend there.

CHAPTER ONE

Connected

Reach into your pocket or bag and pull out your cell phone—if it isn't already in your hand.

Ask yourself: What was my life like before I got connected?

Ask yourself three more questions:

Has this little box changed how I think, or what I do, or who I am?

What is a cell phone *for*, anyway?

Should everybody have one?

Mobile technologies are transforming the lives of people around the world, and they are reshaping countless aspects of human behavior, often in unpredictable ways.

Sometimes it's easy to forget that 2.5 billion people—one-third of the planet's population—don't have cell phones yet. Many of those living in rural, remote regions want mobile service, but they can't have it for reasons that have to do with geography, politics, or economics.

That will almost certainly change over time. In fact, it's already changing, as telecom companies aggressively expand their markets, and as people demand the right to broadband access—what some call the freedom to connect.

This is the story of how one village achieved that freedom.

. . .

During the summer and autumn of 2013, dozens of news reports recounted how a Mexican pueblo launched its own do-it-yourself cell phone network. The people of Talea de Castro, population twenty-four hundred, created an autonomous "mini-telecom company," the first of its kind in the world, without any help from the government or private companies.[1] They built the network after Mexico's telecommunications giants refused to provide mobile service to people in the region, claiming that it would be too expensive to connect Talea to their cellular phone grids. It was a fascinating David and Goliath story that pitted Mexico's largest corporation—América Móvil, which is owned by billionaire Carlos Slim—against indigenous villagers, many of whom were subsistence maize farmers with little formal education.

The reports made a deep impression on me in ways that I still do not fully comprehend. For you see, I spent more than two years of my life in Talea de Castro, living and working as a cultural anthropologist in the 1990s. Gradually, I lost contact with people there.

Reading about Talea's cell phone network inspired me to learn more about the changes that had swept the pueblo since my last visit more than a decade ago. How was it that, for a brief time, the villagers became international celebrities, profiled by *USA Today*, *Agence France-Presse*, *BBC News*, *Wired* magazine, and many other media outlets? I was determined to find out how the people of this face-to-face community managed to wire themselves into the twenty-first century in such an audacious and dramatic way—how, despite their geographic remoteness, they became ever more connected to the rest of the world through the wondrous but unpredictably powerful magic of mobile technology. This book is about how villagers made it happen—and how digital technologies are altering their lives in dramatic ways. Talea's fight to get connected is an object lesson in how ordinary people can use technology to forcefully assert their right to live in a globalized world, on their own terms.

• • •

But this book is about more than just a pueblo's quest to get connected through cellular access. Talea's triumph was not what news reports might lead one to believe—not even remotely. The "do-it-yourself" cell phone network was only made possible after an imaginative group of townspeople undertook years of intense contact and consultation with a colorful cast of characters: a team of scruffy young activists affiliated with two up-and-coming non-governmental organizations, or NGOs; a politically sophisticated lawyer specializing in telecommunications regulation; an internationally renowned culture jamming artist; a small band of wily European hackers; and elected officials from dozens of other Oaxacan pueblos. Most of these people shared a commitment to the idea of access as a human right—that is, internet and mobile phone access.[2] As I got into the story, the plot grew increasingly complex and, at times, bewildering. Without giving away too much of the ending, let me say at the outset that Talea's community-based cell phone network did *not* live happily ever after, as media reports implied. Even before it came into being, there were internal struggles and external pressures that threatened its development. As we shall see later, these conflicts never quite disappeared, and others emerged over time.

In writing this book, I was often tempted to describe the pueblo's cell phone network as an example of how an underdog community fought big business and big government and won. David Graeber has a point when he says that we anthropologists sometimes slip into a kind of populism: "It means you that you must demonstrate that the people you are studying, the little guys, are successfully resisting some form of power or globalizing influence imposed on them from above."[3] But that would be an inaccurate interpretation of what actually happened. It is certainly true that the villagers successfully created the maverick network as an attempt to challenge mammoth telecommunications companies while slipping through the federal government's regulatory loopholes. However, in the end, the villagers compromised with these powerful entities by allowing a transnational mobile service provider to do business in the pueblo. Taleans more or less reached a consensus corresponding to a maxim they have long used to guide them out of conflictive situations: "a bad compromise is better than a good fight."[4]

Despite this, it would be wrong to think of the autonomous cell phone network as an abject failure. Instead, we might hold up the pueblo's homegrown system as a short-lived example of revolutionary action: "collective action which rejects, and therefore confronts, some form of power or domination and in doing so, reconstitutes social relations.... Revolutionary action does not necessarily have to aim to topple governments.... And history shows us that the continual accumulation of such acts can change (almost) anything."[5]

Even though Taleans started abandoning the network they had built just months earlier, they had paved the way for other pueblos that wanted cell phone service and had no other options.[6] The enduring legacy of the village's autonomous telecom experiment includes a cooperative organization of community cell phone networks representing nearly seventy pueblos across several different regions in Oaxaca—not only the northern sierra of which Talea is a part, but also the Mixe Alta, the Mixteca, and the Oaxaca Valley. What is more, as locally based cell phone networks and technologies improve, it seems possible that at some point in the near future, Talea's people might once again return to a homegrown system.

THE PUEBLO

Before going any further, it is worth discussing a bit more about Talea and the region that surrounds it. People who have never lived in a face-to-face pueblo sometimes assume that all such places are more or less alike. That is certainly not the case. Oaxaca is in many ways defined by its variegated cultural mosaic: the state has 570 municipalities (each of which typically includes several affiliated villages known as *agencias*) and is home to more than seventeen ethnolinguistic groups, most of which can be further subdivided by dialect.

Talea is located in a part of north central Oaxaca called the Rincón, literally corner, a place that is hemmed in by mountains on all sides (see figure 1). Even within the Rincón, a relatively small region of the state that includes people who share a mutually intelligible form of the Zapotec language, there is a staggering variety of differences between neighboring villages—in terms of clothing, settlement patterns, farming practices, religious beliefs, and worldviews. There are significant similarities shared between communities—for example, a reliance upon corn and beans as staple foods—but there are also many distinctions that delineate cultural boundaries. The words of Laura

Figure 1. Talea de Castro and its surrounding lands. Photo by the author.

Nader, the first cultural anthropologist to study the Rincón, are still relevant, though intervillage differences are often more subtle today:

> It is not their similarity that is striking, but their diversity. The women from Lachichina wear red waistbands and their wraparound skirt is brown and white striped, with the blouse (*huipil*) tucked inside. The women from Yaviche wear all white with a black waistband. The women from the farthest pueblo to the north, Yobego, still wear a long white huipil over the wraparound skirt, with gay colors covering the side seams.... Taller men with blue eyes come from Tanetze, the shortest of the men come from Yobego, and the men with white shirts and black serge trousers have at one time worked in the cities ...[7]

Among the things differentiating Talea from other Rincón communities is the fact that its townspeople generally have a tolerant attitude toward those visiting from faraway places. Over the years that sentiment has made it relatively easy for outsiders—teachers, physicians, agronomists, anthropologists, photojournalists, and staff from nongovernmental organizations or NGOs—to spend months or even years there as guests.[8]

. . .

I first visited Talea in 1994, drawn by the possibility of conducting doctoral research there. It seemed like a promising site to investigate the impact of unfettered capitalism in an out of the way place. Like thousands of other Mexican pueblos, Talea was undergoing rapid changes in the wake of aggressive laissez-faire policies aimed at further integrating the country into the global economic system by lowering tariffs on many products, including maize—Oaxaca's most important food crop. These changes culminated in the implementation of the North American Free Trade Agreement, or NAFTA, in 1994. As a consequence, many rural Mexicans migrated to the United States because they found it difficult to earn a living. When US and Canadian farmers began exporting cheap, heavily subsidized corn, they inadvertently destroyed the livelihoods of millions of small farmers across the Mexican countryside.

Despite the cataclysmic impact of these policies, many Taleans redoubled their efforts and continued farming the land, cultivating a combination of maize and coffee, a cash crop that grows well in the Rincón's lush tropical climate. After several months, I began working and living with a campesino family that cultivated land in distant fields outside the village. It would be foolish to claim that my adoptive family or hundreds more like them were consciously resisting corporate capitalism. Instead, they were hedging their bets, perhaps anticipating that the system would be unstable over the long run (which, it turns out, it was). Many families had learned from their experience as coffee farmers that international commodity markets are inherently unpredictable, sometimes volatile. Campesinos sometimes told me, "you can eat maize, but you can't eat coffee."[9] Given the circumstances, it made practical sense to keep growing corn and beans, crops that had helped people in the Rincón maintain a relatively high level of food security, a degree of economic self-sufficiency, and limited political autonomy, at least locally.

The more I learned about the pueblo's cell phone network, the more I realized that investigating the topic would mean focusing on a group of Taleans that was strikingly different from the campesinos with whom I had spent time during the 1990s. The cell phone network was orchestrated by relatively young villagers (in their late twenties and early thirties) who had relatively high levels of formal education and had spent part of their lives in Oaxaca City or other urban areas. They tended to come from influential families and typically did not spend much time in the fields surrounding the village. Like many other pueblos in Oaxaca, Talea is home to people who have had wildly divergent life experiences: a welder who learned his trade during a long stint in East Los Angeles lives next door to several campesino families whose members almost never leave the pueblo; a college-educated couple returns to the village from Mexico City to raise their children in a safer, quieter environment; a school teacher from Veracruz and the son of a Talean merchant fall in love, get married, and decide to make their home in the pueblo.

Soon I began wondering whether there was something special or even unique about Talea that might account for its spectacular technological feat. Why, of all the hemisphere's municipalities and settlements, did *this* particular community undertake such a daunting project? Was there something peculiar to the village—perhaps its history or culture or its diverse population—that might help explain its accomplishment? As I explored these questions, it became clear to me that the community cell phone network depended upon several fortuitous factors: the Rincón's legacy of fiercely autonomous villages, ensconced within a state known for its citizens' independent mindedness; the pueblo's deep-rooted custom of cautiously accepting outsiders, foreign ideas, and tools and technologies; an attitude shared by many villagers that may be described as hardheaded pragmatism; and a decades-old pattern of emigration, particularly to the United States.

I also was curious about *how* Taleans were using their cell phones—and eventually, smartphones and social media (see figure 2). This led to a series of questions, some of which reflect the social complexity and heterogeneity of the villagers. Which Taleans use cell phones, in what ways, and for what reasons? For instance, how do campesinos use cell phones as compared to say, merchants, *mototaxi* (tuk-tuk) drivers, or schoolteachers? Is text messaging more common than voice calling? How do junior high students from well-to-do families use these technologies compared to, say, elderly widows, or Taleans who live abroad? To what degree do villagers use cell phones as video games, photo albums, cameras, personal planners, music playback devices, or a means of accessing Facebook, WhatsApp, or YouTube? And what about the dark side of mobile technologies—for example, their tendency to keep users surfing the web or bouncing between social media sites for hours at a time?

Many Taleans often intended to use mobile technologies to stay connected—but not in the superficial way suggested by Facebook's top executives, who naively emphasize that their mission is quite simply to make the world more open and connected. Villagers have indeed used cell phones and social media to facilitate communication, as their ancestors did sixty years

Figure 2. Campesino using a cell phone, with Talea visible in the background. Photo courtesy of Augustine Sacha/Rhizomatica.

ago when they worked with government agencies to build a road linking the village to the state's capital and commercial center, Oaxaca City. But in the twenty-first century they have also used digital devices to stay connected to their own heritage—by downloading weather apps that make farming work a little easier, by posting historic photos of Talea online, by informing outsiders about the village's cuisine, and by recording and disseminating videos depicting fiestas or other communal celebrations. In some cases, they have also used digital technologies to confront and challenge powerful institutions. The swift evolution of locally produced, community-controlled media in Oaxaca has had profound political effects as villagers use radio, cell phone networks, and social media to denounce corporate abuses, governmental fraud, and political corruption.

And yet, despite these changes, many villagers expressed concerns about the ways in which cell phones and social media may negatively affect social life. These people were acutely aware that connections are not the same as conversations, and that connecting is not the same as communicating. Such observations are consistent with those made by critics of digital technologies such as social psychologist Sherry Turkle. She notes that, as people have become increasingly reliant upon text messaging and social media, "we have sacrificed conversation for mere connection.... We can end up hiding from each other, even as we are constantly connected to one another."[10] The word *conversation* has its origins in the Latin verb *conversare*, meaning "to turn together." By contrast, *connection* has its origins in the Latin verb *conectere*, meaning "to tie together" or "to bind together." When we converse, there are many opportunities to improvise and change direction: we can pivot, bend, meander, pirouette, or backtrack depending on the situation. When we connect, we are fastened to others, attached, perhaps even shackled. The difference is significant.

CELL PHONES

As I took a closer look at Talea's cell phone experiment, I wondered how others might be examining this now ubiquitous technology. To my surprise, there was a paucity of anthropological work on the topic; much of the research was being conducted by scholars in other fields.[11] This was puzzling. It seems obvious that anthropology's four-field approach might lead to a better understanding of cell phones and their effects, since the discipline integrates archaeological, sociocultural, linguistic, and biological perspectives. Cell phones are artifacts, pieces of material culture; they are constructed in and absorbed into specific cultural contexts and their use is capable of transforming social relationships

and norms; people use them for oral, verbal, and nonverbal communication (through emoticons, for example); and, when used
habitually, they may have serious biological effects on people—
often negative effects. As an academic discipline, anthropology is
well positioned to contribute to a more holistic understanding of
these technological artifacts.

Several anthropological accounts contradict popular notions
that cell phones necessarily reduce poverty or inequality, or that
they inevitably lead to cultural homogenization. For example,
Heather Horst and Daniel Miller have analyzed the ways in
which Jamaicans of modest means integrate cell phones into their
lives in the early twenty-first century. They note that "technology is used initially with reference to desires that are historically
well established, but remain unfulfilled because of the limitations
of previous technologies."[12] In other words, cell phones build upon
socially established preexisting modes of interaction. Although
cell phones cost money, they provide Jamaicans with a tool for
maintaining and intensifying patterns of reciprocal exchange that
can help them in times of need. Another example of how cell
phones often build upon previously existing cultural patterns can
be observed in the coastal town of Malindi, Kenya. According to
Janet McIntosh, text messaging among Giriama youth is often
done by poetically code-switching between English and local
African languages, suggesting "new ways of being Giriama that
are simultaneously local and modern."[13]

Mizuko Ito has also contributed to a cross-cultural understanding of cell phones. Ito, an anthropologist whose work is
focused on Japan, notes that although industrialized societies
have undergone rapid changes as the result of cell phones,
"social transformations in developing countries, where mobiles
are reaching the hands of those who had no access to telecom-

munications infrastructures, is more radical and broad-based than the earlier wave of mobile adoption in high-tech countries." Like Horst and Miller, Ito and her colleagues observe that cell phones are embedded within particular cultural contexts. In Japan, cell phones are highly personalized artifacts. It is socially unacceptable to look at another person's screen, even that of a spouse. Ito suggests that the Japanese term for cell phone, *keitai* (loosely translated as "portable") stresses "a snug and intimate technosocial tethering, a personal device supporting communications that are a constant, lightweight, and mundane presence in everyday life."[14]

Some anthropologists analyze cell phones within broad historical trajectories of technological change. For example, mobile phones used by Nenets reindeer herders in the Russian Arctic are the latest in a long line of practical innovations introduced over the past half-century including gas stoves, electric generators, snowmobiles, and rubber boots.[15] Florian Stammler reports that among reindeer herders, cell phones are much more than a calling device: "MMS [multimedia messaging], photo-video shooting and sharing, GPS, Internet, chatting, astronomical apps that one can use when looking at the stars, and other applications" have become important features used in everyday life.[16] What is more, the cell phone (like the snowmobile before it) has transformed local perceptions of distance—and behavior. Stammler notes that "it has also changed the pace of nomadic migration for some, which can lead to an entirely new structuration of space into *off* and *on* regions."[17] He listened to reindeer herders complain about a neighbor's camp being located in an "off" region—out of the cell phone coverage zone.[18]

Some anthropologists have focused upon the social and material implications of cell phones across many different cultures. An interesting comparative project analyzed cell phones using three interconnected themes—fetishization, inscription, and intimacy.[19] The researchers considered a vast range of topics including, among others, the political economy of coltan mining in the Democratic Republic of Congo (coltan is a metal essential for cell phone production); concepts of value in the process of repairing damaged cell phones; privacy concerns in Brazil; the curation of museum artifacts using social media platforms; video sharing practices among Australian aborigines; communication patterns in Norway during periods of crisis; and the role of cell phones in romantic relationships in Mozambique.

Yet another recent ethnography examines the introduction and impact of cell phones in Janta, an Indian village in West Bengal. Because most villagers there did not have landlines, they experienced the arrival of mobile phones as a dramatic shift in their everyday lives. At times, villagers used the technology to grapple with other changes that were already underway. For instance, as new agricultural policies made small farms unprofitable, young men used cell phones to look for work outside the village. At other times, cell phones, particularly smartphones, gave some people in Janta the ability to challenge entrenched hierarchies. As noted by anthropologist Sirpa Tenhunen: "Contrary to their hierarchical position, educated young wives and children could become the phone use experts in their families. Low caste people were able to make identity statements simply by possessing smartphones."[20] Tenhunen also argues that cell phones are making a profound impact on strict patrilineal kinship norms. She writes, "I observed how phones offered women a channel to express unconventional ideas and exert their will through networking. For instance, a mother could advise her daughter over the phone to not obey the mother-in-law whose demands were excessive. Thanks to phones, young wives were able to stay in constant touch with their natal families which was unheard of in the past."[21]

Such fine-grained ethnographic accounts, though few in number, give insight into the ways in which different societies are integrating cell phones and smartphones into everyday life. These studies, along with a growing body of anthropological research on the internet and indigenous media, point the way to innovative approaches to the topic of digital communication technologies.[22]

INTERMEDIARIES

This book analyzes another aspect of social life in the Rincón in addition to cell phones—namely, the role of what might be called native intermediaries. These are people savvy in both "the ways of the Indians and the ways of the city" and who are "alphabetically, bureaucratically, and legally bicultural, bilingual, and literate."[23] Historian Yanna Yannakakis compellingly argues that native intermediaries have played an essential role in north central Oaxaca for five centuries. In the early years of the Spanish Conquest, the colonizers were never more than a tiny minority in the remote region, constituting less than 1 percent of the population. In Yannakakis's words, a mere "handful of Spaniards lived in a sea of thirty to forty thousand native people" in the Villa Alta district.[24] Indigenous elites were therefore essential for maintaining the colonial enterprise. Spanish control in the peripheries of empire depended upon the collaboration of indigenous people willing to serve as go-betweens. Translators, middlemen, priests' assistants, and native nobility adroitly positioned themselves along the social interstices between conquerors and conquered.

Another historian of colonial northern Oaxaca, John Chance, has written about itinerant indigenous merchants who spoke both Spanish and Zapotec fluently, who wore European fashions, and who possessed cattle and beasts of burden for carrying commodities and merchandise to and from the sierra. Sometimes these men lived in Antequera (colonial Oaxaca City), as in the case of a Talean merchant named Bonifacio de Chávez. He became wealthy by serving as a middleman, buying cochineal (a valuable red dyestuff) cheaply from indigenous villagers and then selling them salt, fish, steel tools, and other goods at inflated prices. Chance notes that "despite their general poverty, some Indian nobles were willing and able to take advantage of commercial opportunities ... all were highly mobile and had a facility for interacting with different Indian groups as well as with the Spanish."[25]

Much has changed since the days of the conquest, but native intermediaries have endured and even multiplied. They have derived their power from different sources over the years. In the mid-to-late twentieth century many of them were political entrepreneurs, "nation-oriented individuals from the local communities who established ties with the national level, and who serve[d] as 'brokers' between community-oriented and nation-oriented groups."[26] Often they were affiliated with the postrevolutionary government, which is to say the authoritarian Institutional Revolutionary Party or PRI. The PRI monopolized power in Mexico for nearly eighty years, from the 1920s to the end of the century. Sometimes, the cultural brokers served as liaisons between indigenous communities and the state, facilitating economic and infrastructural development programs in outlying rural regions like the Rincón. In 1964, anthropologist Laura Nader noted that "Talean contact with outsiders was gradual and contact with and knowledge of Mexican culture filtered in chiefly through intermediaries—bilingual and bicultural Zapotecs from adjacent regions."[27]

A compelling case can be made for the continuing presence, in the twenty-first century, of native intermediaries—that is, men and women who serve analogous roles at a time when pueblos struggle against and negotiate with the Mexican nation-state, transnational corporations, nongovernmental organizations, and, as has been the case for centuries, each other. These people are well connected. Yannakakis's historical observations can readily be applied to the present: "In the Sierra Norte of Oaxaca, native intermediary figures come from prominent families in native communities, and most are men, although women have also played an active and vocal role in community political life ... [they] spend significant time and energy in transit between the sierra and the statehouse in Oaxaca City, in taking care of 'business' (*trámites*) and 'managing papers' (*manejando papeles*)."[28] In fact, the number of intermediaries has flourished over the past generation, as more and more people have left the region to attend high schools and universities. As adults, many of them shuttle back and forth between their hometown communities and large cities such as Oaxaca or Mexico City, spending weeks or months at a time in each locale.

These changes are particularly relevant for understanding the creation of the community cell phone network. Although it is true that many villagers played a part in planning, constructing, and launching the network, two relatively young and well-educated Taleans were largely responsible for leading and managing the initiative. These modern-day intermediaries were simultaneously connected to their pueblo, on the one hand, and to external entities (nongovernmental organizations), on the other. Their ability to shift easily between different social worlds enabled them to accomplish an intricate series of tasks: to build relationships with technical experts, many of whom were foreign nationals; to persuade their fellow citizens to provide political and financial support for the project; to obtain the endorsement of elected officials from other pueblos in the region; to manage and maintain the network once it was created; and to play the role of engaging, charismatic spokespersons when hundreds of journalists and scholars descended upon Talea in the months following the network's successful debut. The intermediaries were able to do this by deploying a range of abilities and habits, such as linguistic dexterity in both Rincón Zapotec and Spanish, modes of dress that enabled them to approach different audiences with relative ease, and a positive disposition and demeanor that worked in their favor. We shall see that after the autonomous network was established, an older and more established native intermediary intervened. For nearly forty years, this native son of Talea has worked closely with and for the PRI political party (see chapter 5), and his efforts played a part in the eventual demise of the pueblo's homegrown network.

AUTONOMY

Talea's community cell phone system held promise for people seeking a world of creative possibilities, in which local communities might develop bottom-up solutions independently of powerful organizations. Because many anthropologists have worked among hunter-gatherers, pastoralists, and small-scale agriculturalists that maintain a high degree of political autonomy from state institutions, we can potentially provide insight into a radically wide spectrum of human possibilities: different ways of organizing work, or making collective decisions, or distributing goods, for example. Consequently, anthropologists might take a closer look at those who are building alternatives to the state, corporate capitalism, or hierarchical institutions, try to understand the broader implications of their actions, and then offer those ideas back to readers as prospective solutions to common problems.[29] Those contributions may also include warnings, words of caution about potential pitfalls that could hamper the pursuit of viable alternatives. This book is, in part, an effort to document what happened in Talea as villagers embarked on a mission to establish greater connectivity—and perhaps greater freedom.

. . .

Like many Rinconeros, most Taleans place a premium on political autonomy. While it is true that municipalities are formally incorporated into and recognized by the state government of Oaxaca and the Mexican national government, and that villagers enjoy such services as electrical power and public schools that are partly financed by federal entities, there's a preference for maintaining local control over political and legal domains.[30] For centuries, townspeople have elected *cabildos*, or governing councils, to one-year terms of office (see figure 3). Serving in cabildos is obligatory. I never met anyone in the Rincón who was enthusiastic about being elected, since it takes time away from work and family responsibilities. (Until recently, members of cabildos received no salary.) But those who dutifully and responsibly serve in local government gain status and prestige when they participate. The Oaxaca state government legally recognized such systems of local governance in 1995, when it adopted

Figure 3. Talea's *presidente municipal*, circa 2014. Photo courtesy of Israel Hernández García.

legislation protecting *usos y costumbres*, literally the political "practices and customs" of villages throughout the state.[31]

In political terms, the pueblos of northern Oaxaca have remained relatively autonomous, though they have recently struggled to keep state and federal government officials at arm's length. Based on extensive research in Talea, Laura Nader has noted that "local preservation of autonomy using local legal practices has in great part encouraged solidarity."[32] She describes a powerful ideology that still existed in the pueblo in the 1980s that villagers expressed in the following words: "We are peaceful in this village, and by being peaceful and minding our own business we keep control of our village. We keep it in local hands, and by so doing we can maintain a relative autonomy."[33] They were and continue to be fiercely egalitarian. Nader observed that "the mountain Zapotec feel they have a right to challenge authority if it is abused ... [and] the Zapotec are intensely egalitarian about governance.... They believe that people in public roles are accountable and must upon occasion be brought to a public accounting."[34]

Northern Oaxaca has a long tradition of political independence and egalitarianism. Zapotec, Mixe, and Chinantec pueblos of the region were never incorporated into the Aztec Empire. Because of the area's rugged topography and neolithic technology, pueblos were limited in size and were probably small, independent settlements of only a few hundred people. Social hierarchies were relatively flat—in other words, people were more or less equal. Slaves did not exist as they did in the Oaxaca Valley, and there was little difference in wealth between the nobility (*caciques*) and commoners (*macehuales*).[35] According to John Chance, the indigenous pueblos remained autonomous" and "a substantial portion of the indigenous sociopolitical organization survived the [Spanish] conquest years."[36] This changed dramatically by the 1600s for several reasons—namely, the devastating impact of epidemic diseases on indigenous peoples and the abusive labor practices of Spanish colonial officials (see chapter 2 of this book). But the point here is that, given its long history of relative independence, political and economic autonomy is part of the cultural substrate of northern Oaxaca.

And yet the struggle for self-determination is often an uphill battle. For instance, today the Oaxaca state government pays Talea's municipal president ten thousand pesos each month, or approximately five hundred US dollars—more than three times the average monthly wage. Other officials also earn relatively high salaries. While some might argue that such payments are a fair way of compensating cabildo members for lost time, they are also partially financed by means of sales and income taxes collected by the state. These arrangements foster a level of political dependency, and critics suggest that they are undermining local autonomy.

. . . .

Before continuing, it is worth briefly mentioning a recent movement for greater democracy throughout Oaxaca: the Popular Assembly of the Peoples of Oaxaca or APPO. This broad coalition of teachers, workers, students, peasants, women, indigenous people, and urban poor brought the state government to a standstill for six months in 2006. Some have called it the "Oaxaca Commune" in reference to the Paris Commune of 1871.[37] APPO successfully occupied Oaxaca City's *zócalo*, or central plaza, for months. The movement also catalyzed an already vibrant alternative media system when protesters seized a university radio station that summer.

The mass mobilization was eventually crushed. In late October and early November, thousands of federal police brutally cracked down on the insurrection, using helicopters, tear gas, and combat vehicles to tear down hundreds of barricades that had been formed by protesters to keep out government officials. By January 2007, the International Commission for Human Rights reported that over the course of the protests, twenty-three people had been killed, dozens had been disappeared, and hundreds of protest leaders had been brutalized, tortured, and jailed, some in maximum security federal prisons.[38] The movement was forced underground, but an entire generation of young activists had been created. The uprising and its aftermath played a formative role in the creation of Talea's cell phone network.

For more than thirty years, Oaxacan scholars have been fashioning an epistemological concept that reflects the region's historical and cultural legacy of autonomy and self-determination across the region—and its applicability to contemporary society.

This is the principle of *comunalidad*, first articulated and developed in the late 1980s and early 1990s by two anthropologists: Jaime Martínez Luna, from the Sierra Zapotec community of Guelatao de Juárez; and Floriberto Díaz Gómez, from the Mixe town of Tlauhitoltepec.[39] *Comunalidad* is a set of principles and practices that places high value on communal life, collaborative forms of work, locally controlled development, collectively experienced behavior, and human relationships. For both Martínez and Díaz, there are several elements that constitute comunalidad: shared territory (the pueblo, its lands, and the earth mother), shared governance (the *asamblea* or village assembly, and the *cargo* system or cabildo described above), shared labor (the *tequio*, an obligatory day of communal work), and shared enjoyment (fiestas).[40] Martínez Luna, who has described comunalidad as the axis of Oaxacan thought, notes that respect and reciprocity articulate these elements, and that resistance to colonialism and privatization played a vital role in breathing life into it. He also suggests that the concept provides an alternative to the logic of "predatory and now globalized individualism"—that is, modern-day corporate capitalism.[41] Some of those who played leading roles in the creation of Talea's community cell phone network have reflected upon the experience, and have analyzed it as a living, twenty-first-century example of comunalidad in action.[42]

Gustavo Esteva, a Mexican intellectual and activist who founded Oaxaca's Universidad de la Tierra, has elaborated a nuanced view of indigenous autonomy appropriate for the twenty-first century. He notes that "autonomy implies recognition and respect for what the indigenous people already possess.... It is not an ideological proposal or a Promised Land.... [Instead, it] includes an authentic system of government exercised by communities, regions, and indigenous peoples; the implementation of alternate juridical systems for the administration of justice; the application of differential regulations regarding land ownership and use; and the legitimation of the right of self-defense against the interference of the market or the state in the life of the community."[43]

OVERVIEW

The Rincón region has a rich history, and although there is much that we still don't know about the pre-Conquest period, recent scholarship has uncovered new information about the area's earliest inhabitants. Ethnohistorians and anthropologists have used written records, particularly legal and administrative documents prepared by Spanish officials, to create a vivid picture of what life in the Rincón was like. They have used similar sources (though from Mexican government officials) to get a better understanding of postcolonial society, from the early nineteenth century forward. There are several significant patterns or themes that emerge, which tell us a great deal about the Rincón in general and Talea in particular. The points that are most relevant for this book have to do with innovation and creativity.

For complex reasons that we are only beginning to understand—reasons that have to do with the interplay of geography, culture, history, and language—it appears that the people of northern Oaxaca were remarkably resourceful problem solvers. During the pre-Conquest period, Zapotec migrants from the Valley of Oaxaca settled in the region and adapted to the forested terrain; after the Spanish Conquest, they developed survival strategies in the face of epidemic disease and exploitation, including novel farming methods, legal claims, and political arrangements. As a "new town" created after the Spaniards arrived, Talea appears to have been particularly receptive to innovative ideas and practices, probably because it was populated early on by people from different regions in the Rincón and beyond. The fact that the pueblo had relatively little land compared to other Rincón villages may be another reason that its inhabitants were eager to experiment. This attitude of openness intensified during the twentieth century, when influential Taleans actively sought to expand their connections to the outside world. They had benefited from the presence of nearby silver mines, the adoption of a cash crop (coffee), migration to the United States under the auspices of the Bracero Program in the 1940s, and a road linking the community to Oaxaca City.

These transformations did not bring an end to Taleans' long-established ideas and practices; nor has their recent passage into the digital age. Though it's easy to assume that villagers have gradually abandoned paranormal beliefs about mountain spirits, nocturnal enchantresses, dwarves, saints, witches, living trees, sentient crops, departed souls, and spirit attacks, many have continued participating in a host of vibrant rituals, practices, and celebrations, some of which are aimed at quelling troubled supernatural beings. It certainly seems possible that the threat of spectral unrest in Talea is a "constant, perhaps inevitable, corollary" of a society that has relied heavily on compromise and consensus for decision-making, and that the pueblo's persistent enchantment is a manifestation of this situation.[44] On the other hand, it also seems likely that the high value that many townspeople place on connectedness with the outside world occasionally spills over into supernatural realms. In other words, participating in ceremonies, fiestas, and other magico-religious events brings one into close contact and even communion with fellow villagers, with relatives who reside in distant locations, with visitors from neighboring pueblos, and with supernatural beings. When Taleans use their smartphones to post photos or videos to social media sites like YouTube or Facebook, they often highlight images from precisely these kinds of extraordinary events. Sometimes, villagers living in other cities or countries express feelings of nostalgia and longing after viewing such materials.

Taleans often proudly describe their pueblo as a regional trendsetter. When an opportunity appeared to develop a community-based cell phone network, villagers reached a consensus supporting the decision. Chapter 4 provides a detailed account of the events that led up to the creation of the cell phone network in 2013. It began with a chance encounter, then an alliance, between two young villagers interested in community radio and people affiliated with a Mexico City-based NGO seeking to support indigenous media projects. As they worked with a group of hackers and villagers to build the technological network, the Taleans met with elected officials from other pueblos to build a human network that would ultimately provide a base of political and financial support for the initiative. In the meantime, the partners eventually succeeded in formally creating an *asociación civil* (civil association or nonprofit) that would function as a cooperative to support other pueblos seeking to create their own community-based networks. Chapter 5 tells the story of how Talea's network suffered a number of setbacks that weakened and eventually destroyed it. Technical difficulties, unexpected competition, and accusations of mismanagement and fraud drove many villagers away from the homegrown network, and into the hands of a major telecommunication company.

Talea's cell phone experiment is still a work in progress. As villagers make the transition to smartphones, some are expressing concerns about the aftermath of the new technology. Many of these are similar to critiques that have emerged in societies like the United States and South Korea, where people have been using cell phones for more than a generation. Some villagers are worried that digital devices might affect children's physical and social development. Others have observed that cell phones can lead to civic disengagement by drawing users' attention away from discussion of crucial topics at village town hall meetings; they imply that the act of connecting with some people via text messaging or posting messages via WhatsApp may simultaneously be disconnecting citizens from their immediate surroundings and obligations. It is not difficult to imagine how, in the near future, malicious users might use smartphones in the Rincón to generate mass hysteria, as has happened in other parts of Mexico and India, to name but two examples. It seems likely that some villagers have already been subjected to forms of propaganda comparable to what tens of millions of people have experienced in recent political campaigns in the United States. As social scientists delve more deeply into the impacts of cell phones in different regions of the world, we should never lose sight of the fact that the devices are addictive by design.[45] Like most Americans, Taleans are not aware of the fact that many captains of the technology industry—for example, Bill Gates, Jonathan Ive, and the late Steve Jobs—tightly restricted their own children's access to digital devices and the internet for this reason. What the future holds is, of course, an open question.

The book concludes with a brief reflective account about my reconnecting with villagers after having been out of touch for nearly a decade.

CHAPTER TWO

Innovation

For centuries, Oaxaca has been a laboratory for technological and social experiments on a grand scale. Archaeologists working at Guilá Naquitz, a cave site in the Valley of Oaxaca, have determined that the ancestors of the Zapotec were the Western Hemisphere's earliest cultivators. Ancient Oaxacans grew squash there as early as nine to ten thousand years ago. By the time their descendants established permanent settlements around 1500 BC, they were already cultivating many other food plants including maize, beans, chilies, avocados, cactus, and more.[1]

Maize's origins are particularly fascinating. Ancient Mesoamericans domesticated the grain near the Tehuacán Valley in the southern part of modern-day Puebla state, less than a hundred miles from the Rincón.[2] Today, the area spanning northern Oaxaca and southern Puebla has the greatest variety of maize landraces in the world. Though their work is rarely recognized, the region's farmers perform an extraordinary service for humanity. By carefully cultivating and caring for heirloom seeds, they safeguard the genetic diversity of maize, which is among the world's most precious crops.[3]

In the Rincón, campesino farmers are constantly conducting scientific activities. As they go about planting native seeds, and newer ones offered by agricultural engineers or other outsiders, it is obvious that campesinos hypothesize, model problems, experiment, measure results, and distribute knowledge among their peers and to younger generations.[4] The most successful campesinos are enthusiastic about trying out tools, technologies, and crops to see what works, as their ancestors have done for millennia.

But Zapotec experimentation and inventiveness goes beyond agriculture. The roots of creativity extend much further. A number of factors, from ancient times to the recent past, have jointly contributed to what could be called a pragmatic can-do philosophy that inspires many Zapotec inhabitants of the Rincón region.

PIONEERS

As mentioned earlier, the Rincón is situated in a remote area surrounded by mountains. According to ethnohistorian Michel Oudijk, the northern sierra of Oaxaca was first populated in the late postclassic period, between 1350 and 1521 AD. Based on a close analysis of Sierra Zapotec *lienzos* (tapestries depicting maps, genealogical lineages, and other historical materials), Oudijk hypothesizes that political upheaval in the Valley of Oaxaca motivated groups of Zapotec people to flee the region, though it is also possible that their migration was a kind of exodus, a mass defection by émigrés wishing to establish pueblos that differed radically from the rigidly hierarchical society from which they came.[5] It is impossible to know for sure.

During this era, Zapotec and Mixtec groups fought epic battles for control of the valley. By the late 1400s, the political situation was further aggravated by the arrival of Aztec conquerors determined to annex the area as part of their empire. Evidence indicates that some Zapotec nobles migrated from the valley to the northern sierra, accompanied by their followers. It is not clear whether these men and women were forcibly exiled or chose to migrate of their own accord, perhaps seeking to build revolutionary utopias. In any case, Spanish colonial documents referred to the kin groups as *parentelas* or *cónyuges*.[6] We can estimate a population of perhaps one hundred and sixty thousand Zapotecs in the northern sierra in the year 1520.[7]

In this setting, social hierarchies were substantially flattened, though not eliminated. According to historian Yanna Yannakakis, *parentelas* divided land among themselves and created settlements. "There was a basic distinction between nobles and commoners," she notes, "but it appears that the finer social distinctions that characterized indigenous society in the valley of Oaxaca, the Mixteca, and Mexico's central valleys did not exist."[8] The transition from a highly stratified urban center to the uninhabited, thickly wooded cloud forests north of the valley seems to have required a restructuring of the relationships between these Zapotec pioneers. In essence, the frontier had an equalizing effect. Yannakakis argues that an ethos of autonomy emerged among the Zapotec migrants as the result of small-scale, loosely organized *cacicazgos* (estates associated with noble lineages). The fact that the Aztecs never succeeded in bringing the sierra under their direct control probably contributed to this independent spirit.[9]

Although they were never entirely isolated from the Oaxaca Valley (to the southwest) or the coastal plains of the Gulf of Mexico (to the northeast), over the course of perhaps a century or more, the Zapotec migrants and their descendants probably found it more convenient to develop local solutions—informed by knowledge and experience rooted in the centuries-old Oaxaca Valley Zapotec civilization—to make their lives easier. If necessity is the mother of invention, then perhaps necessity is also the daughter of rugged topography.

The migrants certainly would have brought many different kinds of seeds to the northern sierra: maize, beans, squash, chilies, fruits, vegetables. The first Rinconeros would have also brought tools and technologies to clear away the dense pine forests for farming. Although they had extensive experience cultivating subsistence crops in the Valley of Oaxaca, the Zapotec settlers would have had to drastically alter their methods for mountainside farming. Slash-and-burn agriculture was probably the only available means of coaxing food from the soil. The early years were undoubtedly difficult, since campesinos were planting in unfamiliar terrain. They would have also needed to use trial-and-error methods for developing agricultural calendars to guide them as they cultivated, tended, and harvested their crops in an alien environment.

Before Talea was founded at its present site, which likely occurred sometime between 1525 and 1548, there was a nearby settlement located on the opposite side of the Río Cajonos, a river below the pueblo.[10] Long ago, their ancestors or perhaps other beings lived there, in an area called *Sudo'* that is the site of the abandoned community. It lies at a lower altitude, approximately 300 meters below Talea. Today Sudo' is completely covered with coffee shrubs and avocado trees, but you can clearly distinguish the remnants of a massive structure that once existed there. The most significant feature is a stone wall that ranges from one to three feet high, is approximately eighteen inches thick, and is laid out in a rectangular form covering about 250 square meters. Prior to the Spanish Conquest, it was not uncommon for villagers to abandon their settlements to escape disease, dwindling water supplies, or attacks from Mixe warriors.[11] Still, the reasons for and the timing of the abandonment of Sudo' continue to elude us.

. . .

By the time Spanish conquistadors arrived in the 1520s, a surprising degree of linguistic divergence had occurred among Zapotec people in north central Oaxaca. Four strikingly different variants of their language evolved over the course of 150 years or so: in the Rincón, Nexitzo Zapotec; directly south of the Rincón, Cajonos Zapotec; east of the Rincón, Bijanos Zapotec; and in the pueblos west of the Rincón, Serrano Zapotec (see map 1). These variants are about as different from each other as are the Romance languages from each other. The region's uneven topography probably accelerated these processes. Yanna Yannakakis suggests that "the mountainous terrain isolated these Zapotec peoples from one another and most likely contributed to the development of this remarkable linguistic diversity."[12] In addition, two other ethnolingustic groups inhabited the northern sierra, the Mixes in the southeastern part of the region and the Chinantecs in the north, creating an unusually rich ethnolinguistic tapestry in a relatively compact territory.

Is it possible that a combination of linguistic and biological diversity helped to stimulate innovation and creativity? Research bridging the social and biological sciences gives clues that might someday help answer that question. For example, ethnobota-

Map 1. Ethnolinguistic map of north central Oaxaca.

nists and anthropologists are discovering startling patterns of correlation between linguistic and biological diversity in certain parts of Mexico, most notably Oaxaca.[13] Ethnobotanist Alejandro de Ávila suggests that regions of great linguistic variation also tend to be characterized by biological megadiversity, unique biogeographical features, and the influences of cultural dynamics and natural history—particularly the domestication of subsistence crops such as maize and squash.

For decades, anthropologists have hypothesized that language profoundly shapes human thought and action. This idea, first proposed by Edward Sapir and Benjamin Whorf in the 1930s, has recently gained renewed attention as social psychologists have subjected the hypothesis to experimental testing—with impressive results.[14] Given the possible connection between language and cognition, we might ask: to what degree has Oaxaca's linguistic and cultural complexity, particularly in places like the Rincón, influenced myriad ways of understanding the world—and therefore acting upon it creatively, either through technological, artistic, or social means?

NEW TOWN

For many years, Rinconeros have described Talea as a "new town" because it was founded after the Spanish Conquest. Several months after I arrived in the village, municipal authorities invited me to read a tattered document stored in the president's office, titled *Memoria y probanza de la fundación del pueblo de Talea de Castro*—roughly translated as "History and Evidence of the Founding of the Village of Talea de Castro." The account was apparently translated into Spanish from a much older document written in the Zapotec language. The documents relate how Zapotec elders from several Rincón settlements traveled to Mexico City to invite Spanish friars to the region during the early years of the conquest.[15] The Spaniards responded by sending the Mercedenian friar Bartolomé de Olmedo to baptize people in 1525. That year the friars also are said to have founded Talea on the border between two "old" Rincón villages, now known as San Bartolomé Yatoni and San Juan Juquila Vijanos.

At first glance it seems odd that indigenous elders would invite Spaniards to the region. But the Zapotec inhabitants were undoubtedly aware of the cataclysmic changes that other native groups were experiencing as the result of the Spanish Conquest, not only in the Valley of Oaxaca but also in Tuxtepec, a Nahua town near Oaxaca state's northern border with Veracruz. By the early 1520s, Spanish soldiers launched the first of several attacks on Tiltepec, a settlement located in the heart of the Rincón, before finally overrunning it in 1526.[16] Perhaps the elders wanted to forestall attacks on their settlements by establishing peaceful relationships with the conquistadors.

If *Memoria y probanza* is accurate, then we may say that Talea owes its very existence to Rinconeros seeking greater connectedness to external forces. But even if these documents are ambiguous, the fact remains that many Taleans consider them to be authoritative.[17] Ethnohistorians have begun analyzing such texts—which appear to be part of a broader genre of Mesoamerican colonial writing known as *títulos primordiales* or primordial titles. Such documents detail the establishment of communities, land claims, and rural lineages—as foundational elements of colonial memory and a kind of local patriotism.[18] But what scholars think about such matters is ultimately of little consequence to prevailing social knowledge in the Rincón. Thousands of Taleans—resident and diasporic—value connectivity, and it has become part of the collective conscience, partly because of a shared historical understanding about village origins.

. . .

Given the brutality and loss of life initiated by the Spaniards, it's tempting to think of the Zapotec and other indigenous Mesoamericans as little more than victims decimated by epidemic disease and the weapons of war. But despite the destruction—and perhaps because of it—indigenous people often responded shrewdly and creatively. Anthropologist María de los Ángeles Romero Frizzi proposes rethinking the experience of conquest by considering what it might have looked like from the point of view of the conquered: "It is commonly thought that the history of indigenous people during the colonial era was one of constant decline: an inevitable path toward the simplification and impoverishment of their culture. However, what happened was more complicated." She continues: "Contact with the Europeans activated an enormous variety of processes in native society: the capacity for creative selection, negotiation, and adaptation."[19] Indigenous people played a vital role in shaping not only their own lives, but history itself.

This is not to deny the horrific consequences of early Spanish colonialism. In the aftermath of conquest, pathogens ripped through the Rincón, probably killing more than one out of three people in the northern sierra over the next fifty years.[20] Smallpox and *cocolizti* or pestilence—probably a highly lethal form of salmonella—were the most severe epidemics to hit Mesoamerica in the 1500s.[21] Yet, despite the catastrophic destruction of human life, the brutish reordering of the remaining social fabric, and the hastily improvised worlds that were thrown together as the conquistadors attempted to control native populations, the Rinconeros responded with ingenuity.

If the arrival of alien diseases signaled the death of the previous epoch, then the magnificent advent of novel food crops and animals marked the birth of the next. It the midst of this rupture, a world radically different from the one that existed before sprouted from its ashes. As in other parts of Mesoamerica, conquest claimed the lives of most people in the region, but the survivors soon appropriated and acquired tools, habits, and, most importantly, plants and animals to reclaim their place among the region's montane forests. The Rincón Zapotec, who had for centuries considered maize to be a sentient life form—a powerful entity with a memory, a will, and a soul—must have viewed the arrival of hundreds of plant and animal species as a miracle of epic proportions.[22]

We can imagine how, in the newly founded settlement of Talea, Zapotec survivors might have delighted in and rapidly adopted Old World crops: citrus, mangos, apples, grapes, peaches, pears, bananas, and figs; onions, garlic, cilantro, cinnamon, and oregano; rice, wheat, barley, oats, and millet; sugarcane; and much more. And then of course there were domesticated animals: chickens, pigs, goats, sheep, cattle, horses, mules, dogs, cats. Steel tools made farming work easier, and, over time, campesinos used hoes, machetes, and, in some regions, plow blades for working the earth. From the point of view of a Zapotec farmer in the colonial era, many thousands of human lives might have been lost in the wake of *la conquista*, but the period also introduced hundreds of useful and wonderful plant and animal species. These precious beings could make life easier for those who survived the Spanish Conquest.

DIGNITY

As in other indigenous regions throughout colonial New Spain, the Rincón was defined as part of the *repúblicas de indios*—literally, "Indian Republics"—and therefore subject to administrative and legal norms that differed from those applied to the *repúblicas de españoles*, the legal system applied to people of European descent. The Spanish monarchy designed the paternalistic political and legal structure to protect indigenous people from the predations of unscrupulous conquistadors, but it often failed to do so. In the northern sierra of Oaxaca, the segregated arrangement often functioned as a bureaucratic machine that facilitated Spaniards' plunder of labor and commodities from native peoples.[23]

Alcaldes mayores were the highest-ranking officials in the repúblicas de indios, responsible for administering justice and collecting payments in their jurisdictions or *distritos*, literally districts). By the mid-1600s, the Villa Alta district—where Talea was located—had become the most desirable in New Spain because it allowed the alcalde mayor to make more money than in any other district through illicit trading practices called *repartimientos de efectos* (literally, "distributions of goods"). This arrangement enabled alcaldes mayores to serve as monopolists who coercively sold commodities such as cattle, mules, oxen, tobacco, cotton, and wheat to indigenous people in their districts at inflated prices that were as much as twice the market value. Sometimes cash advances were included in repartimientos. On a specified date, indebted natives were required to pay the *alcalde mayor* with harvested crops and cochineal—New Spain's second most valuable export by the mid-1600s—or with finished cotton textiles. Alcaldes mayores routinely valued these commodities at rates that were 50 to 75 percent lower than their true market value.[24]

Throughout the 1500s, alcaldes mayores rewarded former conquistadors with grants called *encomiendas*, which allowed them to collect tribute from one or more villages, often in the form of turkeys, maize, or other foods. More than twenty villages were subject to these payments—including Talea. Those who refused to pay were subjected to beatings or other forms of severe corporal punishment.[25] Alcaldes mayores also had the right to appoint deputies called *corregidores* who collected tribute from indigenous villagers.

Another onerous burden imposed on the Zapotec, Mixe, and Chinantec people of the northern sierra was *repartimientos de labor*, obligatory labor drafts in which alcaldes mayores demanded a specified number of workers each week from a village, typically 2 to 4 percent of the adult male population. During the 1500s and 1600s, Spanish officials used repartimientos de labor to force households to produce cochineal and cotton cloth. Alcaldes mayores paid laborers, but the wages were far below market prices.

. . .

In the northern sierra, indigenous peoples responded to these assaults on their dignity in imaginative ways—sometimes by attempting to subvert structures of power. A case in point comes from the Rincón's mining industry. From the earliest years of the conquest, Spaniards had attempted small-scale mining in the region, but their efforts in this regard never produced much. This changed in 1753 when the Spanish Crown granted a concession to an entrepreneur from Veracruz named Andrés de Berdeja. He established mines at Santa Gertrudis, a mere forty-five minute walk from Talea, and the alcalde mayor of Villa Alta soon ordered labor drafts from Rincón communities to work the enterprise.[26] Berdeja abandoned the mines after only a few years, but a wealthy merchant from Antequera named Juan Francisco de Echarrí reopened them about twenty years later. Echarrí invested a great deal of capital in the enterprise, and the mines became the most profitable ones in the history of the northern sierra. By the end of the 1700s, Echarrí and his brother had become Oaxaca's wealthiest miners.[27]

The Santa Gertrudis mines employed nearly eighty workers by the 1780s, plus an additional ten people who worked the neighboring estate (known as *la hacienda*) that produced food for the workers. But the miners were not free laborers; their work was obligatory, enforced through repartimientos de labor. All the miners working at Santa Gertrudis were from Zapotec pueblos, and each week communities in the region were expected to send work crews equal to 2 or 4 percent of their populations. The mine owners paid their indigenous employees, but the miners had no say in determining their wages, much less in participating in the labor draft.[28]

Indigenous workers detested this system of coercive labor—after all, it was a form of temporary wage slavery—and so they opposed it in many ways. According to colonial-era legal documents, in 1782 miners from the Zapotec villages of Juquila, Tabaa, Solaga, Yojovi and Yaee threatened to kill a Nahua foreman, Antonio Solano, over low wages and dangerous working conditions. The mine workers were so aggrieved over the labor draft and poor treatment that three of these pueblos—Tabaa, Solaga, and Yojovi—filed a lawsuit against Echarrí the following year, in 1783. Several Rincón pueblos field their own suit against him in 1788, paid for in part with *derramas*, or head taxes, which municipal authorities collected from villagers to cover legal fees.[29] If they lost their lawsuits, mountain Zapotec communities occasionally rioted in protest.[30]

Although the workers' actions did not substantially change the repartimiento system, they indicate a sophisticated, multifaceted strategy combining protest, litigation, and direct action.

Rincón villages frequently made use of the courts, much more than other pueblos in the Villa Alta district. According to the ethnohistorian John Chance, their litigiousness can be understood as the outcome of two unusual factors:

> First, since the initial battles of conquest at Tiltepec, the Rincón was always a major area of Spanish exploitation in the Sierra Zapoteca. It contained more than its fair share of encomiendas and corregimientos in the early years.... The cochineal and textile repartimiento demands of the alcaldes mayores may also have been especially onerous in the Rincón. Over time, these heavy demands had the effect of keeping Nexitzo communities divided. Those who could sought exemptions from the various burdens.... The second major reason for the litigiousness of the Rincón pueblos is that as a group they were the most highly acculturated in the district. By the mid-eighteenth century many nobles in the Rincón were fluent in Spanish and dressing (at least occasionally) in European fashion.... Nexitzo Zapotecs had a greater knowledge of and access to Spanish institutions, and this was most evident in their use of the Spanish judicial system to settle their differences.[31]

It appears that Rinconeros' relative facility with Spanish language and culture—perhaps an ironic result of their ruthless exploitation during the early years of the conquest—provided them with additional means of defending their dignity.

IN-BETWEEN

Through all of this, municipal governments or cabildos played a crucial intermediary role in colonial-era power struggles. In the northern sierra, Spanish officials first imposed cabildos during

the 1550s, probably as a means of helping alcades mayores effi-
ciently administer repartimientos and sanction those who
refused to participate. In the northern sierra, cabildos threatened the authority of, and eventually superseded, caciques, the
native nobility. Cabildo officials—indigenous men who were, in
effect, middlemen positioned between colonial administrators
and their native brethren—stood to gain from their positions by
skimming profits off the top, and they often acquired status,
power, and perquisites during their terms of office.

But cabildos could also potentially challenge abusive alcaldes
mayores, *encomenderos* (Spaniards who were granted the right to
exploit Indian labor), corregidores, and others whose demands
occasionally threatened the political stability of the region. In the
case of the Santa Gertrudis mines, "cabildo officers found themselves torn between their communities' expectation that they
would defend them from Echarrí's abuses, primarily through
recourse to the courts, and the expectation of the alcalde mayor
and Echarrí that they would enforce the labor requirements of
Santa Gertrudis. As intermediary figures, these cabildo officers
had little room for maneuver."[32]

By the early 1800s, it appears that cabildos became more democratic and counterhegemonic—that is, they were more likely
to protect the interests of ordinary indigenous people against
the abuses of unscrupulous colonial officials, entrepreneurs, and
labor foremen. Anthropologist Eric Wolf called this a "retreat
from utopia" in which "a tug of war between conquerors and
conquered" resulted in the appropriation of certain European
institutions by indigenous peoples during the late colonial and
postcolonial periods.[33] Though they have undergone many
mutations over the intervening years, cabildos still form the

structural core of indigenous communities in the northern sierra today.

. . .

Cabildo officials are a subset of a larger group of cultural brokers, people who "must serve some of the interests of groups operating on both the community and national level, and they must cope with the conflicts raised by the collision of these interests.... They often act as buffers between groups, maintaining the tensions which provide the dynamic of their actions."[34] In the northern sierra, these intermediaries were people with linguistic talent, intercultural understanding, and sensitivity to the subtleties of communication who stepped into diverse roles such as commercial middlemen, interpreters, priests' assistants, legal agents, municipal governors, and, in the first half of the colonial era, landed noblemen.[35] Yanna Yannakakis notes that native intermediaries were positioned precariously on a tightrope: "As community leaders and cabildo officers, they were responsible for defending their pueblos from abuses *and* delivering tribute to the Crown, for maintaining reciprocal relations between their communities and the gods *and* making sure that their fellow villagers attended Catholic mass.... When the competing constituencies in question called native intermediaries to account, however, the political space closed around them, imperiled their intermediary role, and upset the fragile balance of power that they had negotiated."[36]

These brokers imaginatively used ethnicity, communication skills, and cross-cultural knowledge in ways that might benefit their communities. They might also benefit as individuals. For example, in a colonial-era courtroom, a court interpreter might sympathetically describe a Rincón Zapotec man who dressed in European clothing and spoke Spanish as an *indio ladino*—a Latinized Indian—as opposed to a "barbaric" Indian or *indio bárbaro*. If the Rincón Zapotec man identified himself as a *principal*—indicating that he had served in a high position within his village's municipal government—the court interpreter might be even more sympathetic to the indigenous man's testimony. By constructing a narrative that reasonably explained why certain pueblos appeared to be resisting Church policies, the Zapotec man's testimony might defuse a potentially dangerous conflict and simultaneously raise the status of his own village vis-à-vis regional rivals.[37]

OPENNESS

So far, much of this discussion has centered upon ways in which indigenous people from the northern sierra, especially the Rincón, creatively confronted political, economic, biological, and demographic adversity during the colonial era. Now let us focus on Talea, especially in the postcolonial era.

Talea began changing rapidly in the mid-1800s, when a well-connected mestizo lawyer and entrepreneur named Miguel Castro began buying mines throughout northern Oaxaca. Castro, who was born in Oaxaca City in 1813, eventually acquired the defunct Santa Gertrudis silver mines near Talea during the 1840s, and over the next few decades became one of Oaxaca's most influential *caudillos*, or strong men.[38] By 1880, Castro owned thirty-eight mines throughout Oaxaca—far more than any other person in the state.[39] Miners from the Sierra Zapoteca and the Valley of Oaxaca flocked to the area, and Talea flourished as a commercial center in the late 1800s as villagers began supplying the mines with provisions. The pueblo's newfound prosperity drew outsiders into the village as blacksmiths, brick-makers, weavers, candlemakers, butchers, carpenters, bakers and others began laying the foundation for a broadly diversified economy. Castro's influence even left its mark on the village's name, which was officially changed to San Miguel Talea de Castro during this time.

Castro, who was a close friend of Benito Juárez and a political ally of Porfirio Díaz (each of whom would eventually be elected as president of the Mexican Republic), served briefly as Oaxaca state governor on three different occasions. His political connections brought several influential people to Santa Gertrudis—and presumably Talea. For example, in late 1853 or early 1854, Benito Juárez's wife Margarita Maza spent a brief period in exile at Santa Gertrudis. Maza, who was pregnant at the time and traveling with two young children, was fleeing persecution from military men opposed to her husband's political ideas. After Maza died in 1871, Juárez received heartfelt sympathy letters from Miguel Castro and Juana España de Pérez, the wife of a prominent lawyer and politician named Marcos Pérez, a mentor and benefactor of Porfirio Díaz. Both letters were written from Santa Gertrudis. Another influential member of Oaxaca's political class, Fidencio Hernández, worked as an administrator in Castro's Santa Gertrudis mines before launching his own commercial enterprises.[40] During Díaz's thirty-five year dictatorship (1876–1911), foreign investment poured into Mexico, and caudillos often undertook joint ventures with Spanish, French, British, and American entrepreneurs.

Historians of Oaxaca have noted that at the turn of the twentieth century, Castro, Díaz, Pérez, Hernández and other regional caudillos exercised their economic and political power by controlling trade in commodities, which, in the northern sierra, meant silver, cotton, and, by the early 1900s, coffee. These men often invested their wealth across a wide range of industries. Fidencio Hernández is a case in point: during the late 1800s, he created a factory for manufacturing candles used in sierra mines, helped finance the construction of a road linking the town of Ixtlán to Oaxaca City, and is widely believed to have introduced coffee into the region during the 1870s.[41] Talea benefited both directly and indirectly from *caudillismo* in the mid-to-late 1800s, even as it was subjected to the negative economic effects of the caudillos' trade monopolies. Villagers took advantage of the Santa Gertrudis mining boom by producing and selling goods to the miners, and although they didn't profit directly from the mines, their proximity to the enterprise meant that over time, they would reap other less tangible rewards, such as a rapid increase in population and influence compared to other pueblos in the region. The combined populations of Talea and Santa Gertrudis nearly quadrupled during the mid-to-late nineteenth century, from approximately 520 in 1820 to two thousand in 1900.[42] It seems likely that villagers would have recognized the futility of opposing the reopening of the Santa Gertrudis mines, and pragmatically decided to make the best of the situation.

Because of the political and economic instability leading up to the Mexican Revolution, the Santa Gertrudis mines closed in 1905, and many miners left town. Those that remained established themselves as campesino farmers, while others became merchants. Soon the village became the most important commercial center in the Rincón. The weekly market moved from Santa Gertrudis to Talea, and many of the former miners began to manufacture and sell items needed by people in other villages. By the early twentieth century, Talea had surpassed Yaee as the most important market in the Rincón. For a village with relatively little land compared to other nearby pueblos, these changes were a blessing.

How did Santa Gertrudis's reinvigorated mines shape the outlook of townspeople at the turn of the twentieth century and beyond? Although we cannot know for sure, it is worth considering anthropologist Laura Nader's observations about villagers' attitudes toward change. Written more than a half century ago, her comments were accurate but also seem to have been prescient: "A town that is relatively accustomed to dealing with strangers and incorporating them into its organization is likely also to be a town more willing to accept change from the outside."[43]

· · ·

Many Taleans described the late 1800s and early 1900s as a golden age, characterized by extraordinary accomplishments. For example, the village's Catholic church was built during this period (see figure 4). It is a massive stone structure that was initiated in the 1800s and took decades to complete. According to older villagers, architects modeled it after a painting of an Italian church (the last mine owner was said to have been an Italian entrepreneur named Domingo Tomacelli), and residents constructed it entirely with local materials. Builders hoisted heavy stones, some larger than a cubic meter, into place using a wooden crane powered by oxen. In the early twentieth century, villagers began constructing the municipal palace. They built the stately two-story building—the largest of its kind in the region—with similar materials. Both the church and the municipal palace survived strong earthquakes, and they were proudly cited by many villagers as evidence of the ingenuity, industriousness, and aesthetic sophistication of Taleans.

Figure 4. The village church, built in the late nineteenth and early twentieth centuries. Photo courtesy of Charly Vásquez Chon.

Some villagers took a great deal of pride in Urbano Olivera, an artist who was born and raised in the pueblo during the second half of the nineteenth century. He is probably best known for a series of large oil paintings that were commissioned in the 1890s by Eulogio Guillow, the Archbishop of Antequera, which are still displayed at the San Juan de Dios Catholic church in Oaxaca City. Among his works are *La primera misa en Oaxaca*, depicting the first Catholic mass near the banks of Oaxaca's Atoyac River; *El bautizo de Cocijoeza*, depicting the baptism of a famous Zapotec emperor by Spanish friars; *La Santa Cruz de Huatulco*, depicting a sacred cross said to have been brought centuries ago to the shores of Huatulco by a light-skinned bearded man; *Bartolomé de las Casas defendiendo a los indígenas*, depicting the well-known sixteenth century Dominican friar who championed the cause of New Spain's indigenous peoples; and *Los venerables mártires de Cajonos*, depicting two Catholic Zapotec men who, in 1700, interrupted a pagan ritual and were killed by fellow villagers as a result of their actions.[44] All of these paintings, obviously aimed at predominantly illiterate indigenous audiences, portrayed the Catholic church in a flattering light, as genteel advocates of New Spain's native population.[45]

Olivera's work has been displayed for decades at the National Museum of Anthropology in Mexico City, which is among the world's finest ethnological museums. It is a series of two paintings that depict people from different villages throughout the northern sierra, dressed in *trajes típicas* or "typical" clothing—which is to say that the men are wearing *calzones* (loose-fitting cotton pants and shirts) and *huaraches*, while the women are wearing embroidered *huipiles*, wool skirts, and rebozos. The women of each village wear similar colors and patterns, in contrast to those from other pueblos. Throughout his work, Olivera consistently portrayed indigenous people in a sensitive, respectful manner—as dignified human beings.

In Talea, art collectors could once easily find and acquire Olivera's paintings. Rosendo Pérez García, an intellectual from the Sierra who wrote an extensive history of the region in the 1950s, noted that his art could be obtained at low cost in the pueblo, but it appears that, over the years, buyers have snatched up these works.[46] However, there is at least one Olivera piece that is likely to remain for years to come: a massive painting of Miguel Hidalgo, the priest who sparked Mexico's war of independence against Spain in 1810. The work hangs proudly in the office of Talea's municipal president.

As villagers told me about Olivera and his artwork, I wondered how, over the years, such people could have inspired others—particularly the young—to aspire to greatness. If, despite his humble origins, Urbano Olivera could become a nationally renowned artist, then what could possibly keep them from achieving extraordinary success too?

.   .   .

In the early 1900s, villagers experienced a change that would have massive repercussions in the years ahead: the widespread cultivation of coffee. They probably adopted the crop more quickly than other Rincón pueblos because Talea had relatively little land—and, in the early twentieth century, many unemployed former miners. Throughout the first decade of the century villagers could sell coffee to buyers and purchase maize, beans, and merchandise in exchange. If it had a high enough price, coffee could help the pueblo survive difficult economic circumstances. As demand for coffee soared in the post-World War II period, the Rincón boomed.[47] Rising coffee prices led to an influx of money in the late 1940s and 1950s. Consequently, residents sought manufactured consumer goods: tools, kerosene lamps, hand grinders, cloth, soap, beer, and biscuits.[48]

In the wake of the economic boom, some villagers were determined to build roads for shipping coffee out of the northern sierra. During the first half of the century the Cajonos Zapotec town of Zoogocho was the most important coffee trading center in the region, but things had changed dramatically by the end of the 1950s. A resolute group of Taleans lobbied the government for assistance in building a road connecting the village to Oaxaca City, and eventually succeeded.[49] In October 1959, workers completed the project under the auspices of the Papaloapan Commission, one of Mexico's most ambitious development projects, and Talea quickly surpassed Zoogocho as the most important coffee outpost in the northern sierra.

· · ·

Perhaps no person better exemplifies Talea's spirit of innovation in the twentieth century than Agustín García, a wealthy merchant and coffee buyer whose efforts transformed the pueblo in significant ways. Today, villagers remember him for helping to secure government support for the construction of the road, and for bringing wondrous technologies to his pueblo. García was a visionary who spent much of his money on special projects, including an electric generator used to illuminate public spaces such as streets and the municipal palace in the 1950s—nearly twenty years before the Federal Electricity Commission initiated service in the pueblo. The generator also powered the region's first automatic maize grinding mill. It reportedly harnessed electrical power from a hydraulic water wheel driven by the *Río de la Cantera*, a river located 600 meters below the town center. In the meantime, the pueblo secured its position as the Rincón's predominant market town (see figure 5).

It would be an exaggeration to say that García's technological progressivism is emblematic of all Taleans' attitudes toward science and progress. The proponents of rapid change, who came to be called *progresistas*, tended to have more political and economic power than those who were cautious about new technologies. The latter were sometimes called *cerrados*; in other words, they were "closed" to new ideas.[50] Even so, for most of the past century, a significant portion of the population enthusiastically embraced modernization and economic integration in various forms: the participation of approximately thirty young men in

Figure 5. Talean women selling produce at the weekly market. Photo courtesy of Charly Vásquez Chon.

the Bracero Program (a 1940s and 1950s guest worker agreement between the United States and Mexico); the construction of an airstrip for small planes in the 1960s (now used as a soccer field, since the road has been dramatically improved); and the widespread adoption of electrical appliances from the 1970s onward. More recently, hundreds of Talean immigrants have traveled to the United States and returned to raise families in the relative safety of the village, bringing novel ideas and skills with them: knowledge of homeopathic medicine, which some are integrating with *curanderismo* or folk medicine and Western biomedicine; an appreciation of different styles of music (ranging from classical music to hip hop and reggaeton); and the ability to create parabolic TV satellite dishes by welding aluminum tubing and aluminum mesh.

•   •   •

All of this raises interesting questions about the nature of innovation, a topic that has drawn the attention of anthropologists for several decades. It appears that, among other things, innovation tends to be connected with openness or tolerance: when people from different ethnic, national, religious, or other groups are allowed or encouraged to mingle, "creativity ... may come about as perspectives meet with other perspectives, whether through affinity or discord."[51] Given the evidence, it seems that Talea may also be an environment that fosters openness: the first anthropologist to study the pueblo noted that it "has apparently always been hospitable toward strangers and even accepts people from neighboring villages as citizens."[52]

Although it was founded after the Spanish Conquest, the pueblo is nonetheless a Rincón Zapotec village that shares a common history, language, and culture with other pueblos in the region. Over the course of centuries, people in the northern sierra have faced daunting environmental, demographic, economic, and political challenges with ingenuity and verve. A fortuitous series of events has enabled villagers to build upon that foundation over the past century and a half, transforming the pueblo into the largest Zapotec community in northern Oaxaca. If we think of the place not so much as a geographically remote indigenous settlement but as a bustling village that has for more than century displayed the characteristics of a vibrant, cosmopolitan urban center—a mountain metropolis—then it is easier to comprehend its success in creative problem-solving and innovation over the years.

Yet despite the progressive or forward-looking attitude of many townspeople, Talea is a place where twenty-first century technologies and creative ideas coexist alongside supernatural entities, elaborate rituals, and spiritual beliefs. If people in the pueblo have sought greater connections with people from outside, some have also attempted to establish close nexuses with otherworldly beings. It is to these metaphysical beliefs and practices that we now turn.

CHAPTER THREE

Enchanted

When I visited Talea for the first time in the summer of 1994, I experienced culture shock, which I fully expected and was reasonably well prepared to confront. But I also experienced what might be called reverse culture shock: a kind of confusion or disorientation at finding so many things that were utterly *familiar* to me. During my first twenty-four hours in the village, all kinds of scenarios played out that seemed odd, even bizarre. For example, after receiving me cordially, town officials proceeded to ask if I could help them install software on a used desktop PC that had been delivered to the municipal president's office earlier in the week.[1] As I fumbled around hopelessly with a set of floppy disks, the municipal secretary recounted his experiences in the United States as a *mojado* (a slang term for undocumented immigrant) in the 1980s and explained to me that he learned to love hard rock by listening to 96.1 FM, a Tucson radio station. "Do you like Pink Floyd? Led Zeppelin? Supertramp? The Doors?" he asked.[2]

Later that afternoon, I walked to the pueblo's only phone kiosk to call my parents, who were expecting a phone call from me once I had arrived safely. As I entered the storefront, I was stunned to see a video game arcade with full-size upright consoles including the popular *Street Fighter 2*. Teenagers were playing at all five coin-op machines.

That night, when I was about to retire for the evening, my hosts (a prosperous merchant family) invited me to watch a dubbed episode of the 1990s teen drama *Beverly Hills, 90210*, a fictional Hollywood TV series that followed the lives of good-looking rich kids. I politely declined. It had been a long day.

Before going to bed, I read a passage from Claude Lévi-Strauss's book *Tristes Tropiques*, which is, among other things, an elegy to lost worlds. The villagers I had met appeared, on the surface at least, to be "caught, like gamebirds, in the trap of our mechanistic civilization."[3] Perhaps I would bring back nothing but the ashes of a bygone era from the Rincón.

Similar situations unfolded over the ensuing months. I encountered a campesino who had a reputation for mediocre farming abilities. Yet this man, despite only five years of formal schooling, had read some of Karl Marx's work, and was more familiar with the ideas of Mao Tse-tung and Che Guevara than all but a few of the graduate students I had ever met. On several occasions I met young people who had been born and raised in Talea but had then moved to Los Angeles with their families. Some had lived in cosmopolitan urban centers longer than I had and were fully trilingual in Zapotec, Spanish, and English.

During the topsy-turvy weeks after my arrival, it was difficult to make sense of things. I had expected to enter a world that was rustic, foreign, alien, perhaps indecipherable. Instead, my daily routine included conversations with children who wanted to talk about *The Simpsons*, the Los Angeles Lakers, and *Terminator 2*. Each day the thought crossed my mind: would it be best to drop Talea, and instead do field work in another Rincón village such as Yaee or Juquila? Should I seek out a community that had retained more of *lo auténtico*—literally, authenticity—in order to keep with a long-standing tendency in anthropology to seek out a more radical otherness? I suppose that part of me was drawn to this academic discipline because I craved a social setting where people had valiantly resisted the forces of corporate capitalism and mass consumerism—if they not escaped them entirely. I wasn't naive enough to think that I would find any culturally pristine indigenous villages in northern Oaxaca, but at the same time the prospect of doing field work in a place so profoundly transformed by progress made me queasy.

In 2006, a colleague and I had the opportunity to speak to Annuar Abdalá, an engineer who played a leading role in Talea's transformation during the late twentieth century. As a director of the Papaloapan Commission, he had helped develop the road linking the Rincón to the valley of Oaxaca. But when we talked to him, he expressed grave regrets:

> Initially the road project began with the idea of helping the towns export their products ... [but then] I understood that the road might change everything in the near future. And that's what happened. After nine years, I visited the region again, and I noticed that the clothes people wore were different, the children were different—they were practically contaminated. The external influences were such that there were people who exchanged sacks of corn for sacks of coffee—a truly incredible thing, considering the value of each. This is part of the harm that resulted from that road.[4]

Getting connected came at a price. On the surface, Talea appeared to be a place that exemplified the "disenchantment of the world" described by the eminent sociologist Max Weber nearly a century ago. According to this idea, the rationalization and bureaucratization of modern society leads to a valorization of scientific (as opposed to spiritual, religious, or magical) forms of knowledge—an idea shared by many social scientists in the late nineteenth and early twentieth centuries. Weber famously wrote that in so-called traditional societies, "the world remains a great enchanted garden."[5] I had hoped to find more of that preternatural ground in Talea, but it would be several months before I found out that I had been looking in the wrong places.

AMONG US

Over time, I came to realize that the municipal secretary, the teenagers who spent long afternoons playing video games, and the merchant family that hosted me those first few nights were not representative of most Taleans.[6] The majority of villagers were from modest farming families whose members had never lived in the United States, had no money for video games, and watched precious little TV because they did not have time for it. A campesino friend once joked, "Buying a television obligates you to waste your time!" Many, if not most, of the farmers with whom I spoke shared that commonsense attitude.

After spending time with campesinos in the fields, learning about their everyday lives while working alongside them, it became clear to me that this was indeed an enchanted world. Neither modernization, nor migration, nor the Mexican state had wiped out the *bhni glas*, those mystic beings who inhabited the region before the arrival of the Zapotec. The bhni glas existed in the era of darkness, before the birth of the sun. Some said that these men and women must have been intelligent, for throughout the region campesinos still find finely crafted clay vessels in their tombs. Others told me that the bhni glas were *incultos*, uneducated people who lived like animals. Still others claimed that in the countryside, they had heard the bones of bhni glas whizzing by, and that sometimes the bones collided with trees, making a loud popping sound. Most of those who talked about the bhni glas told me that the ancients built the structures that now lay in ruins at *Sudo'*, on the other side of the Santa Gertrudis River (see chapter 2).[7]

The *bhni gui'a*—literally, men of the mountains—were also largely unaffected by the changes that swept the Rincón in the late twentieth and early twenty-first centuries. These beings, described by some as spirits, appear as well-dressed men who wear slacks, shoes, and a coat and tie. They reside in the forest or sometimes in the rocky recesses of mountainsides. Bhni gui'a manage *dinero encantado*, enchanted money, which means that they may offer a campesino a tempting bargain: financial prosperity. Some say that a campesino who accepts this bargain must also give up his soul. All agree that after the recipient of enchanted money dies, his wealth disappears along with him.[8]

Villagers related other accounts of supernatural beings. The legend of the *matlacihua* is told often in Talea as well as in other parts of Oaxaca. She is a nocturnal enchantress who appears on mountain paths as a beautiful woman clothed in a long, flowing, white dress. Lovesick and inebriated men are especially vulnerable to her alluring calls. Her hypnotic movements are mesmerizing: there are accounts of men who followed her blindly into thickly wooded areas as if in a deep hypnotic trance. Those who are entranced by the *matlacihua* wake up in the morning far from where they encountered her, and they have no recollection of how she transported them there.[9]

Even the earth and her fruits are living, sentient beings for many Taleans.[10] For example, a campesina woman, who, like many of her village counterparts, maintained an astonishingly fertile kitchen garden in a tiny plot outside her home, described her own private ritual:

> Not everybody does this, but I give thanks to her—to the earth. This year, when I cleared away the old plants in my garden and prepared to plant new seeds, I spoke to her, I thanked her for the things she had given us, and I told her that I would take care of her. And I asked her to continue giving us good things. That's my custom. Then I planted my chilies, chayote, cilantro, and other things.

In addition, there are many accounts of maize and the earth punishing people who disrespect it. For example, a person who refuses to share maize with those in need may find that his or her family's supply suddenly disappears. People who unjustly encroach upon the *milpas* of a neighboring pueblo are likely to discover that their ill acquired lands refuse to produce crops.

Other supernatural beings inhabit the Rincón: *duendes*, forest spirits that resemble tiny humans but who, like gremlins, create mischief; mountain spirits who, among other things, protect deer and other forest animals from irresponsible hunters; and a pantheon of nominally Catholic saints who, despite their Spanish-sounding names, play strikingly similar roles to the Zapotec deities of old—if perhaps in somewhat different clothing.[11]

The collective presence of these beings suggests that the world can be a perilous place for those who are selfish, unfaithful, irresponsible, thievish, or disrespectful. What is striking about all this is that the threat of spectral unrest is so markedly different from the apparently harmonious nature of human relationships in Talea.[12] It seems possible that, as in other more or less egalitarian societies that greatly value "communal consensus [or at least its appearance], this often appears to spark a kind of equally elaborate reaction formation, a spectral night world inhabited by monsters, witches or other creatures of horror. And it's the most peaceful societies which are also the most haunted, in their imaginative constructions of the cosmos, by constant specters of perennial war."[13]

RITUAL CONNECTIONS

Apart from the persistent threat of phantasmal activity emanating from these supernatural beings, many Taleans used magic and religion to communicate with other inhabitants of the spirit world that might help them overcome unpredictable situations ranging from reproductive infertility to prolonged drought to the fate of purgatorial souls. In other words, the "enchanted garden" of fiestas, ritual celebrations, and legends enables villagers to connect with the gods and other inhabitants of the spirit world, to deceased kin, to people in neighboring pueblos, and ultimately to each other.

What do these nontechnological efforts have to do with the ambitious quest to obtain cell phone access? Is there a relationship between supernatural and digital forms of connectivity? That certainly appears to be the case. Ritual life in the Rincón generally and in Talea particularly is a deeply integral part of many villagers' sense and state of being, and creating a nexus between the terrestrial world and extramundane realms is both the objective and the result of much of this activity. Cell phones, social media, and digital technologies fit easily within these broader cultural contexts in much the same way that roads did in the mid-twentieth century. There are striking examples that illustrate a close association between supernatural and infrastructural domains, such the roadside Virgin Mary statue located at a site called Maravillas, literally "wonders." This is the place where, in the 1950s, Taleans miraculously conjoined their village with a wider thoroughfare that branches into the Rincón from Mexican Federal Highway 175.

There is another crucial reason that supernatural beliefs and practices are relevant to Talea's cell phone network: decades-old patterns of migration. Much of the pueblo's ritual continuity and survival depends upon financial support from its émigrés, particularly transnational migrants in the United States—some of whom reproduce Talean fiestas, basketball tournaments, and other rituals in Los Angeles, Mexico City, and other cosmopolitan urban centers. The villagers' embrace of cellular telephony and social media becomes more comprehensible against this backdrop. Digital technologies provide an affordable, convenient way of transporting ritual celebrations—imagined traditions—over space and time, while simultaneously archiving those events for future generations.

· · ·

Given these links between supernatural and digital forms of connectivity, it is worth exploring in more detail the ways in which villagers use ritual to promote contact and communion across multiple planes of existence. In my previous work I focused upon aspects of everyday life in the village, many of which revolved around the seemingly mundane routines of farming work and food preparation. Here I turn my attention to extraordinary times: festival days or fiestas. During these communal celebrations, which may last up to five days from start to finish, the village undergoes a remarkable metamorphosis: the tenor of daily life is disrupted by the sensory explosion of the fiesta.

Each year there are two major fiestas in the pueblo, those honoring the Dulce Nombre de Jesús in late January and San Miguel Arcángel on September 29. They attract hundreds of people who have migrated from the village to Oaxaca City, Mexico City, or the United States, and hundreds more who are visiting from surrounding villages. Apart from these events, Taleans also celebrate more than fifteen smaller fiestas. Some of these are sponsored by the village's four *secciones*, sections or neighborhoods; others are religious holidays celebrated throughout Mexico, and sponsored by *padrinos*, patrons who provide a location, food, and drink for the event; and still others are regionally specific fiestas that honor saints that are revered—and sometimes feared—in the region.

Here I describe three annual fiestas, two of which occurred in Talea (San Isidro Labrador and All Saints' Day-All Souls' Day) and one of which was held in the Cajonos Zapotec pueblo of San Andrés Yaa, in honor of a sacred tree called the *Cruz Verde* or Green Cross. During the 1990s I participated as a *músico*, a musician who played the trumpet in Talea's *banda*, "Unión y Progreso." Municipal bands typically consisted of portable brass, wind, and percussion instruments—similar to what one might find in a high school marching band in the United States—and did not include vocalists (see figure 6).[14] Observing the fiestas from a musician's perspective provided me with an insiders' view: live music was and continues to be an essential part of both secular and religious festivals celebrated in the Rincón, and villagers treat musicians respectfully, particularly when they are visiting from other pueblos. Municipal bands that excel at their craft are often contracted by other pueblos to provide music for their fiestas.[15]

Figure 6. *Banda Unión y Progreso* in 1998. Photo courtesy of Gabriela Zamorano Villarreal.

Fiestas captivated me and provoked a sense of rapt enchantment, "a state of wonder" in which "you notice new colors, discern details previously ignored, hear extraordinary sounds, as familiar landscapes of sense sharpen and intensify. The world comes alive.... Enchantment includes, then, a condition of exhilaration."[16] At some point I subconsciously permitted myself to suspend my disbelief and, rather than try to theorize fiestas, I instead decided to run with them.[17] I gave my fellow musicians— and everyone else who planned or participated in the fiesta—the benefit of the doubt. In these moments, I learned a great deal about intervillage relations, about Talean values, and even about myself. I came to understand that fiestas of all kinds are not only "part of an enchanted world" in which "time is transformed to a mythical past or a total present ... as if it were a dream," as the great Mexican poet Octavio Paz so eloquently wrote in *The Lab-*

yrinth of Solitude, but that these communal celebrations are also vehicles for potentially communicating and connecting with others—natural and supernatural others—and, as we shall see later in this book, actual and virtual others.[18] During these exceptional periods, society itself becomes a spectacle.[19] Fiestas are visually arresting events that seem ready-made for us to capture with digital devices. In the Mexican context, they can hold the viewer's attention through sight, sound, and nostalgia.

What follows are narrative accounts intended to evoke a visceral sense of what it is like to participate in three distinct fiestas, each of which can cultivate communication, connections, and communion among and between participants and supernatural entities. By describing events in the first person singular and plural, I hope to evoke a feeling of immediacy, if not intimacy.

CALLING A SAINT

San Isidro Labrador, the patron saint of farmers throughout the Catholic world, is honored by campesinos across Oaxaca.[20] There is a life-sized statue of the saint in Talea's church, and, although it is a light-skinned figure with a thick beard, he is working the land as would any Talean campesino, wearing huaraches and an armadillo-shell seed basket. He carries a simple planting stick and guides a team of miniature oxen tied to a plow. Is it possible that San Isidro is a syncretic version of the Zapotec god of thunder and rain, Cocijo? After all, this fiesta coincides with the beginning of the maize planting season, around the time that the rainy season begins. After talking with many campesinos about it, I came to the conclusion that this fiesta is a way for farming families to thank the deity directly for providing abundant crops—but also to call on him for more. Not participating in the fiesta might mean angering San Isidro, who is capable of influencing the harvest.

This year, the fiesta officially began with a *calenda nocturna*, a nighttime street procession, on May 13. At twilight, I gathered with the other fifteen members of the *banda* "Unión y Progreso" at the top of the village, outside the chapel of San Juan de los Lagos. The site is on the main road into Talea, which, appropriately enough, is called *Comunicaciones*—Communications Street—a testament to the importance placed here on being connected.

We waited for the celebration to begin. A few dozen onlookers gathered around us, mostly neighbors. Nearly all the musicians were full-time subsistence farmers and they seemed especially excited about honoring San Isidro—though they were somewhat tired because they had returned from their fields just a couple of hours earlier. There was a small *miscelánia* or convenience store located next to the chapel, and the owner brought out a case of beer, a bottle of mezcal, cigarettes, and matches as a token of appreciation. Just as we were beginning to relax, a pink fireball zigzagged above us, whistling wildly as it ascended into the heavens, followed by a trail of acrid brown smoke.

BANG!

The church bells clanged crazily from the village center below. And Pedro, the lead trumpet player and de facto director, hissed: "*¡Prepárense, cabrones!*"[21] The fiesta had begun.

Within seconds, Agustín had secured his bass drum, Miguel his timbales, Edgar his snare drum, and Mario his rusty sousaphone. Those of us with smaller instruments took even less time. Then Pedro barked out the title of a well-known *son*. We jumped into a medley of lively *sones* and *jarabes*, rhythms that are the musical heart and soul of the northern sierra. After fifteen minutes, the crowd had grown to more than a hundred, and many had begun to dance in pairs, bobbing to the beat with the restrained, dignified movements characteristic of the region. Then the entire throng descended slowly, almost imperceptibly, towards a hairpin turn known as *la curva* at the northwest corner of the village.

Communications Street was completely unlit, and, except for a few flashlights, the road was pitch dark. As more people joined the multitude, the street got crowded. I was a minuscule speck in an expanding organism that was creeping slowly downhill. Fog began to envelop us, giving an unearthly appearance to the scene. We musicians instinctively formed a double-file line and slowly followed each other down the path, belting out nonstop *sones* and *jarabes* the entire time. My lips were already throbbing from playing so forcefully. Every once in a while Pedro called out a popular *ranchera*—think of it as a polka with a Mexican twist—to vary the repertoire.

Then, another screeching, smoking, spiraling comet...
BANG!

Flocks of kids, full of sugary sweets and soda, swarmed between us, chasing and scaring each other and anyone else in their path. Many of them wore grotesque masks: hairy gorilla masks, and space alien masks, and rubber monster masks, and [then Mexican president Ernesto] Zedillo masks. People ahead of us lit firecrackers, and in the shadows I was able to see more observers as we approached *la curva*: young lovers, taking advantage of the darkness to hold hands or embrace; mothers with sleepy infants tied snugly to their backs; and elderly villagers grinning at the spectacle—leather-faced men in straw hats shaking their heads in amusement; sturdy women in checkered aprons with rebozos pulled tightly against the night air. Onlookers became participants: nearly all of them latched on to the growing human mass, pulled inexorably by the gravitational force of the pueblo's nucleus.

We finally reached *la curva* two hours later. Every few minutes more red, green, pink and orange fireballs lit up the night sky, followed by the sharp stench of sulfur. The church bells had been ringing wildly since we began—in fact, the pace had only gotten more frenetic. From this point forward there were streetlights, and, as we approached a small restaurant called La Morenita, I couldn't believe the size of the crowd—hundreds strong at this point, maybe five hundred or more. Contained chaos. Most people in the streets were dancing; the mood was euphoric. Grown men cried out in sheer bliss—the Mexican *grito* is as popular here as anywhere else in the country—while others expressed their emotion with earsplitting *chiflas*, gleeful whistling.[22]

We continued leading the ecstatic mob down the road, making three more stops for refreshments outside of *misceláneas* and cantinas before we finally reached the *cancha de básquetbol*, the basketball court in the town center, around midnight. The municipal authorities were lined up, looking pleased and proud. They formally welcomed us and then offered more mezcal, aguardiente, beer, and cigarettes. The crowd soon poured into the *cancha* and danced tirelessly for the next two hours. It seemed as if no one would go home—until eventually we called it quits at two in the morning. There were still two more full days of fiesta!

• • •

The next day (May 14) was the *víspera* or eve of the fiesta, and it began with an early morning Mass at the church, where we played the *Misa Oaxaqueña*, a stately, majestic series of compositions that is played by municipal bands throughout Oaxaca.[23] During the most solemn part of the Mass, as the priest recited the words *haced esto en memoria de mí*—"do this in memory of me"—and raised the bread and wine that had become Christ's body and blood, a campesino hammered away at a leather drum from the rear of the church. He was accompanied by a wizened beak-nosed man known as Pedro Periquín (Pedro Little Parakeet) who played a *chirimiya*, or bamboo flute. The church was only about half full for the Mass, and the músicos explained that most men and women could not attend for two reasons: it was a school day, and many women were responsible for getting their children to school; and most men were struggling to keep up with their farm work at a crucial time—the maize planting season—while still honoring San Isidro.[24]

After Mass we went home for breakfast, and then reconvened at a house to escort the *danzantes* who would be performing throughout the fiesta. People had been talking excitedly about *la Danza de los Zancos* for weeks, and it is easy to understand why: the performance was a spectacle that featured gigantic danzantes— most of whom were teenagers—strapped onto stilts more than two feet high. They lampooned colonial-era Spaniards, wearing pink wooden masks, black and white vested suits, and blonde wigs. The danza consisted of about fifteen *sones*, written by a villager who is an accomplished musician.

We and the danzantes filed out shortly before noon. We set up in *El Centenario*, an open-air market building adjacent to the municipal palace. The first performance was more or less a dress rehearsal for the second show, which began in the late afternoon. At this point, more people arrived since school was finally out and men were returning from the ranchos. The audience was entranced by the carefully choreographed buffoonery of the danzantes.

Figure 7. Villager carrying a pyrotechnic *torito* during a fiesta. Photo by Juanjo Juárez/Creative Commons by SA-4.0.

Later that afternoon, men set up tables for *polaca* (also known as *lotería*), a form of Mexican bingo with a strong communal element. Up to forty or fifty people—men, women, children of all ages and social classes—would gather to play. It was a time for them to communicate, talk, gossip, chat, joke. Each card sold for a peso (about fifteen cents), priced cheaply enough for all to play. The prizes were modest, but useful—plastic buckets, bathing tins, pots and pans.

After dinner we returned to the basement of the municipal palace with a group of young men and boys to bring the *toritos*, literally little bulls—bundles of fireworks lashed to a bamboo frame. *Coheteros*, or fireworks makers, design toritos so that the structures can be hoisted on a person's shoulders as he or she runs about like a frisky flaming little beast (see figure 7).

As we played cheerful tunes, teenage boys took turns carrying the toritos to the cancha where by now hundreds of people had

gathered to watch the revelry. Then pyrotechnicians set the toritos alight—sparkling, spinning showers of pure light. The banda
played wildly infectious regional tunes, one after another for
nearly an hour, until the fireworks had burned out. It was a true
spectacle, with green, red, blue, and pink cascades of fire spraying
all over the place; clouds of smoke lifting up; and pungent sulfuric
smells cutting through the air. A wayward spark whizzed onto the
corridor of the palacio municipal where we are playing, skipping
past my feet before it sputtered out. After the sones and jarabes
we played many other pieces: corridos, tropically inflected *cum-
bias*, and more. Hundreds of *paisanos*—that is, fellow villagers—
danced until we ended, well after midnight.

. . .

May 15, the main fiesta day, began with another morning Mass,
but this time the church was packed tightly, standing room only.
Hundreds of campesinos were present—the only ones I didn't see
were the "Evangelicals" (mostly Jehovah's Witnesses and Pente-
costals). This is the first time I had seen Talea's church segregated
by sex, with men on the right side and women on the left. After
the priest's homily, campesinos lined up to offer their gifts to San
Isidro Labrador. I was struck by the elegant simplicity of their
offerings: colorful plastic bags—fuchsia, lime green, lavender,
yellow, purple, turquoise—all containing either maize or beans
grown on Talea's farms. I was impressed by the sheer number of
campesinos, which I almost never saw as a unified group because
they were scattered in the fields six days a week. That afternoon,
shortly after lunch, we played cantos for the procession of San
Isidro Labrador. Men hoisted up the heavy statue on their shoulders and walked counterclockwise around the church, surrounded
by devoted villagers chanting prayers in honor of the saint.

Before the fiesta began, several townspeople told me that this was their favorite celebration because, in their words, "it's for us, not the 'tourists'"—by which they meant out-of-towners, people from other pueblos or the friends of Taleans who have migrated to urban centers. A few mentioned to me that the fiesta of San Isidro Labrador is what the pueblo's major fiestas (in honor of the *Dulce Nombre de Jesús* and *San Miguel Arcángel*) were like before they became overly commercialized.

PERSON TO PERSON

Todos Santos, or All Saints' Day, is a Catholic holiday observed by people in many countries on November 1. All Souls' Day is celebrated on November 2. In Mexico these two holidays are often celebrated together as *Día de los Muertos*, Day of the Dead. Historians and anthropologists have documented and analyzed many aspects of this celebration over the years, including its syncretic Mexican form. Día de los Muertos has links to ancient Mesoamerica and its deities.[25] For example, the Aztecs offered pastries to the deceased and observed a festival in honor of the goddess of death, Mictecacihuatl. Mexican immigrants to the United States have brought the celebration with them, and today some of the largest public celebrations occur in cities like Los Angeles and San Antonio. In a strange twist befitting a globalized Mexico, the 2015 James Bond film *Spectre*, which begins with a fictional procession of skeletal figures through the streets of Mexico City, inspired officials from the country's tourism board to organize the city's first public Día de los Muertos celebration the following year. A quarter of a million people participated.[26]

Villagers typically referred to the celebration as *Todos Santos* (All Saints' Day), even though the main celebration occurs on

November 2, All Souls' Day. In preparation for the festival, all Catholic households in the village—even the most humble— cleaned and prepared the space around the family altar and arranged shelves to hold ritual foods.[27] The most important were *panes de muertos* (breads of the deceased), pastries with a human form. They had small clay faces—complete with painted eyes, nose, and mouth pressed into them. In the campesino home where I lived, members of the family propped up the pastries—that is, they stood them up on their feet—and surrounded them with an elaborate array of food offerings, most of which were sweet. These included plates of candied squash, papayas, and apricots; heavily sweetened bowls of chocolate *atole*, a maize-based drink; bowls of chocolate *mole* (a thick savory sauce made with chilies and chocolate); peanuts, walnuts, pecans, and *pepitas* (roasted pumpkin seeds); fresh seasonal fruits, especially citrus and loquats; and occasionally turkeys or chickens. Many families fastened tall stalks of fresh sugarcane at the edges of the altar as a decoration. Campesinos placed the ritual foods at the altar in late October, several days before Todos Santos. On the morning of the *matanza*, or slaughter of animals, which took place on October 31, every Catholic family sacrificed one or more chickens or turkeys for Todos Santos. After the holiday ended—that is, once the dead had feasted on these delectable foods—household members enjoyed the leftovers.

According to official Catholic doctrine, All Souls' Day is a way of helping to release deceased souls from purgatory so that they can enter heaven, but for many Mexicans, Día de los Muertos serves a different purpose. It is a means of honoring the dead, particularly relatives, by spending time with them. It is a day for communicating and coexisting with the dead, who, as it turns out, never really lose contact with the living. They are perpetually connected.

. . .

In Talea, Todos Santos culminates on the night of November 1, with the "journey of the wounded people" (*recorrido de los bhni hue'*), in which groups of men and women visit the homes of villagers to sing cantos in honor of deceased family members, and to help those that are lost, or reluctant to return to the hereafter, to find their way back. Otherwise, it is possible that those souls may disturb the living.[28] During the 1990s, eight groups of bhni hue' were organized, and each group was assigned to a different part of the village. I was invited to participate as a cantor, and, since it was my first recorrido, I was expected to attend at least one rehearsal. These were held for several evenings in late October in the sacristy of the Catholic church.

Armando, a campesino active in the church, organized the informal rehearsals. He had served as a bhni hue' for many years, and he was assisted by Luis, a young man in his early twenties who also regularly participated in church events. Those attending the rehearsal were almost all teenage boys who were participating for the first time. Armando gave us worn photocopies of five cantos—three in Spanish and two in Latin—and asked us to sing along with him. The melodies of the songs were haunting and difficult to follow, but, as we rehearsed, Armando complimented us for improving. The droning phrases, all in minor keys, did indeed sound like wails of the wounded.

On the night of November 1, the groups of bhni hue' met shortly after dinner and fanned out to their assigned neighborhoods once they had five or six cantors. Each group included a leader, a treasurer responsible for guarding cash offerings, and a person carrying a bucket of holy water and a small cross. Two young men serving as municipal police accompanied each group "to maintain order."[29] As the bhni hue' began traversing the village, other men rang the church bells every few minutes and would continue doing so throughout the night, occasionally fueled by food, coffee, and mezcal sent to them by group leaders.

As we approached the first house—a modern, two-story concrete structure with a TV satellite dish perched atop the roof—we found the head of the household waiting for us at the door. He invited us to enter. As we did, I saw the members of the family standing around the altar, with photos of deceased relatives lined up alongside the pastries, other foods, and candles. We greeted the members of the family solemnly and then entered. As a bhni hue' placed the cross before the family altar, Armando, our group leader, sprinkled holy water and then recited a brief prayer in honor of the dead. After we sang two or three cantos—one of which was requested by the family's matriarch—Armando blessed the altar and then collected gifts offered by the man who had invited us into the house: two human-shaped pastries; two tamales; a pack of cigarettes; and coffee or a small glass of mezcal for any adult interested in imbibing. He also handed the treasurer several bank notes. At this particular house, Armando distributed the food to our group's first-time bhni hue'—"to encourage them to come back next year," he later told me. Older cantors would get their turns once we visited more houses.

Every Catholic home we visited had anticipated our arrival, and residents were waiting for us by the time we got there. Most appeared to be grateful for our interventions, and of the sixty or so families we visited that evening, a handful were still mourning the loss of someone who had died during the past year. In those instances, our incantations provoked intense emotion and sometimes tears of sorrow.

As late night slipped into early morning, our group grew from five to nearly twenty. Most of those who joined us were fathers accompanying their sons. Armando generously shared everything with the children (except mezcal and cigarettes), since the original band of bhni hue' had long since been stuffed with treats. In the meantime, the members of our group began accepting more coffee and mezcal as the morning air got colder. It took us nine hours to complete our sojourn, sometimes traversing muddy, unlit footpaths. By three in the morning, we were a relatively small group again, exhausted, almost giddy with fatigue. Several of the bhni hue' had spent the previous day working in their *milpas*, clearing away overgrowth with machetes. Between homes, in the streets of the village, we had become a tight-knit team, telling jokes and double entendres in Spanish and Zapotec to keep our spirits up through the night.

Our last stop was the home of one of our group members, a man whose wife owned a *comedor* or small restaurant. After we offered cantos and the blessing, we sat down to enjoy a meal of tamales and *chicharrones*. Our hosts offered each of us a generous cup of *mezcal añejo*, aged mezcal, before the meal, and again after. Most of us stayed up until daybreak (though two bhni hue' finally collapsed into deep sleep), discussing life and death in Talea, migration to the United States, the state of national politics, and many other things. Shortly after dawn, we met the other seven groups at the town cemetery, where the village orchestra had already begun playing funeral marches. Then all the bhni hue' walked in a procession from the cemetery to the Catholic church, down Talea's main street. As the priest offered a blessing to Talea's deceased souls, the groups' treasurers deliv-

Figure 8. Talean family members spending time with deceased relatives during *Todos Santos*. Photo courtesy of Gabriela Zamorano Villarreal.

ered cash offerings to the *jefe del templo*, a villager elected by parishioners to manage parochial affairs.

Shortly afterward, families began arriving at the cemetery, carrying candles, *cempazuchitl* (or yellow marigolds), and baskets of food brought from their altars. They spent the morning cleaning the graves of their relatives, sweeping tombstones, pulling weeds, wiping dusty statuettes, repairing broken bits of corrugated tin. As they did this, many people talked aloud with the souls who were visiting Talea on these special days. After helping parents clean the graves, children were free to run around the cemetery squealing with delight, playing hide-and-seek, tag, marbles. Then mothers called their children to sit down alongside the neatly refreshed graves. There they enjoyed either breakfast or lunch—or both—in the company of their departed loved ones (see figure 8).

LONG DISTANCE CONNECTIONS

Several Taleans, including some from the banda, suggested that if I wanted to learn about authentic traditions and customs, then I should make a pilgrimage to the *Cruz Verde* or Green Cross, a sacred tree in the midst of an oak forest near the Cajonos Zapotec village of San Andrés Yaa. They spoke about it with enthusiasm and an almost magical enthrallment.

According to most accounts, the Cruz Verde first revealed itself to a campesino from San Andrés Yaa in the early 1950s. The young man, who was cutting firewood in the forest just above his village, began chopping off a dry branch from an old oak tree with his machete. He was surprised to see dark sap oozing from the cut. The campesino touched the thick crimson liquid, tasted it, and was astonished: it was blood. He looked at the trunk of the cross-shaped tree and witnessed a miraculous apparition: the face of the crucified Jesus Christ, with blood streaming down his forehead from a crown of thorns and tears in his eyes.

The young man informed his fellow villagers about what he had seen, but they did not take him seriously. In fact, he was soon expelled from San Andrés Yaa because villagers thought he was mad. But then others began to witness the apparition, and villagers began to speak of it as a miracle. After three years the campesino was invited back and the people of San Andrés decided to make a fiesta to observe the Cruz Verde in the middle of the forest each May 3. In the Catholic calendar, this is the Day of the Holy Cross. The local Catholic church eventually recognized the apparition. For years, a priest celebrated Mass in the middle of the forest under a canopy of pine and oak trees. By the 1990s, villagers had constructed a small adobe chapel at the site, and, in the early twentieth century, they built a concrete structure for celebrating Mass. The festival has grown exponentially: pilgrims from throughout northern Oaxaca now attend the fiesta—not only Zapotecs but also Mixes and Chinantecs.

In early 1997, the members of Talea's banda decided to attend the fiesta as part of a _promesa_, or promise, for success in future endeavors. As a musician I was obligated to make the pilgrimage. It took our group eight hours to hike to the Cruz Verde, and it was challenging because of the intense heat, the steep, rocky footpaths, and the absence of water along most of the trail. Part of the journey took us through _Matahombres_, literally "man-killer," a precipitous mountainside with treacherous paths and no spring water for most of the year. For many other visitors, especially those coming from the Mixe and Chinantec parts of the sierra, the pilgrimage was an even more grueling experience that involved up to three days of hiking.

As we neared the Cruz Verde, we passed a murky lagoon. Many pilgrims viewed it with as much reverence as the Cruz Verde, even though there appeared to be no Christian symbols at the site. Some pilgrims made offerings that were strikingly similar to those described in colonial-era accounts, according to which rites were performed in honor of the _bhni gui'a_ or other montane spirits. Chicken feathers and dried blood littered one end of the lagoon, and a few eggs lay at the bottom. At another end, a stone altar was covered with cigarettes, votive candles, corn cobs, bread, and tamales. Dozens of people packed the surrounding area, leaving miniature versions of their petitions at the bank of the lagoon as offerings. Those in need of a new home constructed tiny houses made of sticks, mud, and leaves; couples hoping to have healthy children left dolls; campesinos seeking an abundant harvest offered maize, while those wanting a team of work animals left two plastic bulls; merchants hoping to acquire motor vehicles left plastic trucks; and adolescents seeking spouses offered heart-shaped pendants made of tin.

The Cruz Verde was a mere three minutes' walk from the lagoon. It was adorned in a silken sash and covered with many offerings: crimson, orange, purple, and golden ears of maize, and more miniature figurines attached to tree branches. To my surprise, more than a dozen hundred-dollar bills dangled from the lowest-lying branches of the Cruz Verde. I later learned that Cajonos Zapotec villages have higher rates of migration to the United States than any other in the northern sierra, and each year many of these men and women returned to the village to give thanks to the Cruz Verde for their successful peregrinations.

Somewhere between twenty-five hundred and three thousand people made the pilgrimage in 1997. Since there was no permanent housing in the forest site at that time, most people were busy improvising crude lean-to shelters out of tree branches and plastic sheets when we arrived.[30] After presenting ourselves to the village authorities, we immediately began to do the same. The people of San Andrés Yaa were gracious hosts, as are other Rinconeros when their communities celebrate fiestas. Villagers slaughtered several oxen to feed hundreds of hungry pilgrims at a time.

Though the fiesta is nominally a Catholic event that includes Masses said by a priest, the Cruz Verde celebration bears a striking resemblance to agricultural rituals of the pre-Christian past, including the timing (during the maize planting season), the ritual site (in the forest near a lagoon), and animal and food sacrifices.[31] Several classic ethnographies of Zapotec and highland Mixe communities mention comparable rituals. In her 1936 study of Mitla, another important Zapotec site, Elsie Clews Parsons wrote: "On New Year's Day the people of San Dionisio [a settlement not far from Mitla] ascend the Cerro de la Cruz, which is south of the town, to take flowers, candles, and copal to a tree which is in the form of a cross.... It is a miraculous spot." A few years later, Julio de la Fuente observed that in the Cajonos Zapotec village of Yalalag, very near the site of San Andrés Yaa's Cruz Verde, "the trees that deserve reverence are the live crosses [*cruzes vivas*] whose power is somewhat similar to that of the Holy Crosses."[32]

More than a hundred Taleans went to the Cruz Verde in 1997, and even more visit it today—campesinos, merchants, professionals, and students. What does it mean to those who make the journey? As I spoke with people at the site, and as I have spoken with others who have gone, it occurred to me that many experience the place as a kind of utopia. Pilgrims said things such as, "We are all equal here—there are no rich or poor at the Cross," perhaps expressing a longing for an egalitarian world in which there are no rich pueblos and poor pueblos, no immigrants and nonimmigrants, no Zapotec or Chinantec or Mixe, but simply equals. In this enchanted place, everyone slept next to each other in the forest with minimal shelter. Everyone ate the same kind of food in the same communal kitchen; everyone bathed in cold water coming from the same two mountain springs; and (nearly) everyone made the pilgrimage on foot during the sweltering days of early May, the driest time of the year. After the main day of the fiesta, many pilgrims described a palpable sense of transformation, a sense of heightened awareness and admiration of the trees, mountains, springs, and rivers that we had encountered among the way.[33] My companions knew that by traveling the long distance together, we had established a mutual connection that would not easily be weakened over time or space.

. . . .

This is a good point to step back for a moment to consider some implications of Talea's supernatural entities and practices. From one perspective, the fiestas and observances described above might be viewed as attempts to connect with a variety of natural and supernatural beings. For instance, in the May celebration honoring San Isidro Labrador, participants contacted a mighty saint, who, if not treated with respect and proper gratitude, could ruin a harvest or inflict other punishments. The fiesta also put participants into close contact and even communion with other villagers, people with whom they might not interact on a regular basis—those from the other side of town, or from other social classes (see figure 9). The solemn festival of Todos Santos introduces a different kind of communion: sharing food, drink, and time with deceased relatives who have crossed the thin line between this world and the next, but are never far away from the living.

Intervillage celebrations like the pilgrimage to Cruz Verde put participants in proximity to supernatural beings that were tightly connected to ancient deities. Despite the Catholic symbolism associated with the Holy Cross, there are linkages with Zapotec rituals that were practiced before the Spanish Conquest at sacred forest sites. The Cruz Verde also connected people from three different ethnolinguistic groups: Zapotec, Mixes, and Chinantecs. This celebration is at once the newest fiesta, because it began in the 1950s, and the oldest fiesta, since it has

Figure 9. Scene from a village fiesta, with large puppets (*marmotas*) dancing in front of the municipal palace. Photo courtesy of Charly Vásquez Chon.

clear pre-Hispanic elements. Pilgrims created a kind of week-long utopia in which they set aside differences based on social class, ethnicity, or village identity and held a communal celebration in the middle of the forest. This is consistent with a broader historical pattern among indigenous peoples in the Americas in which social distinctions have been negotiated and reformulated by means of panethnic regional utopias.[34]

These revolutionary aspects of the Cruz Verde might be interpreted as a kind of "counterpower [that] often defines itself against certain aspects of dominance that are seen as particularly obnoxious and can become an attempt to eliminate them from social relations completely."[35] Since many Taleans value on consensus and harmony—or at least the *appearance* of consensus and harmony—and energetically try to maintain such appearances, it is worth considering how their enduring connections to the supernatural may be further evidence of counterpower in the Rincón: "It's as if the endless labor of achieving consensus masks a constant inner [spectral] violence.... The invisible worlds surrounding them are literally battlegrounds."[36]

CHAPTER FOUR

Networks

How is it that two unlikely groups—a handful of indigenous villagers and a small international team of hackers and scholars—came into contact, and eventually worked together to create the world's first fully autonomous cell phone network?[1]

As mentioned earlier, Talea has a history of democratic self-government and a degree of political and economic autonomy. Many townspeople have sought to improve their connections with the outside world. Generations of villagers have expressed interest and even enthusiasm for experimenting with novel ideas and technologies, and they have demonstrated a willingness to interact with outsiders.

Given this context, it is understandable why, following a serendipitous series of events, a group of Taleans would want to begin working with a group of outsiders—activists committed to bringing about a different kind of world. The activists included a communications scholar, a lawyer, hackers, engineers, human rights advocates, NGO personnel, and others. They would probably agree with the statement made famous by the Zapatista Army of National Liberation in 1996, two years after its uprising in the neighboring state of Chiapas: "The world we want is one where many worlds fit."[2] The activists would also agree with the notion of mobile phone and internet access as a human right.

There were clearly overlapping interests between the Taleans and their newfound allies. Both groups shared a keen interest in locally based solutions, autonomous political and economic systems, and forms of reciprocal exchange—sometimes called gift economies.[3] Oaxaca's indigenous peoples have practiced such forms of autonomy and reciprocity for centuries, often out of sheer necessity. It seems likely that the hacker community found both inspiration and guidance from the cultural practices and quasi-anarchistic (extra- if not antistate) mechanisms that indigenous peoples had developed and appropriated over the course of hundreds of years.

Both groups also found common ground in terms of technological and social needs. In a sense, what occurred was a kind of reciprocity. The hackers had something that many Taleans desperately wanted: access to and technical knowledge about the hardware and software needed to improve communication using mobile phones. But it also seems likely that the Taleans had something the hackers wanted: a community that might serve as a kind of testing ground, an experimental laboratory for launching the world's first noncorporate open source autonomous cell phone network.

METROPOLIS

When I arrived in Talea for the first time, I noticed that many residents proudly described the pueblo as a small city. Such comments puzzled me, because on the surface the village appeared to be a textbook example of what anthropologists once called the "closed corporate peasant community"—a more or less insulated rural grouping that discourages its members from participating in larger social worlds.[4]

But despite Talea's geographic remoteness, it was not a closed community by any stretch of the imagination. The pueblo had many trappings of urban life and has long enjoyed many amenities: an auto repair shop, a bakery, a credit union, a public health clinic and pharmacy, a modest hotel, more than two dozen private phone lines, and several misceláneas. During the time that I resided in the pueblo, Taleans also enjoyed the services of a private physician and a host of other specialists including a blacksmith, two coffee roasters, three butchers, tailors and seamstresses, a shoe salesman, a *curandera* or folk healer, several midwives, a welder specializing in the fabrication of TV satellite dishes, and a lumberjack who, with the help of an assistant, could expertly transform a fallen pine tree into neatly hewn lumber within a matter of hours using little more than a bright orange Husqvarna chainsaw. As mentioned earlier, Talea had an even more diversified economy during the early to mid-twentieth century thanks to a booming silver mine in the nearby community of Santa Gertrudis. During this period, the pueblo's entrepreneurs distinguished themselves throughout the region as manufacturers of high-quality products who supplied miners with an astonishing range of items (see chapter 2).[5]

For more than a century and possibly longer, many Taleans have prided themselves on being urbane trendsetters, a sophisticated, self-confident people who are ahead of their time (see figure 10). But they have also been pragmatists seeking to get things done—and to get things made—no matter how difficult the

Figure 10. Talean men conversing at a social event. Photo courtesy of Teresa García Bautista.

process might be. During the twentieth century, anthropologists sometimes described peasant societies as culturally conservative and slow to adopt new technologies, but Talea does not conform to this stereotype. The villagers' can-do philosophy has a long pedigree: their ancestors built Zapotec civilizations in the Oaxaca Valley centuries before the Spanish Conquest.[6]

. . .

For many years, Taleans have sought to improve transportation and communication to and from the village for both economic and social reasons. As noted in the previous chapter, part of this has to do with the fact that for about a century, the pueblo has been a regional market hub and merchants have sought ways to ship goods—particularly coffee—to and from the community cheaply and reliably. More recently, migration has also played a role. Many, if not most, villagers have close relatives who have migrated to Mexico City, Tijuana, Los Angeles, and other cities across North America including New York, Atlanta, Seattle, and Madison, Wisconsin. Affordable communication is crucial for those who wish to maintain family ties and cultural continuity over space and time.

I witnessed firsthand the stresses and strains that can afflict families divided by distance. One November evening, after I helped other members of the town's philharmonic band prepare for its annual fiesta in honor of Santa Cecilia, the patron saint of musicians, a trumpet player named Anselmo invited me to have a shot of mezcal. Anselmo was a few years older than I and we had become friends, in part because I too was a trumpeter but also because he had lived and worked in Los Angeles for several years as a young man. He enjoyed talking about his adventures in *el norte.*

As others began leaving the long adobe structure that served as our rehearsal hall, club house, and meeting room, Anselmo became melancholy. Then he recounted a traumatic experience that had happened to him earlier in the year.

He poured another round of mezcal and then quickly gulped down the burning liquid, wincing as it went down. In a gloomy voice, he told me how, earlier that year, he returned from a five-year stint working in the United States, only to find that his six-year-old son had become estranged. "You're not my father—I don't have a father," the boy told Anselmo.

By this point, Anselmo had tears rolling down his deeply tanned face. He confessed to me that he probably hadn't called his wife and two children often enough, and that he had learned his lesson. He vowed to never leave Talea again.

Fortunately, he was eventually able to repair the relationship with his son and daughter (who was older but also became alienated from him during his absence), but Anselmo's story made me keenly aware of the emotional scars that can afflict families in which parents are separated from their children, with limited connection.

．　　．　　．

Earlier, I described how villagers have supported or undertaken many projects to improve communication and contact between the village and the outside world. For example, in the 1950s, Taleans provided much of the labor for a road completed with support from the Papaloapan Commission.[7] They used *tequio*, a centuries-old form of obligatory communal work, to clear the forest for the engineers.[8] To this day, older villagers speak about the event as an accomplishment of mythic proportions. Taleans initiated daily bus service to and from Oaxaca City in the 1980s, and they welcomed the introduction of telephones in early 1994.[9] Although relatively few households were able to afford phone service, an entrepreneurial villager opened a store with several phones available for public use. By the early 2000s, the same store provided internet access using modems and telephone lines.

Many of these changes came about through formal and informal petitioning, in which the village's elected officials traveled to the state capital and presented proposals and requests for services, either from state or national government agents or from private companies. It's a process familiar to indigenous communities throughout Oaxaca and indeed much of the country. Elected officials' requests are often denied—and, in some cases, ignored. More often than not, villagers have been creative problem-solvers because they cannot consistently rely on governmental support.

When government officials have failed to help Taleans, villagers have forged strategic connections with outsiders who possess the technical, political, or economic means to help them bring about changes. Writing more than a half-century ago, cultural anthropologist Laura Nader noted, "Taleans desire modern facilities, whatever they may be ... and many Taleans value, per se, social intercourse with non-Rinconeros."[10] Villagers' attempts at creating a cell phone network are a prime example of this long-standing pattern of collaboration. But before exploring how the network came into being, let us consider the rise of Talea's community radio station.

FROM RADIOS TO CELL PHONES

For more than twenty years, a dedicated group of Oaxacans has led a vibrant media movement. They have promoted efforts to create radio stations and other forms of media featuring indigenous language and cultural programming. An early phase occurred in the late 1980s and 1990s when the federal government's National Indigenous Institute (known as INI) established approximately twenty publicly funded stations such as XEGLO, based in the village of Guelatao. XEGLO can be heard throughout the northern sierra of Oaxaca, including Talea.[11] During the time that I lived in there, I spent a great deal of time listening to the station in the small farmhouses that dotted the fields. During meals, campesinos often tuned in to XEGLO on transistor radios. They enjoyed the station because it broadcast local news in the Zapotec language, and because its musical programming consisted largely of regional *sones* and *jarabes* recorded by some of the finest brass bands in the region.

More recently, many indigenous villages in Oaxaca have launched independent *radios comunitarias*, or community radio stations, sometimes without formal approval from the federal

Secretariat of Communications and Transportation. This movement included several radio stations in northern Oaxaca such as Estereo Comunal in the Sierra Zapotec village of Guelatao and others in the Mixe region east of the Rincón. It grew even more following the massive statewide popular uprising which swept Oaxaca in May and June of 2006 (see chapter 1).[12] The Popular Assembly of the Peoples of Oaxaca, or APPO, began as a militant teachers' protest but soon drew in indigenous peoples' organizations, environmental groups, labor activists, and other civil society organizations, as noted earlier.[13]

In the midst of this political ferment, an outspoken young Talean woman played a leading role in launching Radio Comunitaria Dizha Kieru (the Zapotec term for "our words"), a community radio station. The station was founded in 2007 by Kendra Rodríguez and her husband Abrám Fernández.* Rodríguez is a vivacious and articulate woman, now in her midthirties who exudes self-confidence. Fernández, a powerfully built man who is about the same age as his wife, is the son of a prominent merchant. He is every bit as articulate as Kendra Rodríguez, though he chooses his words carefully and speaks deliberately.

Both Rodríguez and Fernández are extraordinarily media savvy and active on social media. In fact, shortly after they created the radio station, Rodríguez established a Facebook page to promote it. Dizha Kieru included programming that emphasized local concerns and topics, with radio programs such as *La Voz Comunitaria* (Community Voice) and *De Mujer a Mujer* (Woman to Woman). During the early years of the community radio station, Rodríguez created strong relationships with people outside

---

*These names are pseudonyms, as are the names of all living Taleans mentioned in this book.

the region, particularly women associated with the non-profit Palabra Radio, an organization whose members are involved in promoting community radio throughout Oaxaca.[14] These connections later played an instrumental role in the development of the pueblo's community cell phone network.

. . .

In the early 2000s, a small but significant number of Taleans began purchasing cell phones because they traveled frequently to Oaxaca City, Mexico City or other parts of the country to visit relatives or to conduct business. Many of these people were merchants, though some were *campesinos* whose children attended high school outside of the pueblo. These villagers eventually began petitioning Telcel, Mexico's largest wireless operator, for cellular service and became increasingly frustrated by the company's refusal to consider their requests. In 2009 and 2010, the pueblo's municipal authorities submitted formal requests for cellular service to the company.

In response, representatives from Telcel told them that it was too expensive to build a mobile network in such a geographically remote region—this, in spite of the fact that Telcel's parent company, América Móvil, is Mexico's wealthiest corporation, currently valued at more than $71 billion. The board of directors is dominated by members of the Slim Domit family, whose patriarch Carlos Slim Halú is among the world's wealthiest men. Although the Secretariat of Communications and Transportation is obligated to guarantee universal service in rural areas, Mexico's federal telecommunications laws did not require commercial wireless operators to provide cellular service to rural communities.[15]

According to Eugenio Gamboa, who served as Talea's municipal secretary during that time, Telcel responded with a series of requirements, such as guaranteeing ten thousand users—an impossible task given the region's relatively sparse population. In a last-ditch effort, the pueblo's authorities commissioned engineers to find a location on a remote mountaintop where an antenna might hypothetically reach fourteen communities—only to realize that it would require a huge investment. "It turns out that from here to that point there is no road, so we would have had to clear a path through the forest, which would be very expensive," said Gamboa. "We would also have had to provide electricity and that too would cost a great deal of money. We're talking about three to four million pesos [approximately US$250,000–$300,000 dollars] just to prepare the area around the antenna."[16] Gamboa and other elected members of Talea's cabildo, including the pueblo's municipal president, would eventually become staunch proponents of the autonomous community-based network.

．　．　．

Then, in late November 2011, the stars unexpectedly aligned. An opportunity appeared when Talea hosted a three-day conference for people involved in producing, supporting, and broadcasting indigenous media. The conference organizers, affiliated with an international NGO, were particularly interested in providing an opportunity for exchanging knowledge about community-based media. The conference abstract, still available on the internet, is written in the lofty and abstract language that is sometimes used by NGOs to appease funding agencies. It emphasizes the need for indigenous communities to be allowed to develop their "own sustainable media" without "compromising or limiting indigenous communication.... It is important to recognize and support this dynamic of independence between the media and indigenous communication, since it is the communities themselves that define their paths and their development."[17]

Kendra Rodríguez and Abrám Fernández of Talea's community radio station were among those who attended the conference. Also present were two men who would eventually play a crucial role in helping the pueblo establish its cell phone network: Peter Bloom, a US-born rural development specialist, and Erick Huerta, a Mexican lawyer with vast knowledge of the country's telecommunications policies.[18] Although they had never met, the pair shared a common passion: finding a way to provide low-cost cellular phone service to rural communities.

HACKING THE AIRWAVES

Bloom, who is now in his midthirties, received his undergraduate degree in urban studies from the University of Pennsylvania. In 2002, he founded a nonprofit organization called Juntos, which serves immigrants in the Philadelphia area providing them with information about their legal rights and advocating on their behalf. He directed Juntos for seven years, and then began working as a consultant for several NGOs including Amnesty International, the Movement for the Survival of the Ogoni People, and the Stakeholder Democracy Network (the latter two of which are based in Nigeria).

According to Bloom, working in Nigeria inspired him to focus on increasing rural communities' access to cellular phone networks. As he and others began encouraging rural Nigerians to use cell phones to document human rights and environmental abuses, they had to face a difficult question: "Now what should we do with what we have recorded?" In Bloom's words, "It wasn't possible to use existing networks because of security concerns and lack of finances, so we began to experiment with software that would enable communication between phones without relying upon any commercial companies."[19]

When Bloom moved to Mexico to pursue a master's degree in rural development at the Universidad Autónoma de México-Xochimilco, he brought with him the dream of creating an autonomous cell phone network in indigenous regions. Bloom, who wears an industrial piercing on his left ear and speaks excellent Spanish, bears a passing resemblance to Cantinflas—a spectacularly popular and beloved twentieth-century comic film actor who brilliantly and sympathetically portrayed campesino farmers, members of the urban underclass, and other roles representing Mexico's downtrodden poor.

Erick Huerta is a lawyer, but he also holds a doctoral degree in rural development from a Mexican university and a master's degree in social administration from an Australian university. He was an unlikely counterpart to Bloom. Huerta, a slender, clean-shaven man, had more than a decade of experience working with the international government bodies like the United Nations International Telecommunication Union and the Inter-American Telecommunication Commission, an entity of the Organization of American States. He looks equally comfortable in a business suit and a hoodie, and he has the calm, patient, and thoughtful demeanor of a law professor. Huerta and Bloom formed a close bond and agreed to work together under the auspices of Rhizomatica, a nonprofit founded by Bloom in 2010 for the purpose of expanding cell phone service in indigenous areas around the world.

Rhizomatica takes its name from the conceptual idea of the *rhizome* developed by French philosophers Gilles Deleuze and Félix Guattari during the 1970s. In fact, Erick Huerta explicitly cited their work as an inspirational model: "the [cell phone] system does not have a centralized structure. Each part is totally independent and can function on its own, although they rely upon collaborative ties that allow it to operate better. Like the rhizome, each element is a root unto itself from which distinct organizations can sprout."[20]

By his own account, Bloom told Huerta that he had no idea if an autonomous cell phone network would violate federal statutes: "we didn't know if what we were doing was legal, or if it was illegal, for how long we would be imprisoned."[21] Huerta responded that what they were proposing was "not quite illegal, but not quite legal," and he offered to help move things forward on the legislative front.

Even before the Talea conference, Bloom was investigating the idea of building an autonomous cell phone network in Oaxaca. He had been in contact with members of Palabra Radio (see p. 93), an alliance of engineers, technicians, members of NGOs focused on sustainable development, and elected officials from dozens of rural communities. Palabra Radio, which in the past has been supported by the US-based Prometheus Radio Project, connected Bloom with others who had specialized expertise that might be used to link Oaxacan pueblos to mobile networks.

In early 2011, Bloom began exchanging ideas with Kino, a hacker with experience in helping indigenous communities create solutions for evading state controls. Kino agreed to begin exploring methods for building the pueblo's autonomous cell phone network. He mentioned the village's cell phone initiative to a friend, Minerva Cuevas, a Mexican artist known for her politically charged artistic interventions.

Cuevas was intrigued by the idea of a noncommercial, locally based network. Many of her artistic works could be described as anticorporate "culture jamming," and her creations sometimes go far beyond satire. Among her best-known works was a project in which she replaced the original bar codes for items in supermarkets with bar codes for cheaper products. Cuevas supported Kino and Bloom by creating an exhibit (which premiered in Finland) including a $3,000 transmitter that could potentially be used for the network. After the exhibit ended, she donated the transmitter to Rhizomatica. It was later used for preliminary tests of the pueblo's cell phone system.[22]

. . .

By 2012, Kino and a ragtag team of hackers began to overcome a series of tough technical barriers. After researching the problem, they decided to use equipment designed by Range Networks, a San Francisco start-up founded in 2011 with funds from Gray Ghost Ventures and Omidyar Network, a self-described philanthropic investment firm. Range's cofounders, David Burgess and Harvind Samra, had developed an open-source cell phone network program called OpenBTS a few years earlier. (BTS stands for base transceiver station). The free software allows cell phones to communicate with each other if they are within range of a base station or transceiver. It also allows networked cell phones to connect globally over the internet using a method called VoIP, or Voice over Internet Protocol.

From the beginning, Burgess was clear about the company's objectives: "Our goal is to drive the cost of the service down low enough and operate a profitable business to provide low-cost service to literally billions of people, because they're out there and they can't afford the current system," he said. "There are very few people in the world who would refuse telephone service by choice. But there are lots who can't afford it."[23] Range

Networks appeared to be the ideal partner to help advance the freedom to connect.

Burgess and his team successfully field-tested the OpenBTS software at Burning Man and then on Niue, a tiny Polynesian island nation with sixteen hundred inhabitants. Soon afterwards, the Rhizomatica team began discussing in more detail the idea of adapting the Range Network system for use in Talea. Since OpenBTS requires little more than electrical power and an internet connection to enable cell phones to link to the network, it was a prime location. For well over a decade the village had enjoyed reliable electrical service, and it had established internet connections in the early 2000s. Bloom maintained contact with Kendra Rodríguez and Abrám Fernández throughout the year, and they were enthusiastic about Rhizomatica's plan.

According to Bloom, by late 2012 Kino recruited two Italian hacker friends, Ciaby and Tele, to help with the project. They created customized software programs called RAI (Rhizomatica Administration Interface) and RCCN (Rhizomatica Community Cellular Network) that essentially served as a bridge linking the Range Networks system to Talean users—and, eventually, to users in other Oaxacan villages creating similar networks.[24]

In the meantime, Erick Huerta pulled off a coup on the policy front: he convinced government regulators that indigenous communities had a legal right to build such networks. The regulators appeared to be unaware of the fact that although the government had granted the large telecommunications companies access to nearly the entire radiofrequency spectrum, a small portion remained unoccupied. Bloom and his team decided to use this slice of the airwaves for their unprecedented project. They would become digital squatters.

HUMAN NETWORKS

As these technical and legal developments were underway, Kendra Rodríguez and Abrám Fernández were hard at work informing Taleans about the opportunity that lay before them. Rodríguez used the *radio comunitaria*—and its Facebook page—as a means of piquing interest in the possibility of a community-based cellular phone network among her fellow villagers. Fernández, whose father had served as Talea's municipal president several years earlier, was able to complement these efforts by organizing community forums and town hall meetings or *asambleas* in which citizens could discuss the network.

Talea's town hall meetings—and the pueblo's political structure—have much in common with those of other Oaxacan indigenous communities. All male citizens between the ages of eighteen and seventy are required to attend, and municipal authorities fine them if they are absent. During these meetings, all are free to make comments and voice their opinions about political issues or problems facing the community. The asambleas, which occur on Sundays every four to eight weeks, can last up to ten hours. The village's cabildo, a democratically elected council, presides over these gatherings.

Although women have not historically attended Talea's town hall meetings, they have recently been allowed to participate in them. They have always been important political brokers behind the scenes. In practice, men's comments and opinions are greatly informed by the women in their lives—wives, mothers, daughters, confidants, *queridas*. Women generally have a greater presence in the pueblo from day to day and therefore greater knowledge about events that occur there, since most men are busy farming in the fields during the week. Despite many changes that have affected

Figure 11. Rhizomatica's coordinator speaks to Talean villagers about cell phone networks. Photo courtesy of Israel Hernández García.

asambleas over the years—including the intrusion of political parties—the town hall meetings have remained remarkably democratic and durable. Over the past decade—and under pressure from state and federal authorities—various Talean women have been elected to serve in the recently created position of *regidora de equidad y género*, literally "councillor for equity and gender."[25]

Apart from presenting their ideas at Talea's asambleas, Rodríguez and Fernández coordinated several informational meetings open to the general public, which were held in the corridor of the municipal palace. The majority of people attending those meetings were women. Peter Bloom participated in some of the gatherings, and before long a critical mass of villagers began supporting the ambitious project proposed by the team (see figure 11).

Things reached a climax in early 2013. At that time, Taleans held a town hall meeting in which citizens voted to invest

400,000 pesos (approximately US$30,000) of municipal funds in the equipment required to build the cell phone network. By doing so, they also agreed to assume a majority stake in the venture. Talea had undertaken a comparably large commitment in the early 2000s, when villagers created a community-owned bus line to provide daily bus service to and from Oaxaca City. In the weeks that followed, villagers provided labor for the cell phone system based on a version of the *tequio* system described earlier (see p. 90).

Still, Bloom and Huerta took no chances. By this point they had been working closely with Rodríguez and Fernández, who began securing political support from elected officials in other indigenous villages.

While this may seem like a simple undertaking, it was in fact a complicated affair. Travelling from one part of Oaxaca to another can be challenging because of the state's rugged topography. Mudslides frequently block mountain roads for hours or even days during the rainy summer months. Journeying to a village that is fifteen miles away on the map might take ten hours or more by car, since communities are linked by circuitous roads that often have hairpin turns and vertiginous drop-offs.

Another challenge made it difficult for the couple to obtain support from other communities: cultural differences and historical facts. Although the people of the Rincón and the adjacent Sierra region are predominantly Zapotec, there are significant local distinctions that differentiate people from one another. For example, the Spanish language is much less commonly used in some mountain Zapotec communities than in others, and there is a rich range of local inflections and accents. Furthermore, there are many points of divergence between Nexitzo, Cajonos, Bijanos, and Serrano Zapotec dialects.

In other parts of northern Oaxaca, people speak a range of completely unrelated languages, including Mixtec, Mixe, and Chinantec. Profound cultural, economic, and political differences separate the mountain Zapotec and these ethnic groups. For instance, on a visit to Tlahuitoltepec Mixe (a pueblo that later joined the cell phone network), I learned that nearly all families depend on subsistence farming, rather than cash cropping or commerce. In general, Mixe villagers appeared to be much more reluctant than Rinconeros to talk to outsiders. Many Mixe people—also known as the Ayuuk—proudly refer to themselves as *los jamás conquistados* (literally, "the never conquered") because they successfully resisted Spanish, Aztec, and Zapotec conquerors centuries ago.

Finally, each municipality carries its own historical weight, some of which makes it difficult for intervillage dialogue to occur. Nearly all the settlements in the Rincón existed prior to the arrival of the Spanish conquistadores in the 1520s. Consequently, the region's pueblos are sometimes burdened by the legacy of conflicts, typically over access to land, that stretch back for many generations.

I learned this firsthand in 1994, shortly after arriving in Talea for the first time. Three years earlier, a long-standing dispute with San Juan Tabaa over municipal boundaries erupted in violence. Six Taleans were killed in the melee. Such events are not uncommon in the region and in Oaxaca more generally: As recently as December 2017, for example, villagers from the neighboring towns of San Miguel Cajonos and San Pedro Cajonos (both of which now belong to a cellular phone cooperative coordinated by Rhizomatica) clashed over a land dispute, and two people were killed. The communities lie less than ten miles from Talea.[26]

Despite these realities, Rodríguez and Fernández received an overwhelmingly positive response from elected officials throughout indigenous regions of northern Oaxaca. On June 18, 2012, representatives from thirty pueblos in the Rincón and Sierra regions met in Talea's municipal palace. They each signed a letter informing the federal Secretariat of Communications and Transportation of their plan to construct an autonomous cell phone network, and then stamped the letter with the official seals of their respective communities.[27] Such intercommunity statements are not unprecedented or uncommon—they tend to occur in situations where regional alliances can mutually benefit several pueblos simultaneously. Nonetheless, the document is a testament to the young Taleans' skillful organization of an extended human network supporting mobile access.

Rodríguez and Fernández played a crucial role in bringing to life the pueblo's cellular phone network by serving as cultural emissaries or intermediaries who were able to negotiate the relationships and interests of many groups. As cultural brokers, they were able to bridge the gaps between people of different cultural and social backgrounds.[28] Although the married couple had deep roots in Talea, they had also spent a considerable amount of time living as students (and as visitors) in the state capital, a teeming cosmopolitan city of more than half a million people. Their formal education and experience gave them the ability to work productively with Talea's citizens, members of other indigenous communities, and the team led by Peter Bloom.

POWERING UP

At long last, the community cell phone network was ready for a trial run in March 2013. Volunteers had placed an antenna near the center of town, in a location that they hoped would provide sufficient coverage for most of the mountainside pueblo. On the day of the test, the team worked quietly, perhaps hoping to avoid embarrassment or criticism if the network didn't work as planned.

As they booted up the system, the team looked for the familiar signal bars on their cell phone screens, hoping that they would indicate good reception strength.

Success! Members of the group were thrilled, but they were just beginning their work. The next task was to walk through town in order to detect areas with poor reception.

Something seemed strange as they strolled up and down the streets that day. They heard laughter and shouting from several houses. A few people emerged from their homes into the streets, holding cell phones in their hands.

"We've got service!" exclaimed a woman in disbelief.

"What?" asked another.

"It's true, I just called Oaxaca City!" cried a neighbor.

"I just connected to my son in Guadalajara!" shouted another.

Although Kendra Rodríguez, Abrám Fernández, and Peter Bloom knew that many Taleans had acquired cell phones over the years, none of them had any idea about the extent to which they used their devices every day, for listening to music and taking photos and videos. Back at the base station, the network computer registered more than four hundred cell phones within reach of the antenna. Several people were already making calls, and the number seemed to be increasing by the minute, as word spread quickly throughout town. The team was forced to shut down the system shortly afterwards, to avoid overloading it.

As could be expected with any experimental technological system, there were glitches in the early weeks and months. Some houses in the village are located in a neighborhood called *Colonia Virgen de los Pobres*. It is nestled behind a hillside, far from the town center where the Rhizomatica team and its Talean counterparts installed the main antenna. These houses sometimes received poor reception. At times, inclement weather affected service as did occasional problems with internet connectivity.

Over the next six months, Bloom and members of his technical team returned to Talea every week, making the four-hour trip from Oaxaca City in a red Volkswagen Beetle. In September 2013 they installed a larger, more permanent antenna with the help of several volunteers. It significantly improved reception throughout the village and beyond.

The community mobile phone network proved to be immensely popular: more than seven hundred people subscribed to the network within months (see figure 12). By the end of the year, subscription fees had been established at forty pesos (approximately three US dollars) per member. Of that amount, twenty-five pesos was directed to the village treasury—or, more precisely, the Community Cell Phone Committee—and fifteen pesos went to the larger cooperative for network maintenance.

The phone service was remarkably inexpensive: local calls and text messages cost nothing and calls to the US were only 1.5 cents (US) per minute, approximately one-tenth of what it costs using land lines. A fascinating feature, launched in May 2013, allowed villagers to call relatives in Mexico City, Los Angeles, and Seattle for free. This was possible because local numbers in these metroplexes were created as terminal nodes in the network. Phone service was astonishingly cheaper than what existed before. A five-minute call to the United States from the public phone kiosk, connected to landlines, might cost a campesino farmer the equivalent of a day's wages.

Figure 12. Talean children on their cell phones. Photo courtesy of Teresa García Bautista.

The network became so popular that it quickly reached its limits as lines became saturated. The system could handle no more than eleven phone conversations at a time. The village assembly voted to impose a five-minute limit on calls to avoid systemic overloads.

Yet even with these controls, many villagers viewed Talea GSM as a resounding success. And patterns of everyday life began to change, practically overnight: Campesinos who had to walk two hours to get to their maize fields could conveniently phone family members if they needed provisions delivered to them. Elderly women collecting bundles of firewood in the forests above the village now had a way to call for help in case of injury. Youngsters now had the means of sending messages to one another without being monitored by their parents, teachers, or even their peers. And the pueblo's newest company—a privately owned fleet of three-wheeled *mototaxis*—increased its business dramatically as prospective passengers used their phones to summon drivers quickly and conveniently.

Soon other villages in the region followed Talea's lead—first in the Rincón; then in other Zapotec-speaking regions of northern Oaxaca; and later to adjacent regions where Mixe and Mixtec languages are spoken. By the end of 2015, nearly twenty villages had obtained service with the help of Rhizomatica, including many of those that had signed the 2013 letter. They formed a new cooperative non-profit, Telecomunicaciones Indígenas Comunitarias (TIC), in October 2015.

. . .

Talea became a media sensation in the months following the successful launching of its community cell phone network. Journalists from around the world flocked to the village during the summer and fall of 2013. Dozens of international news organizations published sympathetic reports, typically feel-good accounts that portrayed the pueblo as a quaint, unified community that had successfully beaten back a greedy, callous telecommunications giant.

However, the cell phone network ushered in a new and, in some ways, tumultuous era. By rapidly adopting cell phones, hundreds of Taleans would transform local patterns of communication and interaction, sometimes in surprising ways. For example, an image of the pueblo—a virtual village—began to take shape online, as villagers and Talean emigrants began to create Facebook accounts, post YouTube videos, and write blogs about different aspects of life there. Although many of the changes made life more interesting, easier, safer, and more convenient for many people, they also opened a Pandora's box of concerns about privacy and security in a community where reputation matters. As if this were not enough, some began asking questions about management and maintenance of the community network. Who could be trusted with overseeing this critical innovation upon which villagers had quickly come to depend? What forms of oversight would be needed to safeguard such an important part of the pueblo's nascent digital infrastructure? These were difficult questions, but for the moment, Taleans were basking in the glow of their glorious technological achievement.

CHAPTER FIVE

Backlash

The morning of May 12, 2014 began like any other Monday in Talea—energetically. By daybreak, dozens of merchants had arrived to display their wares at the weekly market. In the chilly morning air, a few could be seen descending upon the mountain village by foot alongside cargo-laden mules. But most merchants rode in on the beds of clattering pickup trucks, huddled with dark *rebozos* or wool *zarapes* clasped tightly against their bodies.

The open-air market, which in Mexico is called a *tianguis*, had once been a much busier place. In the mid-twentieth century, the marketplace roared with activity and people literally rubbed shoulders throughout the central plaza and adjoining streets. The number of visitors who come to buy and sell things has diminished over the years, in part because it is easier than ever to travel to Oaxaca City's gargantuan market.[1] Even so, Mondays are still an extraordinary time in the pueblo. The variety of merchandise at the market is astonishing: Here one can buy local and imported produce, fresh meat, live farm animals, eyeglasses, handmade huaraches, electrical appliances, machetes and other steel tools, knockoff Nike sneakers and Levi's jeans, DVDs, electronic gadgets, and countless other items. Some come to Talea to collect money wired from relatives living in the United States, since the village has a telegraph office that receives Western Union cash transfers. Still others come to purchase medicine at the town pharmacy, repair musical instruments, or sell sacks of coffee.

As hundreds of people from neighboring villages slowly streamed into town on this bright spring morning, the central plaza came alive as Rinconeros sought to take care of business—and pleasure. By midmorning, the pueblo's *comedores* and cantinas were full; some were even overflowing. For many visitors—the vast majority of whom were from campesino families that spent long hours working in the fields or in their homes—the *tianguis* provided a welcome opportunity to socialize with others over coffee or perhaps a shot of mezcal.

• • •

Few could have predicted how things would take an unexpected turn today. As streams of marketgoers bustled frenetically through the streets, a voice blared over the speakers of the village's public address system:

> *Attention: The municipal presidency of San Miguel Talea de Castro informs you that in thirty minutes there will an informative presentation regarding a new cell phone service in the pueblo. We invite the general public to attend this event, which will take place in front of the municipal palace.*

The announcement boomed across the village again fifteen minutes later. Curious onlookers began to congregate around the perimeter of the town's basketball court, drawn by the sounds of a brass band playing festive marches in the corridor of the municipal palace. As music filled the air, two young men in white polo shirts set up inflatable "sky dancers" at the edges of a public space that was usually reserved for official ceremonies. Then they assembled tables, positioning them directly in front of the municipal palace, a stately building that for more than a century has stood as a proud symbol of village authority. The youths draped the tables with bright blue tablecloths, each imprinted with the corporate logo of Movistar, Mexico's second largest wireless provider. Six men then filed out of the municipal palace to sit behind the tables and faced the growing audience.[2]

What followed was a ceremony that was unusual, even bizarre by Rincón standards. It was part political rally, part corporate event, part advertisement—and, as we shall see, part public humiliation. Sitting at the tables were Candelario Carranza, a native-born Talean and longtime politician who had served several times in the federal Chamber of Deputies (Mexico's lower house of congress); Gustavo Monterrubio, the pueblo's municipal president; Adalberto Gómez, a current member of the state legislature representing Talea's district; and three others, apparently employees of Movistar. Carranza and Gómez were affiliated with the Institutional Revolutionary Party or PRI, which has dominated Oaxacan state politics since the 1920s. The men were flanked by two young, attractive, local women who stood awkwardly near each end of the tables, wearing tight jeans and Movistar T-shirts.

The politicians and company men had journeyed to the pueblo in order to inaugurate a new rural mobile phone program developed by Movistar, the Mexican subsidiary of Telefónica, a multinational corporation based in Madrid. Various PRI politicians—including Carranza and Gómez—had lent support and encouragement to Movistar. The initiative, called

Franquicias Rurales (literally, rural franchises), was based upon a franchise model. Movistar would rent a telecommunication tower to an investor or group of investors, and these franchisees would sell service plans to local customers in turn. Initial reports indicated that profits would be divided evenly between Movistar and the franchise owners, but it appears that, in reality, Movistar's share was 60 percent.[3]

To launch the program, they announced the installation of a telephone antenna that would soon have the capacity to provide villagers with Movistar cell phone service—years after a group of Taleans had unsuccessfully petitioned the company for precisely that. After thanking the municipal president and reciting the usual formalities, one of the politicians, Adalberto Gómez, squarely took aim at the community cell phone network. Gómez, a thirty-five-year-old with Chinantec roots, claimed that the network had operated outside the law, was fraudulent, and had depleted the pueblo's municipal assets. He provided no evidence to support his claims, but rumors had been circulating in the village about the possibility of financial mismanagement.[4] Hundreds of onlookers—many of them from neighboring villages interested in possibly developing their own community-based networks—listened intently to Gómez's remarks. Some villagers probably felt embarrassed by the claims. After all, Gómez was making them in a public forum, with many visitors present as the Monday market was drawing to a close. According to several accounts, the event later became a fiesta where Movistar sales representatives gave away cell phones, T-shirts, and other bits of swag as they enrolled villagers in the company's mobile phone plans.[5]

· · ·

The Movistar event came at a rough time for the pueblo's cell phone network. From the beginning, Talea GSM had experienced technical problems, but these shortcomings were well known to the public, and subscribers "were clearly conscious [of the problems] and understanding" about the situation.[6] In a press statement, Rhizomatica explained that Talea GSM's frequency band couldn't provide adequate service for the overwhelming demand, and therefore had requested that the Federal Telecommunications Commission grant a new experimental concession for additional bandwidth—which it eventually did. But even with these improvements, the system faced serious challenges. Since it worked using Voice-over Internet Protocol (VoIP), it relied upon a stable internet connection, which, in the case of Talea GSM, was provided by a Oaxaca-based company called Protokol. Though service was usually adequate, it sometimes crashed. In the words of Erick Huerta, "It's possible that our system doesn't have a single problem, but if the internet fails, then the call can't be made."[7]

Villagers had a seemingly insatiable demand for Talea GSM in the weeks after it went online, which further complicated things. To meet this demand, the municipal authorities acquired a higher-capacity system, which cost 380,000 pesos—approximately US$40,000. To recoup the investment, Talea GSM increased its rates to thirty pesos per month, and then, later, to forty pesos. If some villagers didn't understand the reasons behind the rate hikes, it is likely they may have begun to doubt Rodríguez and Fernández's ability to manage the network. Yet, as demand continued to grow apace, the problems continued, even with a more powerful system supplied by Canadian company Nutaq/NuRAN Wireless.[8] When too many users saturated the network, it crashed. When the electricity went

Figure 13. *Dizha Kieru* community radio, Talea GSM's headquarters. Photo courtesy of Augustine Sacha/Rhizomatica.

out, which is not uncommon in the Rincón during the stormy summer months, technicians would have to painstakingly reboot the system from the network's base of operations (see figure 13).

In early 2014, Talea GSM encountered a different threat: opposition from community leaders. By this time, it was clear that popular support for the network was waning. There was a growing perception among villagers that those in charge of maintaining the network were mismanaging the entire enterprise. It is impossible to know for sure whether there was any truth to the rumors, but people from very different political persuasions—ranging from supporters of the PRI to those backing the leftist MORENA Party—complained that Rodríguez and Fernández were less than transparent when it came to questions of financial management. Even some members of the cabildo that had supported the network in its infancy began backing away from it.

According to one account, "technical problems such as cut calls and network crashes, as well as the debt that the municipal government had assumed, became the arguments that Talea's newly elected officials used to hurt the telephone project.... They obligated the young staff from the community radio [responsible for managing Talea GSM] to repay the 380,000 pesos that had been invested."[9] The pueblo's officials would eventually use these funds to pay for the installation of Movistar's antenna.

. . . .

Adalberto Gómez's attacks and allegations were shocking, but they undoubtedly fed into the concerns of villagers who had experienced technical difficulties when using Talea GSM. It seems likely that Gómez's claims were effective, especially when combined with Movistar's aggressive marketing strategy and the persistent perception of financial mismanagement and lack of transparency. Over the next several weeks, dozens and then hundreds of villagers began pulling out of Talea GSM and subscribing to Movistar. According to one source, Talea GSM lost more than half of its members in the months following the company's arrival, even though the overall cost of a Movistar telephone was more expensive.[10] In other words, somewhere between 250 and 350 villagers chose to abandon the homegrown network within months, despite the fact that it had brought the pueblo international acclaim and wide media coverage.

The architects of Talea GSM were dismayed by the turn of events. Abrám Fernández claimed that many villagers were dazzled by Movistar: "Fifty users left us, they went with the idea of something new and corporate that they saw on TV." When asked about Adalberto Gómez, he said, "He did it for political purposes, he wants to take credit for something that someone else did. They're getting rich from the needs that exist in rural communities."[11] But some villagers were mentioning similar things about Fernández and Rodríguez—namely, that they were using Talea GSM to advance their own political careers and perhaps even to benefit financially.

Kendra Rodríguez noted a bitter irony: Rhizomatica, the NGO that had helped Talea GSM get off the ground, had proposed a partnership with Movistar just months earlier. "That's just what hurts the most," she said. "At the beginning [Peter] Bloom and Erick Huerta approached the multinational to present the proposal for coverage in rural communities, which they rejected. Then afterwards, they copied Rhizomatica's system and applied it in communities."[12]

In a similar account, Peter Bloom noted that in late 2012, Rhizomatica contacted representatives of the company with the idea of working together, so that the pueblo's network might make use of some of the company's excess bandwidth. "They were very indifferent, but it seems that they have gradually come to like our project, because from what little we know, they are copying it," he said. Then he added: "It doesn't matter whether they do it or we do it. What's important is that all the communities get connected."[13]

Though I have not found any direct evidence that Movistar's rural franchise program was inspired by the Talea GSM-Rhizomatica network, it certainly seems plausible given the timing. By February 2013, Movistar had announced *Franquicias Rurales* to the world and Latin American media covered it extensively in the following months and years. Movistar, faced with cutthroat competition in Mexico's telecom industry, was pulling out all the stops in an effort to increase its user base. At the same time, the company's rural franchise program provided favorable PR: Movistar could portray itself as a wireless provider that was truly concerned about the plight of Mexico's rural people, millions of whom had been ignored by the other two big telecom companies: América Movil and AT&T. By 2018, the firm announced plans to export the program to other Latin American countries: "Movistar Has a Plan to Close the Digital Divide," read one headline.[14]

.   .   .

Why did this corporate coup d'état succeed? What factors made it possible? And what, if anything, does it tell us about Talea, about Oaxaca—or perhaps even about ourselves? There were various elements that led to Movistar's successful campaign, including local politics, ideologies of mass consumption, and what might be described as a reactionary reflex against an autonomous community-based technological system.

At least one PRI adherent had been working behind the scenes months before the Movistar event was staged. In early February 2014, just weeks after taking office, Talea's recently elected municipal president, Gustavo Monterrubio, publicly discredited the community cell network. According to Talea GSM's supporters, he manufactured a crisis by claiming that the network had irremediable deficiencies and was practically non-functional, and declared that village funds would no longer be used to finance the system.[15] But others claimed that Rodríguez and Fernández were converting Talea GSM into their own family business, and that the presidente municipal was simply looking out for the pueblo's interests by calling them to account.

Official support for Movistar extended beyond the free use of municipal space. Hernández provided company representatives with an opportunity to pitch their proposal to citizens at a town hall meeting. According to Abrám Fernández, Movistar's salesmen promised efficient service and internet access on their cell phones—which, in the short term, they were unable to deliver. Municipal president Gustavo Monterrubio then reportedly convinced a majority of citizens to commit the equivalent of nearly US $40,000 in order to obtain a Movistar rural franchise.[16] Ironically, these funds came from the money that Talea GSM had returned to the village coffers just months earlier. Village officials also allowed Movistar to install its transmission antenna atop the municipal palace at no cost—not even for the electrical power it needed to function.

But the community network was trapped in a downward spiral. By early 2017, fewer than 10 percent of Talea GSM's original customers remained.[17] A year later, a Talean friend told me that "the community telephone [system] doesn't really function anymore." She was speaking to me from her Movistar cell phone.

. . .

It seems counterintuitive, even ironic, that Candelario Carranza and Adalberto Gómez—both indigenous Oaxacans (Zapotec and Chinantec, respectively) who should be seen as native intermediaries in their own right—would work hand in hand with a Spanish multinational corporation to undermine the pueblo's autonomous cell phone network. Some might even view this as a twenty-first-century conquest—high tech colonialism in the digital era. But their collaboration with Movistar makes more sense if we consider the fact that both Carranza and Gómez were loyal devotees of the PRI party, which, for more than twenty-five years, has strongly supported a corporate-friendly form of capitalist development—and has often opposed indigenous communities seeking greater political or economic autonomy.[18] A more sympathetic interpretation might be that they simply wanted to help remedy a complicated situation.

The two politicians may also have been reacting against a proposal offered several months earlier by a federal senator from Mexico's most powerful progressive party, the Party of the Democratic Revolution or PRD. In September 2013, just months after Talea GSM got off the ground, PRD senator Benjamín Robles formally proposed that the system serve as a model for indigenous communities throughout the country. By early 2014, work was underway to grant concessions over sufficient bandwidth to make this a reality.[19] It's possible that Carranza and Gómez, seeking to stop the momentum of the community cell network model, appealed to Movistar for help.

Since his election to the lower house of Congress, Gómez had antagonized people from other indigenous communities in Oaxaca. In 2014, just weeks after Gómez's performance in Talea, elected officials from the Chinantec town of San Miguel Maninaltepec accused him of fomenting a conflict between their village and his much larger hometown of San Juan Quiotepec. They claimed that in 2011, when Gómez was serving as Quiotepec's municipal president, he aggravated a long-standing land conflict by promising that he would grant Quiotepecanos access to a disputed section of Maninaltepec's territory. The conflict culminated in an armed confrontation between citizens of the two communities. Fortunately, only one man was injured in the standoff, but the conflict continued to simmer for months after the incident.[20] More recently, in early 2016, representatives from the Liberal Union of Municipalities of the Northern Sierra, an alliance of Sierra Zapotec villages, held a press conference in which they accused Gómez of politically destabilizing the region by manipulating asambleas to benefit his own economic interests. They also claimed that in the communities of Yotao, Lachatao, and Comaltepec, he attempted to appoint municipal authorities without respecting the wishes of the citizenry.[21]

Although it is difficult to determine the extent to which these reports are true, it seems clear that Gómez's primary allegiance is to his political party. Upon his election for a second term as a state representative in 2018, Gómez publicly emphasized his experience as a PRI operative above all else: "I've worked eighteen years working militantly in the PRI, eighteen years serving Oaxacans and countrymen from the Sierra Juárez as a PRI delegate, secretary of political operations of the PRI in Oaxaca, secretary general of the CNOP [National Confederation of Popular Organizations, an arm of the PRI] in the state capital," he said.[22]

Another PRI functionary present at the Movistar event in Talea was Candelario Carranza, who had been a mentor to Gómez for several years. Carranza, now in his late seventies, was born and raised in Talea and is fluent in Nexitzo Zapotec. He left to attend secondary school in the 1950s and has not resided in Talea since then. By all accounts Carranza is a man of humble origins, the son of a fireworks maker. Carranza was recruited by the renowned anthropologist Salomón Nahmad to work for the Secretariat of Public Education (SEP) in the early 1970s; and he later worked for the National Indigenist Institute (INI). Nahmad was a controversial figure because of his efforts to radicalize SEP and INI, both of which had functioned for many years as highly bureaucratic, even sclerotic institutions.[23] He launched a series of ambitious projects, including innovative bilingual education programs that relied largely upon the talents of indigenous researchers, including Candelario Carranza.[24]

By the 1980s, Carranza was offered several posts in the Oaxaca Department of Indigenous Education. The state government, which was almost entirely dominated by the PRI, became a launching pad for Carranza's political career. In 1991, voters elected him as a representative to the lower house of the congress for the first time, and he has since become an increasingly influential member of the PRI party in Oaxaca.[25] One columnist described him as a "grand boss [*cacique*] of the PRI" who is "repudiated in his own [political] districts.... He is rarely seen in the Sierra."[26] Over the course of his career, Carranza has been embroiled in numerous scandals ranging from simple nepotism, to accusations of electoral fraud, to a federal investigation into exotic animal trafficking.[27] More recently, Carranza was accused of illegally diverting resources during his directorship of the Colegio de Bachilleres de Oaxaca (COBAO), a prestigious and highly competitive public high school.[28] What emerges from such scenarios is a picture of a career politician who fits old stereotypes about corruption within the PRI. Despite Carranza's reputation, he is currently serving once again as a representative to the lower house of the Mexican congress.

During the 1990s, when I was conducting research in the Rincón, it seemed that everyone had an opinion about Carranza. Although there were some Taleans who seemed to hold him in high regard, many villagers described him disparagingly as a dyed-in-the-wool *priista*, or PRI party member—at a time when citizens generally viewed the PRI as a morally bankrupt one-party dictatorship. Many people in the Rincón despised Carranza because they perceived him to be a staunch opponent of Pueblos Unidos, a cooperative association of seven villages (not including Talea) formed in the late 1970s. He and other PRI officials seemed particularly upset by the cooperative's bus line, Autotransportes Pueblos Unidos, which provided daily service to and from Oaxaca City. In an open letter published by a national newspaper, more than fifty people and civil society organizations accused Carranza and other state officials of seeking to terminate the cooperative bus service to open a path for private bus lines.[29] If this is true, it would be consistent with Carranza and Gómez's support for Movistar. In both cases, PRI politicians seeking to pave the way for private companies were undermining independent indigenous cooperatives.

I met Carranza on a couple of occasions in 1996. The more substantive conversation took place over a lavish breakfast at his home in the upscale neighborhood of San Felipe del Agua, in which he made several remarkable statements that revealed much about his worldview. Carranza was clearly proud of his indigenous heritage and of his hometown's many accomplishments, and he spoke with nostalgia about his childhood. At the same time, he chided campesinos who did not seek the highest possible formal education for their children. Carranza said he thought it foolish for a campesino father to tell his son, "This is how I work, son. Watch closely; do as I do so that you can learn to work well." I was appalled by his comment, for the family that had essentially adopted me in Talea had no intention of sending its children to high school, and I thought that perfectly appropriate given their situation. But for Carranza, progress was necessarily linked to the nation-state, particularly a growth-oriented, capitalist nation-state. He showed little understanding or patience for those who had alternative visions of what Oaxacan society might look like.

At another point in our conversation, Carranza referred to Talea as having "a higher stage of social development than other villages in the region," and he described other communities as "envious." He also implied that in the sierra, there were significant and unfortunate differences between the state government (dominated by the PRI) and INI initiatives.[30]

Looking back on my meetings with Carranza, I am not surprised that he would oppose Talea GSM, even if it hadn't been riddled by accusations of mismanagement. Although the autonomous cell phone network put his hometown in a sympathetic media spotlight, it also cut directly against Carranza's ideological leanings. Many reports about Talea GSM implied that the Mexican state was failing to provide indigenous people with tools for modern telecommunication. The network also demonstrated that indigenous villagers had a continuing capacity for economic and political autonomy, even in the twenty-first century. What is more, the potential political power of an intervillage multiethnic telecom cooperative (Telecommunicaciones Indígenas Comunitarias or TIC) might well have been interpreted by Carranza as a challenge to his own legitimacy. After all, he had served on the federal Committee on Indigenous Affairs, and by 2015 had become its president.

• • •

Although it is tempting to scapegoat Carranza and Gómez for their roles in undermining Talea GSM, that would be giving them too much credit. There were other reasons, some subtle and some not so subtle, behind the pueblo's turn to Movistar. Apart from the efforts of Talea's municipal president and the ambitions of the PRI politicians, we cannot rule out an important, though insidious, factor behind Movistar's success: the cachet of a globally recognized brand. No one forced hundreds of Taleans to turn their backs on the autonomous cell network that had brought them a level of international fame. Villagers have never been passive victims—in this case, they were actively involved in Talea GSM's downfall. It is likely that Movistar's success had partly to do with factors that had been years in the making.

These processes began at least as early as 1957, with the completion of a road linking Talea to Oaxaca City. As noted earlier in this book, that road allowed people and products to move to and from the village much more quickly than before. The engineers who designed it—and some villagers—saw it as a hallmark of what industrial societies call progress. Since that time, many things that were once produced in Talea have diminished, and so have many forms of knowledge.[31] The pueblo's lands are perfectly suited for growing tropical fruits, but for decades merchants have imported these and other goods from elsewhere. During the same period, knowledge about indigenous healing practices has withered away. I was astonished to find that since the early 2000s many families have made tortillas, the most important culinary staple in Oaxaca, with cheap corn imported from the United States, disrupting a centuries-old system of locally sourced food. As a colleague and I noted several years ago in a documentary film, standardized educational techniques make the young strangers to their own roots.[32]

However, it is more than the educational system that is undermining knowledge. Since television arrived in the 1970s, two generations of villagers have been exposed to a relentless barrage of commercial advertising.[33] When the young are growing up corporate, we shouldn't be surprised that so many have been allured by Movistar. The most widely viewed television events in the pueblo (as in much of the rest of the world) are World Cup soccer matches. Even as Movistar employees were

Figure 14. Movistar's shop in Talea, which sells cell phones, data plans, selfie sticks, and other accessories. Photo courtesy of Teresa García Bautista.

signing Taleans up for service during the summer of 2014, members of the Mexican national soccer team wore training jerseys prominently featuring the telecom company's logo emblazoned on the front (see fig. 14).[34]

There was yet another factor that would drive villagers, particularly young villagers, toward Movistar: a strong desire for mobile data services such as internet and email access. Over the years many teenagers, particularly the sons and daughters of merchants, have attended high schools in Oaxaca City where they have become accustomed to the internet and all that it offers. A significant portion of them return to their hometown once they have completed their studies. An American researcher, arriving in Talea for the first time in the summer of 2014, provides a sense of just how popular virtual worlds have become there:

> We get the sense that we have emerged in a world far removed from the hustle and bustle of the capital city, its pace and rhythm of life sheltered not just by its remote location, but also by the strength of the people who have lived here for generations. Yet along with the sense of traditions long preserved in this lush mountain village, the first thing we see as we walk the main street are two internet cafes, not two blocks from each other, teeming with people of all ages, faces lit up by screens, reflecting the fleeting promises of technology, of connections to far away worlds at their fingertips.[35]

According to Israel Tonatiuh Lay, a researcher at the University of Guadalajara, since the Oaxaca community networks "don't yet have fiber optics, as of now the service offered by TIC is only for phone calls and [text] messages, which puts it at a disadvantage compared to Movistar's 'packages.'"[36] By 2015, hundreds of Taleans were active on social media, and the prospect of having access to WhatsApp and Facebook on a cell phone was enough for many to jump on corporate bandwagons, even if that meant dropping Talea GSM. Movistar's successful conquest of the pueblo was due partly to the prestige and status afforded by an international brand along with a significant technological advantage: the ability to access the internet and social media from cellular devices—the quantum leap from 2G to 3G, and then perhaps someday to 4G and beyond. But it was also undoubtedly linked to a mounting crisis of confidence in those managing the homegrown network.

There are of course different ways to interpret this historical juncture. From one perspective, villagers were making practical choices, leapfrogging into twenty-first-century virtual worlds for the sake of convenience and digital connectivity. From another perspective, the pueblo was abandoning its aspirations of local autonomy in order to embrace a raw form of consumer capitalism.

. . .

By the summer of 2014, even people who had once been staunch supporters of the community cell phone network were becoming disillusioned with the apparent lack of accountability. Talea GSM's demise becomes much more comprehensible when we take those perspectives into account.

Tomás, who took over his father's bakery in the pueblo several years ago, was an ardent supporter of the community network in its early months. He is a politically sophisticated man in his midforties who, throughout his adult life, has been an enthusiastic supporter of radical movements and left-leaning political parties, including the 1994 Zapatista uprising, the 2006 APPO (Popular Assembly of the Peoples of Oaxaca) movement, and the recent rise to power of the MORENA party. Tomás said that he was disappointed to hear that *la pareja*—"the couple" (by which he meant Kendra Rodríguez and Abrám Fernández)—had taken the entire apparatus to Oaxaca City when the citizenry began asking tough questions. Given his ideological leanings, I fully expected that Tomás would have lamented the loss of the community cell phone network, especially since PRI politicians that he loathes appear to have played a part in orchestrating its demise.

Talking about the events obviously stirred up disagreeable memories for Tomás—he expressed regret about the situation, but he expressed more rancor toward "the couple" than he did toward those from the PRI who may have helped broker the Movistar deal. Tomás suggested that Rodríguez and Fernández had used Talea to further their own personal political ambitions.

To support this claim, Tomás reminded me that Kendra ultimately entered the world of Oaxaca state politics: she ran as a candidate for the Oaxaca state congress in 2018 under the banner of *Juntos Haremos Historia* (Together We Will Make History), a coalition of left-leaning parties. Although the coalition fell apart, Tomás was still galled at the fact that Rodríguez and Fernández would (as he put it) "use" the village to promote their own careers. By contrast, he expressed great admiration for Peter Bloom, whom he described as "a truly great person." Tomás told me that he was honored to have hosted him one night in his home.

Another person with strong opinions about the situation was Guillermo, an articulate fifty-seven-year-old Talean, who, after having lived in Mexico City for a decade, decided to return to the village to raise his two young children. Guillermo had long been a politically and socially conservative person who had typically supported the PRI. He served as municipal secretary in 2013, the year the community cell phone network was launched, and he and other members of the cabildo strongly backed the initial proposal. Once the citizenry expressed willingness to support the community network, the cabildo facilitated the process.

When I asked Guillermo to describe how townspeople went from solidly supporting the initiative to near total abandonment of it, he responded bluntly: "In this case, there was a great deal of politics and even corruption." From his perspective, Abrám Fernández's father, who had served as municipal president a few years before the village launched Talea GSM, had been meddling in the network's day-to-day operations. When I asked Guillermo to compare what happened in Talea with what happened to the intervillage alliance of seven Rincón pueblos known as Pueblos Unidos (see pp. 122–123)—which collapsed in the early 2000s due to apparent corruption and mismanagement—he said: "Precisely the same thing happened in Talea. That family thought that they could fool the pueblo, but the citizens woke up and protested." Like Tomás, Guillermo had a different view of Peter Bloom. "I got to know Peter Bloom and have respect for him—I know exactly what he was trying to do, but what happened was really beyond his control," he said.

. . .

Several years after Movistar's debut in Talea, Kendra Rodríguez was still bitter. When a journalist asked why she thought Taleans had dropped the community-based network, she responded acidly: "It's because of the damn mentality [*la pinche mentalidad*] that many people have, who think that what comes from outside is better than what we have here." On another occasion she reportedly said: "Lamentably the people are accustomed to what arrives from outside, and even more if it is a big transnational corporation."[37]

Rodríguez's harsh words conjure up the idea of *malinchismo*, a concept that has a long history in Mexico and probably in New Spain before it. Throughout the country (and across other parts of Latin America), malinchismo is a pejorative term referring to a preference for foreign things—for example, people, culture, or products—and the simultaneous rejection of one's own. A *malinchista* is more than just a sellout; he or she is a self-loathing, opportunistic traitor. According to its early theorists, malinchismo is rooted in a deep inferiority complex that stretches all the way back to the Spanish Conquest.[38] The word is derived from Malinche, the indigenous woman who served as a translator for the Spanish conquistadors and became Hernán Cortez's consort.

Here I will not review these debates; nor will I explore a series of related questions: whether or not Malinche (also known as Malintzin and Doña Marina) was a traitor or a heroine; whether she helped facilitate the conquest or temper its excesses; or whether or not she has served as a convenient female scapegoat—a victim of intellectual misogyny.[39] But I will say that Rodríguez has probably never used the term malinchista, because, as someone who is working in the worlds of media and politics, fields that have been dominated by men in Mexico (as in many other countries including the United States), she has faced gender stereotypes and discrimination, and has written eloquently about these experiences.[40] Rodríguez's own career and her many accomplishments illustrate just how dramatically gender roles are changing in Talea and in many other parts of rural Oaxaca.

In any event, Taleans are certainly not malinchistas—at least not any more so than Americans who buy German or Japanese luxury cars, or, for that matter, American anthropologists with a penchant for French philosophers. In our country, we don't assume that our fellow citizens are racked with self-hatred when they express foreign preferences. But, more to the point, the pueblo has not hesitated to create its own autonomous organizations when it has needed them. Perhaps the best example of this is the municipal bus cooperative, Autotransportes SAETA (Servicio de Autotransportes Ecológicos Talea), which was launched nearly twenty years ago to provide daily service to and from Oaxaca City. Villagers created the bus line after withdrawing a concession that had been granted to the unscrupulous owner of Servicio de Fletes y Transportes (SFTSA), a private bus line that had previously provided transportation service to the pueblo. Shortly thereafter, a group of villagers pooled their resources to create a locally owned cooperative. They bought brand new buses that were safer than SFTSA's. Autotransportes SAETA has thrived ever since. The practicality of Taleans seeking a reliable, affordable, locally based service may mean that villagers will once again opt for a locally based, locally managed cell phone network.

. . .

Some have described Movistar's gambit as a shrewdly calculated move designed to crush the dream of an autonomous network. On the surface, this seems entirely plausible. It is hard to think of a better way to kill a fledgling competitor than by dumping products or services on the market at a relatively low price. In the case of an innovative community-based network, this may also have a powerful psychological effect by crushing the aspirations of those who designed it. For example, some have suggested that the corporation had ulterior motives:

> Why would a transnational telecom company compete with a community of 1500 people where the cost of cellular service is less than fifty pesos? Perhaps it has to do with blocking the proliferation of thoughts about collective autonomous interests.... The logic of TIC [cooperative] is that when a community joins, it acquires its own equipment, it administers it, and once it recuperates its investment, the community decides how to use the profits: whether to increase its coverage with a second antenna; to support community projects; to return the investment to the community coffers; or to purchase new equipment.[41]

Was this, then, Movistar's goal? To smash an incipient system of community-controlled communication, destroy a bold vision for an alternative future, and prove that villagers are incapable of managing affairs themselves? While these possible objectives may have been behind the moral and material support granted to Movistar by PRI politicians, it seems likely that the company's goals were more modest: to increase market share by extending its tentacles into a remote region of the country.

But despite the decline of Talea GSM, the idea of community-based cell networks had taken hold firmly across dozens of other communities throughout the region and beyond. The pueblo's early struggles had paved the way for significant legal and regulatory changes. Mexico's Federal Telecommunications Institute enacted reforms in July 2015, granting the country's first social concession to indigenous communities for cell phone service. Erick Huerta of Rhizomatica notes that the change was historic, "not just because it is the first time that an indigenous community has been granted a portion of the cell phone spectrum, but also because it represents a transcendental step in the larger struggle for indigenous peoples seeking to acquire, administrate, and operate their own media—a fundamental element in their processes towards autonomy."[42] The regulatory agencies would not have granted such a concession without a prolonged struggle from the TIC cooperative and the NGOs with whom it worked.

Israel Tonatiuh Lay agrees: "In spite of efforts to minimize the achievements reached by the village in the area of community-based telecommunications, we can recognize Talea as a pioneer for similar projects throughout the world. The self-sustaining and self-managed project serves as an example to the other twenty communities [forming TIC], who are replicating what has been done in Talea."[43] At this moment, TIC now includes approximately four thousand users in over seventy villages, covered by nearly twenty community-owned networks.

The decline of Talea GSM was probably impacted by several factors: extremely high demand and rapid growth; a series of thorny technical and legal obstacles; Movistar's clever marketing tactics and global prestige; the machinations of local and state politicians; villagers' preference for convenience rather than local control; and, not least of all, a perception of mismanagement and a lack of transparency related to the community network. But apart from everything else, many Taleans have long been open to people, ideas, and technologies arriving from outside their village, and have generally maintained a pragmatic attitude that has led to a kind of permissiveness and willingness to experiment with innovations that are relatively unusual in the wider region.

The same outlook that led villagers to enthusiastically embrace the dedicated team of foreign hackers that helped create Talea GSM also led the pueblo to give Movistar a chance to redeem itself after having ignored the pueblo's earlier appeals for service. You might say that villagers are ecumenical when it comes to technology. Peter Bloom thoughtfully reflected on that peculiar aspect of life in the pueblo. In an email, he noted that, "compared to other towns in the Rincón, Talea being more open to innovation actually led them to adopting the Movistar network and leaving the community network quite weakened. Basically, they opted for the corporate offering over the community one."[44]

While some might interpret Talea's eventual abandonment of the community cell phone network as evidence of a lack of commitment, I'm not convinced that villagers have a tendency to trivialize autonomy and self-governance. Their legal system, their cooperative bus line, and many of their other institutions are evidence that villagers can staunchly support local ownership and control when necessary.

At the same time, many Taleans are also very pragmatic people who value convenience and communication. As I tell undergraduate students at my university, which is located in the heart of Silicon Valley, villagers have for many years longed to be reliably and conveniently connected to each other—and to the wider world of which they've always been a part. In other words, Taleans want cell phones and internet access because they want to be like you.

CHAPTER SIX

Posts

Several months after Talea launched its community cell phone network, the British Broadcasting Corporation (BBC) posted a story, complete with a video, about it on the portion of its website devoted to news in Latin America. The video started with dramatic images of pueblo's lush cloud forests, and then the narrator's voice began: "Talea de Castro has been disconnected for decades...."[1]

I watched the video, entranced by the architecture of the village that I had gotten to know so well. But then I drew back at the sight of two boys, perhaps ten years old, standing side by side with their backs against a wall. Each held his own cell phone, tapping his fingers on its screen, fixating his eyes on the tiny glass portal. Were they sending text messages? Reviewing photographs for a school project? Playing video games? They seemed to be together, yet somehow also alone in their respective virtual worlds.[2]

Tangled thoughts filled my head at that moment: exhilaration at seeing the pueblo in the global media spotlight; a sense of awe at the villagers' stunning accomplishment; concern about the

long-term consequences of Taleans' impending entry into the
virtual world; and a profound feeling of disenchantment at
the idea of these two children passing the time in more or less
the same way as so many millions of other youngsters worldwide: heads tilted down, unblinking eyes transfixed before a
handheld luminescent video display.

Memory is an elusive—and often selective—thing.[3] For
nearly twenty years, I had subconsciously filtered my recollec-
tions of children in the village so that they conformed to the subject matter that most interested me. When I remembered Talea's
youth, they were for the most part doing light farming work—for
example, picking coffee, spreading maize kernels out to dry, or
helping to gather firewood. In retrospect, it is not coincidental
that I chose these images to illustrate my first ethnography of the
pueblo. My memories of children also included scenarios in
which they participated in *danzas*, learned to play musical instruments, or played games like marbles and basketball. It took
significant effort (and a careful rereading of my field notes) to recognize that I was deceiving myself. After all, from my earliest
days in the village I had observed children playing video games
and, in some households, watching TV for hours on end. Over
time I came to realize that in order to get a more complete understanding of the ways in which Taleans are connected today, I
would need to look beyond the actual village.

I struggled to find research methods for exploring this subject. For the better part of a century, cultural anthropologists
had traveled to remote sites for months or years at a time in
order to make sense of "the native's point of view" by carefully
observing and participating in the daily routines of foragers,
farmers, fishers, or pastoralists.[4] For better or worse, being there
often gave anthropologists the confidence to write and speak

with authority about the lives and customs of others, and this differentiated the discipline from the other social sciences. Even today, academic anthropologists will occasionally advise graduate students to choose conventional (actual, not virtual; foreign, not domestic) fieldwork sites in order to hone their face-to-face ethnographic skills—and to establish their credibility. But the discipline has had to change. As many millions of people spend their waking hours in virtual spaces—and as virtual communities take shape—anthropologists have had to develop methods for researching online worlds.

In preparing this book I learned that a small but growing minority of Taleans frequent virtual worlds, spending parts of their lives online. Most of these people are city dwellers, but there are also resident Taleans—including some young campesinos—who use the internet and social media. Although I never imagined I would someday be doing research using Facebook, YouTube, WhatsApp and other programs, I now recognize that "studying virtual worlds 'in their own terms' is not only feasible but crucial to developing research methods that keep up with the realities of technological change."[5] The arrival of internet service, cell phones, and, now, smart phones in Talea is ushering in a brave new world of possibilities—and perhaps also of pitfalls.

VIRTUAL VILLAGE

By the late 1990s, when limited internet service began in Talea, a virtual version of the village began to take shape. Today, you might say that the pueblo exists in two different respects: there is an *actual* village located amid the mountains and cloud forests of northern Oaxaca, and there is a *virtual* village located in the ethereal domain of the World Wide Web. Even before the advent of smart phones, townspeople were using the internet—including social media—for their own ends, sharing and displaying communal celebrations, cultural events, and performances. Today, virtual Talea can be found on thousands of online sites: Facebook pages, YouTube videos, Instagram accounts, Flickr photo albums, and other platforms and apps.

The virtual village is ephemeral and its inhabitants are a widely dispersed and heterogenous group. They include those who were born in the pueblo but who now reside far away, especially in the United States; those who have never visited the village but who have an ancestral connection to it; one-time visitors to the actual Talea or others who have an interest in following events there; and, of course, those who are residents of Talea but spend part of their time visiting the virtual village.

My own introduction to this online world occurred relatively recently. Several days after I gave a classroom lecture about doing (actual) fieldwork in the pueblo, a student told me that she had seen a YouTube video featuring Talea's version of *Danza de los Aztecas* (literally, Dance of the Aztecs), one of a dozen or so plays performed by young villagers during Talea's festival seasons. These historical reenactments are a kind of street theater typically depicting the triumph of Spanish Catholicism over Islam, represented by the Moors, and Mesoamerican religions, represented by the Aztecs. Spanish friars imposed the *danzas* on indigenous communities in the 1500s, and, over time, the pueblos made them their own. Throughout Mesoamerica, danzas represent an important part of indigenous identity and some anthropologists argue that they are a form of cultural resistance—though this probably overstates the case.[6]

I was intrigued by the possibility that Talea's danzas might be available online and I asked the student to email me a link to the

YouTube video, which she did promptly. I clicked on the link, and for the next three and a half minutes, I was transported through space and time—back to my years in Talea. The video was simple but captivating: It provides a front row view of a carefully choreographed dance in which a dozen Aztec warriors, played by adolescents, bound, skip, and pirouette as the village's brass band merrily plays an intricately metered, repetitive melody. The warriors wear elaborate costumes. Some wear feathered headdresses and carry shields and faux obsidian-tipped clubs, while others don leopard or tiger suits. The scene was familiar to me: nearly two decades years earlier, I had participated in *Aztecas* as a musician, playing trumpet with the village band. Between rehearsals and actual performances, I had seen this particular danza more than twenty times.

In the video, two young boys suddenly appear in the foreground. The diminutive *danzantes* are apparently confused. One is dressed as a World War II-era soldier, clad in drab olive military fatigues and a khaki-colored rucksack. He carries a miniature rifle in one hand and a tin pitcher in the other. His partner is a soldier from the Napoleonic era, sporting a bright blue shako and epaulets (see figure 15). I laughed aloud as a young man called back the tiny conquerors—*¡para 'tras, güey! (get back, dude!)*—for they aren't supposed to appear until after the Aztecs have finished their dance.

The video abruptly ended. I felt as though I had awoken from a dream. I impulsively scanned the webpage: viewers had seen the short clip more than twenty-five hundred times. The person who posted the video has the unusual surname of a prominent Talean merchant family. I spent hours that afternoon binging on YouTube videos featuring danzas from Zapotec villages throughout the Rincón. Then I found out more about the person who

Figure 15. The cast of *Danza de los Aztecas* includes Spanish conquistadors, Napoleonic soldiers, American GIs, and Aztecs. Photo courtesy of Teresa García Bautista.

posted the *Aztecas* video. A quick Google search revealed that he was a young man, now probably in his early thirties, whom I instantly recognized as the son of a prosperous shoe salesman. He works in Oaxaca City as an electrical engineer and apparently produced the video during a visit to Talea, where he was born and raised.

· · ·

These experiences led me to ask: If a growing number of villagers are avid users of the internet and social media, then how are they using these powerful technologies? And, what are some of the ways that virtual Talea differs from actual Talea? To help answer these questions, I immersed myself in the virtual village for a month by probing social media sites—mostly Facebook pages and YouTube channels—to find people who live (or once lived) in actual Talea, to learn more about how they use these media for connecting with each other and the outside world.

It would be misleading to say that Taleans or Rinconeros or Zapotecs have craftily outsmarted these technologies or the people who designed them. My point is not to argue that "they are not fooled, not crushed, not homogenized," much less to convince readers that "they are creatively appropriating or reinterpreting what is being thrown at them in ways that its authors would never have anticipated."[7] Such arguments are disturbingly similar to those espoused by tech industry executives who claim that when people in so-called developing societies are given the ability to freely use Facebook, or WhatsApp, or Instagram, their lives necessarily improve. The picture is far more complex, for even as these tools allow people in places like Talea to create and circulate culturally valuable representations and productions, they also render them vulnerable to algorithmic modes of governance. Like us, they are being transformed into digital consumers, tracked and eventually targeted by online advertisers. And someday, they may also be subject to governmental surveillance through their handheld devices.

STATUS UPDATES

As I embarked on this research, I realized that I would need to create a Facebook account, something I had never done before.[8] I had no idea where this would take me. At times it was an intensely disorienting process in which I would lose myself for hours, compulsively scrolling through Taleans' Facebook pages and posts, reviewing lists of their "friends" for familiar names, or shuttling back and forth between a computer screen, hand-

written field notes from the 1990s and early 2000s, and internet
search engines in order to meaningfully collate and contextual-
ize social media posts. It was a bizarre experience for someone
new to social media.

My preliminary journeys across Facebook's blue-bordered
two-dimensional world were clumsy efforts to locate villagers
whom I had befriended during the 1990s. I began by searching for
campesinos who had invited me to their farms, but I should have
known better. After several failed attempts I realized they were
the least likely to have the time for, or interest in, social media.
So, I decided to try searching for their children. After combing
through my field notes, I was able to compile a short list of names
of people who, according to my calculations, would now be in
their late teens or early twenties. Here I had a little more success,
which is all it took to begin locating many others using a crude
form of social network analysis.[9] Within days I had tracked down
literally hundreds of people who had either listed Talea as their
hometown or whom I recognized from my actual fieldwork.

Most Taleans' Facebook posts contain the kind of material
that habitual social media users in the United States have come
to expect (and promulgate): status updates, inspirational quotes,
baby photos, memes, crude jokes, cute videos, political rants,
food photos, and, of course, ubiquitous selfies. If CEO Mark
Zuckerberg "built Facebook to help people stay connected and
bring us closer together with the people that matter to us," it is a
strange kind of togetherness that has coalesced in these virtual
spaces.[10] Among Taleans—as among Americans—it is a kind of
togetherness built on an economy of "likes" that tends to promote self-expression over self-reflection; boasting and bravado
over empathy; the sensual over the ascetic; coarseness over
courtesy.

Although it is difficult to precisely quantify such things, it became apparent to me that the pueblo's most active Facebook users are those hundreds of native sons and daughters living and working in the United States—in places like Grandview, Washington, Chambersburg, Pennsylvania, Madison, Wisconsin, Gainesville Mills, Georgia, and, most of all, in Greater Los Angeles (including Anaheim and other parts of Orange County). Assuming that their self-reported locations are accurate, one can map migration settlement patterns using Facebook profiles as a source of data. Many Taleans who reside in Tijuana or other parts of Baja California, the west coast state of Jalisco, Mexico City and surrounding areas, and Oaxaca City also regularly post "status updates" and other materials to Facebook. Presumably they have more reliable internet access than those living in rural areas. A modest number of resident Taleans—probably about a hundred or so—have Facebook accounts, but they typically do not post materials as often as their urban counterparts do. They are more likely to respond to posts created by nonresidents who live in cities. Many resident villagers who have accounts have never posted anything other than a profile photo. I was struck by the fact that many users, particularly those who claim to reside in the pueblo, have profile photos portraying emblematic or iconic village symbols: a statue of Talea's patron saint, San Miguel Arcángel; the church tower; a branch laden with coffee beans; a panoramic photo of the municipal palace. Few villagers had enabled Facebook's privacy settings—photos, posts, and videos were typically available to anyone else with a Facebook account, myself included.

Information that I gathered from Facebook was often confusing, though I was able to collect a great deal of basic data about Taleans' lives: for example, where they were living; where they had traveled; if and when they were married; when they had become parents or grandparents; and (for migrants living outside the village) when they had last visited the pueblo. While perusing these Facebook pages, I sometimes had the uneasy feeling that I might be snooping into the personal lives of villagers who presumably hadn't read Facebook's four-thousand-word terms of service—but then I quickly realized that little of what I saw would be radically different from the kinds of things to which I had access as an anthropologist living and working in actual Talea.[11] I was often surprised by posts that bluntly revealed a person's values, stylistic preferences, or political opinions, because in the actual pueblo people tended to be more subdued about such things. For every time that I encountered an image I thought the user may not want me to see, I found other materials that were remarkable in either historical, anthropological, or aesthetic terms: a high-resolution photo of a wedding reception from the 1950s; an image of a grandmother living in actual Talea, tenderly holding an infant born to her daughter who has lived in Los Angeles for more than fifteen years; brashly aggressive selfies taken by a young man with earplugs, nose rings, and many other facial piercings, born and raised in the village but who, according to his Facebook profile, now manages a tattoo parlor in Mexico City.

•   •   •

Anthropologist David Edwards, in a recent book on sacrifice and suicide bombing in Afghanistan, notes that Facebook, which was famously created by privileged young men in a Harvard University dorm room, is a platform with many culturally embedded assumptions and concepts. For example, the notion of publicly displaying one's face would hardly be considered controversial among the vast majority of people in the United

States. But in Afghanistan, where face has historically been synonymous with reputation, "Facebook has been central to redefining the cultural significance of the human face" in unpredictable ways. Among those who are online enthusiasts of the Taliban—that is, "Talifans"—the most commonly displayed faces on Facebook are those of young men, soon to be martyred as suicide bombers.[12]

Another assumption is the idea of "friends"—in the United States, there tends to be a general sense that "friends" are good to have, and that on Facebook, the more "friends" the better. Yet Facebook has transformed the responsibilities of friends in the United States, and in other societies as well. Edwards writes: "we must consider how much more dramatic and far-reaching might be the implications of Facebook when transplanted to other cultures, which have their own established friendship ideals and sometimes conflicting expectations related to other social matrices, most importantly kinship and religion. "[13]

This chapter is, in part, an effort to explore what happens when Facebook is transplanted to the Rincón, specifically Talea. Rather than give an exhaustive summary of villagers' Facebook use—which would be impossible given the massive quantity of material posted to the platform—I will present four fragments to illustrate some of the ways that Taleans are using this technology.

. . .

Let me begin with a Facebook post uploaded by Julio Baltazar, a man in his late fifties, several days after the pueblo's biggest annual fiesta in January. The four-day event attracts thousands of visitors, mainly native sons and daughters who live in other parts of the country or the United States. Resident villagers often told me that the fiesta had evolved into a celebration for migrants returning to visit relatives and friends. Julio Baltazar was among those people—he and all but one of his siblings have lived in Mexico City for most of their lives.

Baltazar's post is a status update that includes a photo portraying a campesino sitting down at a table, wearing a loose-fitting yellow polo shirt and a dark blue baseball cap. The man, who appears to be about sixty years old, has a bowl of refried beans and a small cup of coffee in front of him, and in one of his prominently veined hands he delicately holds a piece of tortilla that serves as a spoon. A bowl of tomatoes and chilies are on the table, along with a bag of dry black beans, several gourds, some plastic bags, and a bottle of cooking oil. His back is propped up against the back of a neatly made adobe wall. The man's face has a somber expression—one eyebrow is slightly raised, and he is staring straight into the camera. The caption reads: "In the farmhouse enjoying some delicious refried beans on Tuesday, January 23, my brother Beto."

I was fascinated by the post and the photo for several reasons. To begin with, I immediately recognized the man in the photo as Beto, Julio Baltazar's oldest brother. I had gotten to know Beto well; in fact, he was the first campesino to invite me to pick coffee with him, in early 1995. The year before, another one of his brothers, Rogelio (who has since moved to Mexico City) had invited me to the family's farm at a site called Xaca, and we had eaten meals in the very same ranch house depicted in the Facebook post. Xaca is located almost four hours from the village. As children the Baltazars often went with their father to work the land there.

The post was remarkable for another reason: It was followed by many comments, apparently written by close family members, particularly siblings living in Mexico City who expressed nostalgia for Xaca and Talea. A total of thirty-seven comments and replies followed Julio Baltazar's status update—too many to include here—but a sample of them will illustrate the point:

TENCHA BALTAZAR [*JULIO'S SISTER*]: What a beautiful photo Julio, thank you for sharing

JUANA BALTAZAR [*JULIO'S SISTER*]: All of us siblings should go, it would be fantastic and with our children too so that those who haven't been there can get to know it.

. . .

CAROLINA GONZÁLEZ [*JULIO'S SISTER-IN-LAW, ROGELIO'S WIFE*]: Mmmmmm, if I go tell them that I went to leave tortillas for my father-in-law, may he rest in peace, [when I went to Xaca] he served me boiling coffee for the heat and I felt as fresh as lettuce, ha ha

EVA GÓMEZ [*RELATIONSHIP UNCLEAR*]: Pop, at least bring us a few tortillas ha ha

LAO SALINAS [*RELATIONSHIP UNCLEAR—COUSIN?*]: When I go [to Talea] invite me to the farmhouse, relative

. . .

YADIRA BALTAZAR [*JULIO'S SISTER*]: Brother, that is in Xaca right? So many beautiful memories. My heart beat faster, I shed tears. You're so lucky to be there. Enjoy it. Take lots of photos and share them please.

TENCHA BALTAZAR [*JULIO'S SISTER*]: Yadi, when we go I'm really looking forward to remembering beautiful times that we spent there

YADIRA BALTAZAR [*JULIO'S SISTER*]: Let's go! And eat beans with ice cream beans ha ha [from the pacay tree]

. . .

JULIO BALTAZAR: I'll send you more [photos]

YADIRA BALTAZAR *[JULIO'S SISTER]:* Thank you for the other photos!! What's incredible is it's just like I imagined it!!

VERÓNICA CASTILLO *[FAMILY FRIEND]:* Yadira, I remember well when you went your mami

YADIRA BALTAZAR *[JULIO'S SISTER]:* Yes Vero!! There I spent a big part of my childhood!! Oh and how could one forget when we went for a whole week to pick your grandma's coffee!! Samy and Leti would go too. Do you remember????

VERONICA CASTILLO *[FAMILY FRIEND]:* Yeeees, beautiful memories when "Flatface" would go all the way to *loma yagcua* for bread, I can't image who he wanted to impress ha ha

The messages express a sense of longing for an idyllic past, which presumably still exists in Xaca. There is also an expressed desire for their children to know this place. Notably absent from the exchange is Beto, who, like most Talean campesinos, does not have a Facebook account. In fact, he is mentioned only once in the lengthy series exchanges, even though he is the subject of the photo.

Ironically, in the 1990s I listened to Beto bitterly complaining to a group of close friends about the fact that of all of his siblings—two brothers and three sisters—he was the only one who worked the land. He was a melancholy man and something of a black sheep in his family. His brother Rogelio had finished high school and secured an office job in Talea, but only rarely went to the fields. Beto acknowledged that he had gotten into trouble as a young man traveling through different parts of the country and had even been jailed for a while in northern Mexico, but he expressed frustration about his burden: "If I didn't do this work, then who would? What would become of the land that my *jefe* [father] sacrificed himself for? It would all go to waste." He also regretted relying on his mother to prepare his tortillas and wash his clothes—though from what I saw, she needed him just as much to help maintain the house since she was a widow. It wasn't entirely clear to me why Beto stayed in the pueblo. It's possible that his parents expected him to remain there, maybe because he never married, or because he didn't finish junior high school, or simply because as the oldest son he was expected to farm the land.

I couldn't help but wonder whether Beto was even aware of the fact that the photo led his siblings to wax nostalgic about their childhoods—or what he would think about their comments if he found out. Knowing Beto, he would probably respond with a faint smile and a simple invitation: "Anytime you want, *carnalitos.*"[14]

. . .

As mentioned above, there are probably a hundred or so Taleans who live in the actual village with Facebook accounts, but few of them regularly post photos or other materials online. Although not many use the platform for publicizing their innermost convictions, there are exceptions. For example, Kendra Rodríguez's personal Facebook page includes many posts in which she openly and eloquently discusses her political activities and ideology, in her own words. For example, she posted this message on March 8, along with a photo in which she is posing before the Zapatista army's "Office of Women for Dignity" in the Chiapas town of Oventic:

> *On this day when we commemorate International Women's Day, I express my greetings and admiration for all those women, anonymous or not, visible or*

*invisible, from all latitudes of the entire world. To those who have made a
path for new generations, those who have passed on their knowledge, those who
have encouraged us to keep growing. Because the role of women in society
offers an array of functions: friend, companion, mother, worker, professional,
educator, housewife, artist, athlete; and now more than ever, present and
future protagonist among the people of the earth. There is still a long path
ahead, because the gender divide is still great, but accompanying one another,
together in sorority we will continue advancing.... Thank you to all.... I
send you an embrace from the beating heart of the Sierra Juárez.*

In another post, Rodríguez includes the following comment,
accompanied by an article published in one of Mexico's most
popular daily newspapers:

*Once more, decisions are being made without informing the principal [coffee]
producers, with the [economic] crisis and need that exist in the coffee sector
of our state—not only Nestlé wants to take advantage of this, but also Star-
bucks, which is beginning to advance on the Sierra Norte, to try to hoard coffee and to impose its genetically modified coffee varieties that are of poor
quality.*[15]

Here I do not wish to imply that most villagers use Facebook
to communicate lengthy or elaborate messages such as this—in
fact the opposite is true. As in the United States, Taleans' posts
are typically short, mundane entries that don't do much more
than bluntly express a feeling to friends—nostalgia, surprise,
alarm, frustration, irony, pride, affection—"I share, therefore I
am."[16] But there are exceptions, and Rodríguez's posts illustrate
the political potential that exists when social media is used to
communicate more complex, nuanced ideas over space and time.

. . .

I reviewed many Facebook posts that were apparently created
to transmit or perhaps reinforce a sense of civic pride. As I

expanded my list of users from the village, I encountered the profile of Abel Santillano, a man now about forty years old who lives in the state of Mexico. In the 1990s I had gotten to know him well because we were both musicians and had the opportunity to perform together on many occasions. Although he was only sixteen years old at the time, Abel was wise beyond his years, probably because of the fact that his father had gone blind and depended on him for many things.

At first, I had a difficult time believing that Abel was the man in the Facebook profile. Time—and city life—had completely transformed the wiry, clean-shaven boy I had known twenty years ago. He looked like he could be an anthropology professor on the cusp of middle age: He was now muscular, sporting a thick beard, a handlebar mustache, perfectly spiked hair, and stylish horn-rimmed eyeglasses.

Although most of his Facebook posts included photos of his wife and child, Abel returned to his hometown four years ago for the annual fiesta in honor of San Miguel Arcángel, and he posted several dozen photos of the pueblo's landscape with the heading "My Talea." The most captivating photos portrayed women preparing *comidas típicas*, typical foods, which villagers often describe as the most authentic in the region: *atole de cacao* (a corn-based chocolate drink), *yht gu* (bean tamales wrapped in banana leaf), and other delicacies (see figure 16). The caption for one of his status updates read as follows: "The dough for bean tamales. Women working—in the rehearsal hall of the BUP [Banda Unión y Progreso]."

The responses from Abel's Facebook friends demonstrate how social media facilitates communication among Taleans living in different cities across North America. Here I include the location of those commenting on the photo:

Figure 16. Facebook photo of Talean women preparing *yht gu* (bean tamales). Photo courtesy of Andrés Pérez Gerónimo.

ADRIAN CHÁVEZ *[INGLEWOOD, CA]:* Thank you for sharing the photos.... I just saw my dear mom

ABEL SANTILLANO: Sure thing, bro, thanks for visiting my profile, later I'll upload more....

...

GUILLERMINA MENDOZA *[TIJUANA, BAJA CALIFORNIA]:* I WANT BEAN TAMALES MMMMMMM HOW DELICIOUS

LUIS LUNA *[XALAPA, VERACRUZ]:* BEAN TAMALES HOW DELICIOUS

MARÍA ALANIZ *[OAXACA CITY, OAXACA]:* My ex-mother in law is a total sweetheart

Another set of entries posted by Abel expresses enthusiasm about the pueblo's community cell phone network. During the summer of 2013, Abel posted a photo of a newspaper resting on his lap. The newspaper headline reads, "They Created Their Own Cell Network" and includes a page-long story with photos of Taleans using mobile phones. Abel posted the following caption, which garnered more than fifty "likes": "As I was getting my shoes shined, I borrowed a newspaper … and oh, what a surprise … I found this." In a series of other Facebook posts, Abel posted screen shots of a TV news program reporting on the village's autonomous cell phone network. The news report appeared on the Televisa network, which dominates Mexico's pay TV market. He and others were beaming with Talean pride, even from hundreds of miles away.

. . .

Villagers sometimes use social media to provide some of Talea's most cherished institutions with a means of chronicling and archiving their activities and accomplishments. For example, among the pueblo's most vibrant Facebook groups are "Alma Taleana" and "Unión y Progreso," organized by the village's two philharmonic bands, each with more than a thousand Facebook followers. The websites include photos, announcements, and links to video clips featuring the bands' public performances.

Similarly, other organizations and businesses use Facebook to promote their activities or products, inform followers about special events, and forge alliances with other organizations. For example, in 2013, growers created a cooperative called Oro Talea to commercialize locally produced coffee. The cooperative's Facebook page has nearly a thousand followers and includes a post that was published in late 2018, at a time when global coffee prices had sunk:

Many of us complain about the miserably low market prices for coffee and we don't do anything about it, even though we all have the solution: to consume coffee that comes directly from our fields. This organization will initiate the commercialization of Talean coffee products; we hope that those Taleans who live outside of our community will consume it; this way we can guarantee fair prices for our working people.

In a relatively brief period, the cooperative has established a nursery for the cultivation of trees and has established relationships with coffee roasters and exporters. Like so many other Taleans, the youthful director of the cooperative has worked to cultivate relationships with outsiders in order to advance the village's interests.

Other organizations with Facebook pages include the cooperative Autotransporte SAETA, which has provided daily bus service to and from Oaxaca City for nearly twenty years; a family-owned *panadería* or bakery that occasionally posts photos of its wares online; Hotel San Carlos, a privately owned business; and Mototaxis Talea, one of several tuk-tuk companies that has benefited greatly from the introduction of cell phone service in the pueblo.

• • •

It would be a mistake to suggest that villagers' social media posts are mostly filled with social significance, economic importance, or cultural weight. In fact, a great deal of it is sheer horseplay, *puro relajo*—good fun. Many Taleans pride themselves on their keen sense of humor, and even the most reserved villagers enjoyed telling jokes or playing pranks once I got to know them better. I experienced a prank firsthand several months into my field work, after I had volunteered to serve as a municipal policeman. One drizzling night, my fellow *policías* sent me on a frantic

Figure 17. Talea's basketball team posing for a photo, circa 1993. Photo courtesy of Daniel Bautista.

mission to catch a runaway thief, who did not actually exist. After about fifteen minutes of scurrying up and down the pueblo's steep, slippery cobblestone streets, I realized I was on a snipe hunt. I was lucky not to have fallen on my face.

Talean humor translates well on social media. Take, for example, this Facebook post, uploaded without any written commentary by a merchant's son who is now in his late forties (see figure 17). He is the tallest person in the photo (on the far right side, wearing number 11), and was often called *güero* (fair-skinned) by his friends and relatives because of his fair complexion and light brown hair. The photo depicts the pueblo's basketball team— that is, a group of young bucks—posing uncomfortably with a *real* young buck after winning second place in a tournament during the early 1990s. Several of the teenagers awkwardly hold plastic bags containing large tacos. It is customary for fiesta organizers to send off visiting teams with bundles of food as a token of gratitude and good will. (Later in this chapter I will discuss the significance of basketball—and deer—in the Rincón.)

ADRIEL ALARCÓN: What place did the team come in, güero? Poor Pablo *[see fourth player from the right, wearing a jersey with the number 6]*, that dude was really chubby, no? Haha!

FRANKIE BOCANEGRA: Second place in an epic final against Jaltianguis, a double match, there you'll see one of the old men that you can't outrun now, dude haha

ADRIEL ALARCÓN: But now you don't even want to play, dude

NOE PEÑA: Couldn't you all leave the tacos to the side? ha ha ha ha, cool picture,,,there's one to remember, congratulations!!!!

. . .

BHNI YATÓN: Friends if I'm not mistaken it was in San Bartolomé yatony *[Yatoni]*, help me remember!

FRANKIE BOCANEGRA: It was in Talea in January 93, if I'm not mistaken, but that deer was given to us for winning first place in Yatoni the year before.

BHNI YATÓN: Great times, it's been a long while, hasnt it

MARIO VILLAREAL: Number 4 and number 11, all beans . . . hahaha

OSCAR LUNA BOCANEGRA: Damn you, güero, you're just making fun of our loincloths, dude

LORI GOMEZ: Great photo, puro muchachón *[pure strong young men]*! Those are really athlete's legs!

It's impossible to draw any grand conclusions from the ways in which Taleans use Facebook, other than the fact that those who live in the actual village tend to use it much more sparingly than those who live outside of it, and that it is quite rare for campesinos to use the medium. Another tentative observation is that photos posted to Facebook appear to function as a means of preserving memories and distributing nostalgic photos. YouTube often serves a similar purpose in virtual Talea.

CREATING CONTENT

Compared to Facebook, YouTube was a relatively easy medium to analyze. To begin with, there are fewer posts—there appear to be between 150 and two hundred videos set in Talea, plus several dozen news reports about the village's community cell phone network. As it exists in YouTube videos, the virtual village can be organized into roughly five themes, most of which are associated with annual fiestas. In order of popularity, these are *danzas*, musical performances (particularly by the village's bands), *calendas*, fireworks displays, and basketball tournaments. Another category might be called *la vida cotidiana*—scenes from everyday life such as the preparation of regional foods, aspects of agricultural work, or the pueblo's picturesque surroundings. Most of the time it is relatively easy to confirm the identity of the person who posted the video (the "content creator" in YouTube parlance) by comparing his or her name with another social media account.

Viewing Talea through the lens of YouTube gives a distorted picture of the village, since so many posts portray extraordinary moments. As Octavio Paz famously noted in *The Labyrinth of Solitude*, "The fiesta is by nature sacred, literally or figuratively, and above all it is the advent of the unusual. It is governed by its own special rules, that set it even apart from other days."[17] From another perspective, YouTube provides a window into events that are hyper-realistic. In many cases, the viewer finds himself or herself right in the middle of the action. These are almost never staged productions—they are typically eye-level recordings of culturally significant events.

Analyzing videos of basketball tournaments can provide insight into life in the Rincón and beyond. For nearly a century, basketball has been the most popular sport in indigenous communities throughout the state of Oaxaca. Most pueblos have a basketball court located in the town center or plaza, and Talea is no exception: its court is located directly in front of the municipal palace.[18] An essential part of fiestas throughout the state are tournaments between teams representing different villages. Men's and women's teams participate in separate contests. Winning teams receive prizes including cash, oxen, deer or other valuable animals. The most prestigious tournament of all is Copa Benito Juárez, held in the village of Guelatao, where up to two hundred teams compete. Tournament finals often attract an audience of hundreds—women and men, young and old are equally drawn to the sport. During the 1990s, the Sierra Zapotec village of Macuiltianguis constructed a state-of-the-art indoor stadium at a cost of more than half a million dollars. The *torneos de básquet* provide an outlet for villagers to compete with each other in a way that allows them to express civic pride, discipline, and camaraderie within the framework of indigenous values.

Outsiders often find it perplexing that basketball, rather than soccer, is so popular in Oaxaca, and the historical reasons for this are not entirely clear.[19] There are several hypotheses about how basketball, which originated in the northeastern United States during the 1890s, arrived in rural Oaxaca: some claim that schoolteachers brought the game with them when the first public school opened in the 1930s; others think that miners brought the game to the region early in the twentieth century; still others credit President Lázaro Cárdenas for promoting the construction of basketball courts.[20] Oaxaca basketball is now a global phenomenon: many indigenous villages, including Talea, have corresponding teams in Los Angeles that participate in the Copa Oaxaca, a tournament that has taken place every summer for more than two decades. Some of these matches have been posted on YouTube, spanning the borderless ether of the internet.

YouTube videos of basketball games sometimes reveal tensions that go beyond sport. For example, in the Cajonos Zapotec village of Santo Domingo Yojovi, a recent fiesta tournament culminated in a final match between Talea and the neighboring village of Tabaa. As I watched the video, there was a palpable sense of excitement and emotion among the athletes—and the audience. An announcer barks out a tense play-by-play account of the half-hour game. Even the weather adds to the drama: in the background, looming overhead just above the nearby church, are leaden storm clouds. At one point, a referee calls a foul as two players shove each other, struggling over control of the ball. Men in the audience jump up and bellow in frustration—and then play resumes again. In the end, players from the two teams congratulate each other.

Most adults from the Rincón who watch this video would immediately recognize the deeper significance of the game. For decades Talea and Tabaa have had a strained relationship, even though they lie less than five miles away from each other. Like so many other villages in Oaxaca, they have had territorial conflicts over disputed lands. In the early 1990s, the conflict turned violent—several men were killed during an armed confrontation between villagers. Since then there has been relatively little interaction between people from the two communities.

.   .   .

The Talea-Tabaa basketball video was created by Velasco Productions, a cottage industry that creates short YouTube videos of fiestas and other community events in the northern sierra of Oaxaca. To my surprise I learned that the company has more than nine thousand subscribers to its YouTube channel, and its videos have been viewed more than 2.5 million times.

I was even more astonished when I learned about Oaxaca City-based VideoRey, which was founded in 2005 by a retired industrial engineer, a man from the Sierra Zapotec village of Xiacui. He created VideoRey to document fiestas "so that the inhabitants of the communities can pass them along to their descendants and awaken in them a love for their native towns."[21] The engineer claims to have covered more than a thousand fiestas and notes (quite plausibly), "I possess the largest and most original library of videos of the festival life of Oaxacan communities." Apart from selling videos in the communities he visits, his popular YouTube videos earn royalties. VideoRey's YouTube channel has more than twenty-one thousand subscribers and its videos have been viewed more than 15 million times. He has filmed numerous events in Talea, including its largest fiesta, held every year on the third Sunday of January. That video has now been viewed more than sixteen thousand times.

Comments posted by viewers give a sense of how important the virtual village can be in reestablishing a sense of identity: *"greetings to talea from juan and greetings to noemi fernandez. from usa, what a charming video i'm not from talea but how beautiful it is."*

Another writes, "*upload more videos of the dance i was getting excited but i don't remember . . . they took me there when i was very small but my father was born there and maybe one day i'll have the pleasure [of returning] it looks charming*"

Although VideoRey does brisk business with people living in rural Oaxaca, it is clear that its target viewing audience includes indigenous Oaxacans who have migrated to the United States. Among the company's clever advertising slogans is "*no les mande mole, mándeles un videorey de su fiesta*" (don't send them *mole*, send them a VideoRey of their fiesta). The tagline plays on a decades-old practice in which rural Oaxacans hire local drivers to ship dried *mole*, *chintezle* (chili paste), *panela* (unrefined brown sugar), *chapulines* (toasted grasshoppers) and other delicacies to the US-Mexico border. Once the shipments arrive on the Mexican side of the border, they are delivered to couriers (usually either US citizens of Oaxacan descent or Oaxacan Green Card holders) with vehicles registered in the United States.

There are other video production companies that also specialize in filming fiestas and other events in Oaxaca's indigenous communities, though these appear to be limited to YouTube broadcasts. They include Valencia Tradiciones de Oaxaca, San Cristobal Films, and Yaee Films.[22]

* * *

Companies are not the only entities that create YouTube videos set in Talea. Tomasa Cruz, a native villager who resides in Mexico City, is a remarkably prolific producer and returns to the Rincón frequently. Cruz, who is in her midforties, began posting videos on YouTube eight years ago. Since then her videos have been viewed more than 1.8 million times. She specializes in producing high-resolution videos featuring public performances by the pueblo's municipal band and highlights from the village's largest fiestas, but she has also produced many other works, some of which were made in other Zapotec communities. Although it is difficult to calculate a precise figure, Cruz's work has probably earned her somewhere between US $3600 and $5400—comparable to a thousand days of work at Mexico City's official minimum wage.

I was intrigued by Cruz's most popular posts (she filmed half of her top ten in Talea), but the video that most captured my imagination was a twelve-minute video filmed in the early morning hours of Día de los Muertos, the Day of the Dead, in her home. It depicts the *recorrido de los bhni hué* (see chapter 3), a ritual in which a group of men sing cantos in honor of the dead. The video begins with six *bhni hué* or cantors entering the main room, which has a large, intricately decorated altar adorned with fruit, food, candles, and a large photo of Cruz's deceased parents. Then the men methodically sing the cantos. What made the images especially compelling to me was the fact that two of the bhni hué were men who had become close friends of mine in the 1990s. The video, which, coincidentally, I found on November 1, exactly a year after it was filmed, brought me great joy and nostalgia, for I had volunteered to serve as a bhni hué more than twenty years earlier.

During my sojourns in the virtual village, I encountered several odd or remarkable YouTube videos that didn't fit into the typical categories. For example, a three-part series of short videos depicted a wedding in which a man who is a Talean native marries a woman who is clearly an outsider: her father and mother, featured in the video, appear to be of Euro-American and East Asian ancestry, respectively. A few minutes of internet research revealed that the young couple are residents of Vancouver. In the video, the young couple and their relatives appear to be thoroughly enjoying themselves, and though the reception is lavish by local standards, the events include many elements common to most Talean weddings: the preparation of *comidas típicas* (there is striking footage of women preparing hundreds of *memelas*—toasted cakes made of maize and beans—before the reception begins); the procession of the bride and groom to the Catholic church; music from the banda municipal; and presumably the brideprice: a symbolic exchange of turkeys, tortillas, and other gifts. If, in the past, observers have described Talea as a place that welcomes outsiders, then this YouTube post provides visible evidence to support that claim.

Another unusual video, produced by VideoRey, is entitled simply "Talea de Castro, Tequio Enorme" and features footage in which dozens of men sling huge buckets of wet cement upon their shoulders, then climb a long ramp rising more than twenty feet into the air, eventually reaching the top of a building. The rooftop is covered with wooden beams and rebar. As the men pour cement onto the rebar, the flat roof takes shape. This is a relatively new kind of event called a *colado*.

Many YouTube viewers in Mexico or the United States would probably be puzzled both by the video and by the fact that it has been viewed more than five thousand times. For someone who has participated in a *tequio*—a kind of communal work in which all able-bodied male citizens are expected to participate—such a video can bring back feelings of deep nostalgia. While living in Talea, I spent several days participating in *tequios* exactly like this one, and seeing the video evoked vivid memories. I immediately remembered the chalky, salty smell of wet cement; the heavy gray goop that quickly dried out our fingers and hands; the crunching sound of rocks being shoveled into the rumbling cement mixer; the endless stream of double entendres as we climbed up and down the ramp, over and over again, over a six-

hour period; the throbbing pain that would affect my shoulder
and back for days afterwards; the pleasure of hearing first the
clinking, then the popping open of brightly colored soda and
beer bottles at the end of the day—fizzy, frosty tokens of appreciation from the municipal authorities once our work was done.

. . .

During my last few days in the virtual village, I found a gem on
YouTube: *Linda Taleanita* (Lovely Talean Woman), a slick music
video featuring approximately forty young musicians from the
municipal banda Alma Taleana, ranging in age from about eight
to eighteen (see figure 18). They are dressed in clothing that
would have been popular in Talea a century ago. Boys sport spot-
less ivory-colored *calzones* (loose fitting pants and shirts made of
coarse cotton), black broad-brimmed wool hats, and pointy-toed
huaraches from the Cajonos pueblo of Yalalag, still commonly
worn by Talean campesinos. Girls don *huipiles* (embroidered cotton blouses), long pastel-colored skirts, and black *rebozos* wrapped
around their heads. Dramatic clips of Talea's cobblestone streets,
majestic church, and municipal palace are interwoven with close
up shots of the protagonist—a beautifully poised teenage girl
expertly picking coffee and patting tortillas. The song also features a gifted singer, a Talean man known locally as "el gran
Pavarotti" because of his operatic voice.

At first I didn't know what to make of the elaborate production. It seemed ironic that Talean children who normally wear
T-shirts, blue jeans, and sneakers were decked out in clothes
that their great-grandparents would have worn many years ago.
But these youngsters—with lots of encouragement from their
parents and Taleans everywhere—are performing traditions
for the whole wide world to see. I couldn't help but think of the

Figure 18. Scene from *Linda Taleanita* video, featuring Banda Alma Taleana. Photo courtesy of Ulises Canseco Peña/Banda Muncipal de Villa Talea de Castro.

saying, "If you've got it, flaunt it!"[23] The video was coordinated, and presumably underwritten, by a successful Talean engineer and benefactor who has lived in Oaxaca City for many years. He owns the pueblo's only hotel, which happens to be the setting for some of the scenes in the video.

. . .

Trying to make sense of the virtual village highlights some of the contradictions of digital technologies. These potent tools provide a seemingly indestructible medium for documenting, curating, and distributing images, sounds, and sentiments that are culturally anchored and socially valued. Anthropologist Mary Good, who has studied the impact of social media among Polynesian youth, suggests that "the introduction of Facebook does not become a Western technology behemoth ruthlessly steamrolling across a passive new territory of eager users ... adopting new media and incorporating it into their lives is a process, and sometimes facilitates the maintenance of more long-standing traditions."[24] In virtual Talea, a comparable process is unfolding in which villagers are able to celebrate communal life, a shared sense of aesthetics, and individual opinions and attitudes among peers. It is possible to acknowledge the potentially constructive aspects of digital media without accepting the naive and unsettling techno-utopianism of industry executives such as Facebook's Mark Zuckerberg and Google's Sundar Pichai.[25]

At the same time, when it comes to social media, Taleans have joined the ranks of literally billions of other users around the world who, in exchange for free access to platforms and apps, are subjected to the same forms of surveillance and algorithmic processing that have enabled Facebook, Google, and Amazon to become the world's most powerful advertising firms. Like you, and me, and about half of the planet's population, Taleans—or, more precisely, the data they generate along with the rest of us—*are* the product.

Villagers have long sought to maintain a measure of autonomy in the face of powerful forces that tried to impose coercive, repressive power from the top down: Spanish conquistadors and colonial administrators; the army of the Second French Empire during the 1860s; and post-revolutionary Mexican governments, for example. Today, however, control is more capillary, and power more pernicious. Social networks often feel good because they are unquestionably connective.

But *are* they?

A relatively small but growing body of psychological research suggests that social media paradoxically connects *and* disconnects people from each another. Jamil Zaki of the Stanford

Social Neuroscience Laboratory argues that "social media allows us to connect with anybody but makes it more difficult to truly connect with anybody [who is] right in front of us.... In terms of its effects on the brain, we don't really know, because there's no control group.... We're in the middle of a vast longitudinal study but we don't know what will happen."[26]

As Facebook, YouTube, and other social media are giving shape to people's sense of self in Talea, they are also "producing certain forms of dependency and subjective bonds to authority ... [while] enabling rather than simply opposing agency."[27] The interactive nature of social media—and the internet more broadly—seductively draws in users as they skip from one post, page, or site to another, often losing track of time, space, and perspective. Documenting the consequences of Talea's cell phone revolution inevitably leads to a difficult question: What kind of connectivity is being created—and at what cost?

CHAPTER SEVEN

Aftereffects

When I began writing this book, I naively thought it would be the Mexican version of a familiar plot line that has driven many successful Hollywood films, from *It's a Wonderful Life* and *Harlan County, USA* to *A Civil Action* and *Erin Brockovich*: small town men and women fearlessly take on big, bad company. Townspeople undergo trials, tribulations, and then ... triumph! And they all lived happily ever after.

Talea's cell phone adventure was a much more complicated story—and, as it turns out, it would have no definitive ending. The latest phase in the pueblo's centuries-long effort to expand its connectedness to the outside world is still very much a work in progress.

Understanding the complexity of the story requires, among other things, a familiarity with the nuances of local history. As noted earlier, Talea may have been founded by Spanish friars invited to the Rincón by Zapotec elders from the region during the early years of the conquest. Regardless of whether they were motivated by trepidation, hospitality, or some combination of the two, it seems that the Zapotec *wanted* to connect.

Villagers may value connectivity—but they value hard-boiled pragmatism even more. One way or another, Taleans would get a weekly market; they would get telegraph service; they would get a road built to Oaxaca City; they would get electrical power; they would get radio and TV broadcasts; they would get land lines; they would get the internet; they would get cell phones and then smart phones. A pragmatic outlook means it doesn't really matter whether you get there with the help of the government, a non-governmental or nonprofit agency, a multinational corporation, a regional cooperative, or none of the above. And if it *is* none of the above, then you do it yourself—that is, collectively as citizens. That practicality often spills over into the political domain. Talea has always had its ideologues, but the pragmatic majority— whether campesinos, merchants, students, or professionals—have tended to be wary of them.[1]

Many questions remain about the long-term consequences of the Rincón's digital technologies. How will politicians and federal regulators deal with the rise of community-based cell networks? To what extent will users experience the kinds of chronic distraction and behavioral addiction that have been observed in the United States, Europe, East Asia, and other regions?[2] Is it possible that face-to-face communication in the Rincón will eventually give way to face-to-screen communication—as has happened in so many parts of the world? And how might the cell phone network make villages more susceptible to digital surveillance, online profiling, political manipulation, and algorithmic modes of governance that have become normalized in so many countries?

UNCERTAIN FUTURES

It is unclear what the future holds for Talea and the other villages that boldly launched Oaxaca's community cell phone networks. In late 2017, *Telecomunicaciones Indígenas Comunitarias* (TIC), the cooperative organization that has helped nearly twenty Zapotec, Mixe, and Mixtec villages create autonomous networks like the one built in Talea, was dealt a blow. Less than two years after being granted a license for accessing the radio frequency bands used for their networks, Mexico's Federal Telecommunications Institute demanded that TIC pay nearly one million pesos (approximately US $50,000) for continued use.[3] This threatened the network's very existence. Although the government agency had originally exempted TIC from paying concession fees, the cooperative now found itself spiraling into what one journalist called "the abyss of Mexican bureaucracy."[4] Regulators decided that TIC's operations fell under the jurisdiction of Mexican commercial law and were therefore within the regulatory domain of the Secretariat of Finance and Public Credit; in other words, they were subject to federal taxes and back taxes. The fact that all of TIC's income was destined for either the villages' municipal coffers or the cooperative for maintenance and reinvestment was apparently dismissed by regulators. In many ways, the decision was consistent with a long pattern of state and federal government policies that have sought to undermine indigenous peoples' attempts to maintain political, economic and cultural autonomy in Oaxaca.

If federal regulators thought that TIC would surrender, they were badly mistaken. From the beginning, the men and women involved in building the Rincón's mobile network had to navigate a bewildering and sometimes contradictory tangle of regulations and laws at local, state, and federal levels. Sometimes they directly appealed to such laws in order to justify their actions. For example, in 2012, elected officials from thirty Zapotec communities petitioned a top official at the federal Secretariat of Communications and Transportation, or SCT, requesting support for the proposed network. They cited the Mexican constitution (most importantly Article 2), which states, among other things, that the federal government is obligated to "expand the network of communications so as to permit the integration of the communities through the construction and expansion of channels of communication and telecommunication ... [and] establish conditions under which indigenous peoples and communities may acquire, operate, and administer means of communication."[5]

Soon after federal regulators levied the concession fee, TIC appealed the decision. The cooperative's legal advisors—most notably Erick Huerta and his associates at the Mexico City-based NGO Redes A.C.—were able to get a hearing before a federal tribunal in early 2018. By March of that year, the tribunal declared that the imposition of the fee contradicted the legal principle of *pro personae*—the notion that the law that most favorably benefits all individuals should be applied in a given circumstance. For the moment, then, TIC's future appears to be secure (see figure 19). But there are certain to be more legal challenges in the years ahead. In the words of one observer, "A bureaucrat accustomed to dealing with millionaires in an industry that generally requires a great deal of capital for operations, will tend to believe that the ocean is full of sharks, and forget that poverty and marginalization still exist in Mexico."[6]

•   •   •

Figure 19. Workers assembling a mobile antenna in a Cajonos Zapotec village. Photo courtesy of Israel Hernández García.

In August 2018, the nongovernmental organization Rhizomatica announced that TIC would begin providing internet access and other data services to its users. This service links smart phones to the internet via satellite. According to Huerta, TIC successfully forged an alliance with the federal Secretariat of Communications and Transportation, which allowed it to use government satellites to reach remote regions served by the cooperative.[7] Assuming that TIC is able to provide this service at an affordable cost, perhaps some Taleans might decide to return to an autonomous, community-based cell phone network. As mentioned earlier, villagers did something very similar in the early 2000s, when they pooled their resources to create a locally owned bus line, Autotransportes SAETA, which has thrived ever since (see chapter 5).

DISTRACTED

When I first visited Talea in the summer of 1994, the *norteño* supergroup Los Tigres del Norte had just released a song entitled "El Celular" ("The Cell Phone"). It was among the most popular songs in the region. The bouncy polka could be heard blaring from the windows of people's homes, on the bus that provided daily service to and from Oaxaca City, and even in the fields as campesino children sang the song at the top of their lungs. Even though Tigres wrote the tune more than twenty years before Taleans had built their own cell phone network, the composition clearly articulates the double-edged nature of mobile technologies. Among other things, the humorous song alludes to the ways in which cell phones can control their users and end privacy. It also suggests that habitual cell phone users have a difficult time thinking clearly.

Among the many Facebook posts I viewed during my month of social media immersion, some caught my attention because they suggested preoccupations that villagers have about cellular technology. They were usually hilarious. For example, a Talean schoolteacher reposted a video (almost certainly staged) in which a campesino shouts at his teenage sons, each of whom is holding a cell phone, and then chastises them for sending text messages instead of working. The three are surrounded by ripe sugarcane plants, when the frustrated father suddenly stops and faces one of the teenagers:[8]

FATHER: Throw that worthless crap away, man, throw it away!

[Points at Teenager 2, who is texting.]

AND WHAT ARE YOU DOING, MAN?

TEENAGER 2: *[Mumbles indecipherably while holding cell phone.]*

FATHER: *[Faces Teenager 1 again and gesticulates wildly.]*
YOU TOO, WITH THE LITTLE TELEPHONE IN YOUR HAND?
[Grabs Teenager 1's phone and throws it to the ground.]
THAT PHONE IS WORTHLESS, WORTHLESS!
[Stomps on the phone.]
YOUNG PEOPLE ALL HAVE TELEPHONES IN THEIR HANDS,
LOOKING FOR WORK, TAPPING AND TAPPING THEIR
PHONES!
[He mockingly pretends to be texting.]
THAT'S WHY THE YOUTH DON'T PROGRESS, BECAUSE THEY
HAVE TELEPHONES IN HAND! UNDERSTAND ME—THE
TELEPHONE DOESN'T GIVE YOU WORK . . .
[Stomps on the phone again, then points to it.]
NOW THERE'S YOUR TELEPHONE! . . . TOMORROW I'LL RUN
YOU OUT. . . .
[Points to Teenager 2.]
THERE'S YOUR TEACHER. *[Then, in a high-pitched mocking
voice.]* TIME TO GRAB MY LITTLE TELEPHONE! HOW
INTELLIGENT HE IS. . . . I'M BETTER OFF GOING, I'M GOING!
[Walks away angrily.]

As someone who spent several weeks toiling in the pueblo's
sugarcane fields, harvesting cane, extracting its juice, and helping to prepare *panela* or unrefined sugar from it, I could appreciate the father's frustration. The sugarcane harvest is by far the
most difficult farming work done by villagers. When a campesino cuts cane during the hottest part of the year, his skin is easily irritated by the finely serrated leaves and sticky, hairlike
spines covering the stalk. The end products are delicious, and

the conviviality between campesinos reinforces strong bonds, but the labor is intense, monotonous, and physically punishing. The video is riotously funny because a person familiar with the harvest would probably prefer to do anything rather than cut cane. But, of course, as the infuriated father reminds us, there is work to be done.

•   •   •

Do Taleans face such problems today? I wanted to learn more about villagers' attitudes toward cell phones. Among those I spoke with was Jacinto Chapa, the campesino who had become a mentor to me. He explained that although he doesn't have a phone, his teenage son does and that it is often useful. They regularly use the phone to send messages to Marta, Jacinto's wife, asking her to send fresh tortillas, coffee, or other staples when an opportunity arises—in other words, the next time a campesino travels from Talea to nearby fields. Before cell phones, Jacinto had to return to the village himself for such things. The six-mile hike down a mountainside and up another is not as easy as it once was, for he is now more than seventy years old and he suffered a serious foot injury several years ago. He also told me that if a campesino gets injured or bitten by a snake or other dangerous creatures, cell phones can be used to call for help.

For Jacinto, this is a significant advance. When he was a young man, a black widow spider bit him and injected enough venom to make him feel feverish and partly paralyzed. Fortunately, a neighboring campesino was able to help by taking him back to Talea on a mule. Once he returned to the pueblo, Jacinto got help from his father (a *curandero* or healer) and eventually a physician. If this kind of situation arose today, Jacinto explained, a campesino could call for help and a mototaxi could be dispatched from the village, perhaps with a doctor on board. "There are many advantages now," he said.

When I asked about potential problems that the cell phones may bring to the village, Jacinto paused for a moment, deep in thought. His voice grew a bit tense: "Well, we're already seeing them. There are many young people who are distracted—that can cause problems. A youngster almost got run over by a car because he wasn't paying attention to where he was going." Earlier in our conversation, he mentioned in passing that one of his grandchildren—a five-year-old girl who is healthy and smart— is also *terrible,* by which he meant mischievous: she has a habit of picking up her parents' cell phones to play video games.

I thought about how I might make a comparable observation from my own experiences, since Jacinto seemed to always enjoy hearing about my life in the United States. So I talked with him openly about an everyday fear: "You know Jacinto, my office is more than sixty kilometers away from home and I have to drive my car on the freeway to get there; every day I see lots of distracted drivers around me, talking on their phones, tapping the screen, not watching the road, driving dangerously."

He paused again, and said, "It's difficult, no? That's how accidents happen."

"Many accidents," I replied. "Thousands of people die that way in my country every year."[9]

. . .

There is another kind of twenty-first century distraction observed in Talea, and presumably in other villages as well, and it even came about before the advent of cell phone service: it might be referred to as civic disengagement. As noted earlier, adult citizens are expected to participate in various aspects of political life. These responsibilities include mandatory attendance and participation in *asambleas*, which are convened every four to eight weeks depending on the urgency of the issues at hand. The two largest meetings are for the *ciudadanía* or citizenry, which adult men are required to attend, and for the *comuneros* or commoners (landowners), a group that includes both men and women. For asambleas extending beyond four hours, the group takes a long lunch break and reconvenes in the afternoon. In Talea, the municipal police close the doors of the meeting hall to prevent villagers from leaving, and the young men station themselves at the doors to ensure that no one leaves. Villages throughout rural Oaxaca typically have comparable systems for democratic discussion, dialogue, and debate.

On several occasions, village leaders allowed me to attend these asambleas. After two or three hours it was sometimes difficult to stay focused. To stay alert, people often stood up and walked to the bathroom, or occasionally smoked cigarettes, or else engaged in hushed conversations with their neighbors about the topics at hand, sometimes gossiping about the person speaking into the microphone, sometimes telling jokes. In the case of all-day sessions, some men spent a portion of the lunch hour at one of the nearby cantinas for a quick mezcal or a beer, often talking politics at the bar. As a result, the bathroom visits, the cigarette smoking, the conversations, and the jokes were more frequent in the late afternoon.

But for the past several years, cell phones have become the latest source of distraction. According to Peter Bloom, some Taleans have observed their fellow villagers playing video games and texting during asambleas.[10] This shouldn't come as a surprise to anyone who has attended a college lecture or been to a theater in the United States over the past decade. The question is: Given the fact that citizens have been so vigilant about enforcing attendance at these meetings, will they ban cell phones from asambleas in the years ahead?

Others worry about the ways in which cell phones can erode the secure, confidential nature of asambleas, which, historically, only citizens were allowed to attend. In the words of a villager, cell phones mean that "people who are present can send out messages immediately about what is happening or being discussed.... The internal life of the pueblos is now more public than it was in the past."

COMING OF AGE ONLINE

I am looking at a blurry Facebook profile photo of Fidel, a fifteen-year-old Talean boy who is the youngest child of a campesino friend. His profile appeared haphazardly, as I was searching through hundreds of "friends" listed under another Talean's Facebook page. I instantly recognized his face, though it has been more than twelve years since I last saw him. He has a faint smile. On his Facebook page he has no "friends" of his own listed, no "time-line," no "check-ins," no movies, no books, no TV shows, no posts, no nada. Just a blurry profile photo posted in May 2017 and nothing before or since.

Nothing, that is, except for comments, which appear to be meaningless chatter between two other adolescent boys. Kid One says, "Like that or more scared?" Kid Two replies, "Leave the kid alone, dude." The response from Kid One: "Now you scared him." Reply from Two: "You think so, dude?" and so forth. My immediate sense is that pranksters created this page and are maybe telling Fidel that they're posting crap about him online. For a moment I feel an overwhelming indignation, and an almost instinctual need to protect Fidel. What does this mean?

I do a quick Facebook search and find Kid One. He wants to portray himself as a thug, mean looking wannabe gangsta face and baggy hoodie and photos of himself posing with a bandana and sunglasses, LA cholo style. Misspelled his own maternal surname, nice detail. Lots of "friends" who attend(ed?) Talea's secondary school. Kid Two looks nerdy and has only posted to his

Facebook page once or twice but visits other students' pages and frequently
"likes" their posts.
  Has cyberbullying reached Talea? Pueblo chico, infierno grande . . .[11]

· · ·

I originally intended to include this entry from my raw "virtual
field notes" alongside other Facebook posts (see chapter 6), but it
made more sense to include it later, since it foreshadows the
impending arrival of a host of problems associated with frequent
social media use, especially by young people: anxiety, disrupted
sleep patterns, depression, loneliness, and other possible effects.[12]
And it seems likely that social media will also aggravate another
aspect of Talean life: economic disparities.

For many years, Talea has been marked by sharp class distinctions, most notably between *gente humilde*, humble folk, and
gente rica or rich folk. *Gente humilde* included subsistence farmers
who spent most or all of their time growing maize, beans, and
other food crops. *Gente rica* included merchants, professionals,
and farmers who spent relatively greater amounts of time growing coffee.

Taleans often learn these class distinctions painfully, during
the adolescent years and sometimes earlier. On more than one
occasion I spoke with a subsistence farmer who, as a teenager, had
been attracted to the daughter of a wealthy family. Even though
the couple was deeply in love, the romance went nowhere. Often,
both sets of parents discouraged their children from marrying
across class lines. Well into the mid-twentieth century, these class
divisions were reinforced through institutions like bride price,
which was typically payable with turkeys and tortillas.[13]

There was an instance in which I witnessed the hidden injuries of class firsthand.[14] As I was returning to Talea from the

fields one summer evening with Filiberto, a twelve-year-old campesino boy, I was surprised to hear him suggest that we take the long way home, around the perimeter of the pueblo. My young companion, who was from *gente humilde*, wore huaraches, a straw hat, and, like me, muddy pants after having worked on the farm all day. "*¿Por qué, Filín?*" I asked. "Why?"

He answered sheepishly: "I don't want Yoli to see me like this," he said, waving his hand downward, over his earth-covered pants and muddy, sandaled feet. Yoli was the daughter of a well-to-do merchant and she worked in the family store every evening, right on the pueblo's main street. He obviously had a crush on her. I got the message. We silently took the long way home.

As Taleans increasingly inhabit virtual worlds including social media, will teenagers from families with internet access and smartphones begin to think of *gente humilde* as living anachronisms? Until the advent of cell phones, all young villagers had to negotiate their social lives in public spaces to which everyone had equal access: the classroom, the schoolyard, the basketball court, the music rehearsal hall, the streets. The children of *gente rica* and *gente humilde* had to face each other regularly—cooperating, conflicting, working out differences, getting to know how the other half lived. But now, a different kind of social space is emerging online. It is segregated by class, to the extent that wealthy kids have greater access to the internet and social media than those from cash-poor families. To put this slightly differently, a kind of digital divide may be emerging in which young Taleans like Fidel—completely dedicated to farm work rather formal education, with little time or money for online worlds—may become unwitting targets of ridicule at the hands of their peers.

Early on in Talea's experiment with the autonomous cell phone network, some expressed concern over the impact of digital technologies on children. In fact, children younger than sixteen years old were not allowed to subscribe to the network. Abrám Fernández made the following comment about the decision to place this restriction:

> At the beginning of all this, the phones were available to the public. It didn't matter if it was a child, a young person, or an adult. Then we began to ask: Really, why does a child need a cell phone? We didn't want to make mass consumers out of them, or at least we had that idea because many parents started to buy phones for their children. But why spend money on a phone for a child if he or she really doesn't need it?[15]

In the end, however, the community network didn't survive, and Movistar prevailed, without placing any such restrictions on subscribers. Time will tell what sort of long-term impact smart phones will have on Talea's youth.

DISINFORMATION

As villagers make the transition from ordinary cell phones to smartphones, they are likely to spend more of their lives online—and therefore to be subject to all the potential forms of political and commercial manipulation that go along with it. During the summer elections of 2018, many Taleans used their Facebook pages and WhatsApp and Twitter accounts to post, tweet, and retweet news reports and articles from legitimate media sources. But, like tens of millions of other Mexicans, they were inundated with fabricated news stories both before and after the elections, many of which appear to have been generated domestically.[16] For example, shortly after the newly elected Mexican president-elect Andrés Manuel López Obrador won the July 1 elections, an official-looking document on letterhead appearing to be from MORENA (López Obrador's political party) circulated widely on WhatsApp, Facebook, and Twitter. It suggested that López Obrador, a left-of-center politician, would impose draconian measures after taking office: the federal government would supposedly take control of the internet, remove biased or defamatory news stories, prohibit junk food, ban ownership of more than one car per person, and cap the salaries of private sector employees.[17]

In the weeks and months before the election, trolls (paid online agitators) and bots (automated programs designed to act like human internet users) overwhelmed Mexicans' social media accounts with propaganda. The Spanish newspaper *El País* reported that trolls were often college students seeking extra income. Some earned as much as twelve thousand pesos (approximately US $590) a month for managing dozens of fake Facebook, Twitter, or WhatsApp accounts.[18]

Living in a global village—or a mobile village—means being exposed to the same forms of mass manipulation and propaganda that we experience in our own society. Sometimes, the same companies do the manipulating. In July 2017, Cambridge Analytica—the political consulting firm that would later be embroiled in a massive US data mining scandal—acknowledged that it was exploring business opportunities in advance of the 2018 Mexican elections.[19] Many believed that the company helped Donald Trump win the 2016 US presidential elections, though there is little evidence that it had a significant effect, and its CEO hinted that it could deliver comparable results in other countries using its "psychographic" methods. The *New York Times* reported that Cambridge Analytica approached Mexico's ruling PRI party with a fifty-seven-page proposal outlining a "dirty campaign" strategy. The company outlined a plan to

improve the PRI's poor public image while attacking the reputation of López Obrador. The proposal stated that by "using
similar techniques that were employed against Hillary Clinton
in the 2016 US presidential election," Cambridge Analytica
would wage "a powerful negative campaign strategy to undermine" López Obrador. PRI officials ultimately decided that they
could run their own campaign, but they paid the company anyway to *not* assist its opponents.[20]

· · ·

To what extent might Taleans' differences of political opinion be
aggravated by cell phones and social media? For example, will a
village long characterized by "harmony ideology" be transformed by social media's tendency to politically polarize people,
even as it interconnects them?[21] I could find only a single case in
which villagers publicly aired their views about local politics
using social media. In that instance, a Facebook page representing one of the village's mototaxi companies posted several
entries denouncing elected officials, including the municipal
police—young men elected to serve without pay for a year, to
patrol the streets without weapons or uniforms—as "stagnant"
and ineffective at maintaining order. It led me to wonder whether
minor internal squabbles that typically either fizzle out or simmer harmlessly for long periods of time might one day escalate
into uncontrollable conflagrations spread via social media. And
then there are the ancestral intervillage conflicts over territorial
boundaries that plague so many Oaxacan pueblos. I cannot help
but wonder whether Talea's long-standing dispute with the
neighboring community of Tabaa might be reignited at some
point in the future, perhaps as the result of rumors circulating
on WhatsApp, Facebook, or some other platform. As mentioned

earlier, when the conflict erupted in the early 1990s several Taleans were killed (see chapter 6). Villagers who recalled those events were deeply traumatized by the violence.

•   •   •

Yet another troubling possibility is that smartphones and social media might be used to trigger episodes of mass hysteria or even mob violence. If that sounds outlandish or paranoid, consider the case of Acatlán de Osorio, a Mixtec town located in the southern part of Puebla state, near its border with Oaxaca. On the afternoon of August 29, 2018, people began gathering outside the municipal police station—a few at a time, until a crowd of more than a hundred had assembled.[22] A police car arrived carrying two men, whom officers promptly whisked away to the town jail. As more villagers joined the mob, voices from the crowd accused the men of being *robachicos* or kidnappers.[23] Municipal officials told the crowd that the two men, twenty-one-year-old Ricardo Flores and his fifty-six-year-old uncle, Alberto Flores, were being held for the minor offense of disturbing the peace. Unbeknown to the police, the mob was acting on a different story: the angry throng was convinced that the two men, neither of whom resided in Acatlán, were organ traffickers looking for young victims. They were responding to a message that someone had circulated earlier that day on WhatsApp:

> Please everyone be alert because a plague of child kidnappers has entered the country. It appears that these criminals are involved in organ trafficking.... In the past few days, children aged four, eight, and fourteen have disappeared and some of these children have been found dead with signs that their organs were removed. Their abdomens had been cut open and were empty.[24]

Figure 20. High-tech lynching in Puebla state: Acatlán de Osirio, August 2018. Photo courtesy of Idalia Medina/Agencia Enfoque.

As more people arrived, a man scaled the pueblo's campanile and began ringing the bell to draw more people to the center. Another, using a loudspeaker, implored his fellow townspeople to contribute money for gasoline. Still another began broadcasting events in real time using his smartphone and Facebook Live, a real-time video streaming service.

Within minutes, the mob descended on the police station and forced the door open. A group of men hauled Ricardo and Alberto Flores out of the building, brutally beat them, and then doused them with gasoline. Then they set the bodies aflame. Macabre photos depict more than a dozen people holding up their phones, recording images of the burning bodies (see figure 20). It is a scene worthy of the TV series *Black Mirror*, a contemporary version of the *Twilight Zone*—though it is perhaps more terrifying, since this is not fiction.

The next day, in the pueblo of Santa Ana Ahuhuepán, in the central Mexican state of Hidalgo, villagers accused two more people of being *robachicos*. As in Acatlán, they were falsely accused, but the facts did not prevent a mob from brutalizing them and setting their bodies on fire. A spate of WhatsApp alerts circulating among villagers served as a catalyst for the crowd. Because of WhatsApp's encryption system, designed to protect users' privacy, it is impossible to trace messages shared on the app.[25]

Although I am not aware of any lynchings that have occurred in the Rincón in the recent past, they do occasionally happen in Oaxaca and other parts of the country—and are generally not connected to the major drug cartels that have wreaked havoc in Mexico since the late 1980s. Lynchings are not a new phenomenon in Mexico, but the rise of social media makes it easier for false accusations, rumors, and disinformation to go viral in communities and neighborhoods—potentially opening the way for a high-tech form of vigilante justice.[26]

BALANCE

In the summer of 2006, I journeyed to Talea with a colleague to document the rapid changes that were transforming villagers' lives.[27] We were especially concerned about the loss of local knowledge and asked: "Is it possible that fifty years of 'development' has done more unraveling than five hundred years of conquest? Are the Taleans ... knowing more and more about less and less?" As people in the United States were becoming dependent on Google, Wikipedia, and YouTube for everything from grocery shopping to parenting tips, we wondered about the extent to which the pueblo might be negatively impacted by technologies of convenience.

Initially, I approached this topic with the assumption that accelerating technological change would have a detrimental impact on the people of the Rincón. Even after having chronicled the boundless creativity and resourcefulness of campesino families in my previous work, I wondered how villagers would deal with the turbulent transformations of the digital age.

I underestimated the adaptive abilities of the Zapotec. As we gathered footage for a documentary film, we discovered a complex situation in which some kinds of knowledge—for example, *curanderismo* or healing—were disappearing, while other kinds of knowledge, such as architecture, were being creatively adapted and updated with techniques and ideas borrowed from elsewhere. "If there is a crisis of losing knowledge occurring in Talea today, there is also a process of finding new knowledge that isn't exclusively rooted in indigenous cultures," we concluded.[28]

Talea's cooperative mobile network illustrates the point. At times, villagers have borrowed and appropriated outside knowledge and technology largely on their own terms, harnessing it to maintain social and kinship networks across national borders. As a villager posted on Talea GSM's Facebook page: "Let's adapt technology to our needs, not adapt ourselves to its needs."

In practice, the appropriation of cell phones is taking complex forms as the technology becomes entangled with social structures like cabildos. For example, within a few years, cell phones have become crucial tools for elected officials and, simultaneously, a burden. Instead of visiting a municipal president in his office, a villager, politician, or state regulator may send him a message using WhatsApp—and expect a swift reply. The pressure to speed up political life has grown in recent times, to the extent that more and more time is spent in virtual realms. "The days of a *presidente* without a cell phone or a *municipio* without a Facebook account are long gone," noted a villager who had served in various elected positions.

Many questions remain about the long-term impact of these devices. Like gambling machines, smart phones and apps were intentionally engineered in such a way as to make them as appealing as possible to users, and therefore extraordinarily difficult to put down.[29] These are habit-forming technologies by design, and there is no reason to believe that Zapotec users are any more immune to their aftereffects than are South Koreans, or the British, or North Americans, or Brazilians.

And yet the Rincón Zapotec experience is evidence of the tantalizing prospects offered by locally created technological networks. Ramesh Srinivasan reminds us that even though the vast majority of the world's population has no say in the internet's future, or in the design of virtual technologies, experiments in rural and indigenous societies hint at the possibility of a decentralized, locally oriented internet. Such systems might foster a radically distinct alternative—collaborative, bottom-up connectivity.[30]

Perhaps the people of Talea can maintain vigilance and caution as they become ever more tightly (and virtually) connected to the rest of the world. It is not implausible to think that they may ultimately be more successful than the millions of people who have succumbed to the magnetic attraction of compelling digital technologies—not only phones, but video games, social media apps, and the internet itself. But it is not necessarily a foregone conclusion. A Zapotec friend who lives in the sierra (a region adjacent to the Rincón) recently told me about a face-to-face conversation he had with a group of teenagers, all of whom had cell phones. Most of the youngsters were concerned about the ways in which the technology might affect relationships in their pueblo, since using cell phones often requires periodically disconnecting oneself from daily life. At the same time, many acknowledged that the devices can greatly facilitate communication and enable political and social mobilization. Their sophisticated understanding and ambivalent sentiments about digital media suggested a kind of existential anxiety. If the younger generations have absorbed these connective technologies into their everyday lives, will indigenous cosmologies and cultures eventually collapse?

As I was completing this book, I corresponded with Salvador Aquino, a Sierra Zapotec man with a doctorate in cultural anthropology from an American university. In a series of thoughtful email messages, filled with lighthearted jabs and even a few emoticons, he reminded me that technology ultimately rests in the hands of its users. Trial and error methods allow people to experiment, but they also permit people to modify things or reject them altogether. In Capulálpam, Aquino's hometown, villagers largely abandoned agriculture in the 1980s as they turned to forestry and ecotourism. Now, more than a generation later, the pueblo has reflected on its unacceptably vulnerable position: all its food now comes from Oaxaca City. Although it is a difficult process, the people of Capulálpam are now seeking to revive subsistence farming, using a combination of old and new technologies to cultivate native varieties of maize, wheat, and beans from their region.

As he gently chided me for my glum assessment, Aquino offered an optimistic and self-assured perspective—bolstered by the weight of history:

My good Talean ... experience and the method of trial and error that you mention are crucial. So don't be sad! We *serranos* [mountain Zapotec] historically have been leaders! People will have to tame the virtual media; real communities will undoubtedly overlap with virtual ones; social identities will be transformed; and so too will the meaning of what it means to be serrano. But in the end, the villages will remain. If we've endured for a millennium, then why not endure for one more?

This fragmentary glimpse into what a digital future may look like in the Zapotec pueblos of northern Oaxaca makes sense on many levels, and it reveals an underlying sense of cultural confidence and creativity. Aquino seemed to be saying: Our pueblos have survived conquest, colonialism, contagion, capitalism, and other calamities—surely we can adapt to virtual life without sacrificing the things that we cherish the most.

And yet there are concerns and—at least among some Zapotec people—care and caution. In a public forum held in Oaxaca City, a leader from the Rincón community of Yaviche summarized a town hall meeting that took place in his pueblo as it was weighing the pros and cons of cell phones: "Some said, it's going to break with our customs, because now we won't be able to talk directly to my neighbors.... But others said, cell phones can't take that away from us—as long as we are secure in our [collective] identity and values. We must teach our children and youth the proper way to use phones when the devices arrive in our community."

· · ·

In 1980, an influential Talean elder who had served in nearly every elected position in the village, had this to say about technological innovation: "We've all become comfort lovers ... [but]

what can be bad about new things is not knowing how to use them properly. I'm not against progress; I'm for it. But I think there must be a balance."[31]

Finding that balance in the midst of digital media technologies will likely be among the biggest challenges confronting Taleans—and the rest of us—in the twenty-first century.

CHAPTER EIGHT

Outro (Reconnected)

This is a fleeting account of how I got reconnected to Talea.

Although it isn't directly related to the events or the people described in other chapters of this book, I include it because it has a great deal to do with telephones, long-distance communication, and human relationships. It also touches on some of the trickier aspects of doing anthropology that rarely get written or talked about—even though they probably should.

It was hard to write this epilogue, not because I didn't want to share my experiences with others, but because I had a tough time finding the right voice with which to do it. I'm not sure I ever did.

If my words help to encourage an anthropologist or two to use the magical, glowing devices that we carry in our pockets to get back in touch with people that opened their homes to them and maybe even their hearts, then it will have been worth the effort.

• • •

During the time that I lived in Talea in the 1990s, I was introduced to Jacinto, a campesino whom villagers generally described as one of the best farmers in town. *Está muy metido en el campo*, they said admiringly: "He's deep into the countryside." Within a few months I grew close to him and his family—that is, to his wife Marta and their five children, ages two to fifteen—and they eventually took me under their roof, fed me, and invited me to accompany them as they worked in the fields and the forests surrounding the village. Jacinto became a mentor who taught me the intricate details of subsistence farming. Day in and day out, he and his wife patiently explained to me why they did things as they did. Although they must have been puzzled by my endless questions, they never expressed irritation or annoyance.

Eventually, after Jacinto had taught me more than I ever thought possible about agriculture and life, I knew that my research project was ending, and that it would soon be time to return home. I left the pueblo as the twentieth century was drawing to a close, and I felt an inexplicably overwhelming, unexpected sense of sorrow. My hosts' final words to me were: "Our door will always be open for you." Once I departed, I knew that nothing would ever compare to the life that I had enjoyed but never taken for granted: the fragrance of smoldering firewood and roasted coffee beans; the delicate pit-a-pat of fresh rain on cobblestone paths; the brilliant emerald hues of corn fields, coffee trees, and sugarcane; the mystical ancient cloud forests blanketed in thick quilts of fog; and, most of all, the humor and hospitality of the villagers.

Most families had to work hard to put food on the table. Even children were expected to toil with their parents in the maize fields during summertime and the winter coffee harvest. But the regularity of farming life was punctuated by fiestas and life-cycle celebrations such as funerals, weddings, and baptisms where there was lively and intense social interaction and human connection. In this place, the rhythm of village life continued to follow the seasons more than the clock. ___

As the years passed, we began to lose contact—or, to be more precise, *I* began to lose contact with *them*. At first, I was methodical about keeping in touch with the families that had put up with me for more than two years. But over time, I found it more and more difficult to write letters or to coordinate phone calls. When I left the pueblo in 1999, there were approximately twenty telephones. These were all landlines owned by relatively prosperous families. Phoning my campesino friends was an excruciating process. I had to first call the village's phone kiosk during the six hours that it was open for business; then ask a messenger to summon the person with whom I wanted to speak; and then, after that person had paid the messenger, phone the kiosk once again to finally connect. If the intended recipient of my call was not home, then I would have to try again another day.

As my own work and family responsibilities grew—and when I gradually stopped writing letters to *anyone* as I became dependent on e-mailing and text-messaging colleagues, relatives, and friends—I lost touch with the villagers. I guess you could say I let them slip away. Month after month, I kept postponing the simple task of writing a letter. The demands of a tenure-track position and eventually fatherhood seemed to consume all my time. This was a period of heartfelt letters begun but never finished, calls intended but never made, conversations imagined but never realized. In retrospect, it was a time of disconnection, separation, isolation. Before I knew it, eight years had passed.

I don't know if these situations are common among cultural anthropologists—or if what happened to me was an unusual phenomenon. Of the many conversations that I have had with colleagues over the years, the subject of what happens to the human relationships we establish during the course of our research almost never comes up. Perhaps I formed closer bonds during my time in the pueblo than most other anthropologists do. Or maybe I was less prepared than others to take leave of my hosts. Or maybe lots of us subconsciously scrape through these painful moments, suffering in silence.

. . .

When I finally reestablished contact with my Talean friends, it was not by cell phone but via Skype (on my end) and landline (on their end)—more or less as I had done years ago. I had no idea if the phone kiosk was still operational, but it was the only number I had. I dialed nervously, then listened anxiously to Skype's cheerful, staccato, six note trademark. To my surprise, a woman answered immediately, as if expecting a call.

I assumed that I would have to go through the same routine as before, asking for a messenger to summon a member of Jacinto's family, then call back a half hour later. But the voice at the other end of the line sounded vaguely familiar.

"Who is calling?" asked the woman after I asked if a messenger could be dispatched to Jacinto's house.

"A friend of the family—my name is Roberto." I replied.

Five interminable seconds of silence.

"Roberto! González! Flores! Where have you been?" she exclaimed, in a mock scolding voice. I immediately recognized the woman as Eloisa, Jacinto's second child—now a thirty-seven-year-old woman, apparently employed at the phone kiosk. "We've been wondering what happened to you!" I could tell from her voice that she was smiling.

Words cannot describe the sense of relief I felt as Eloisa and I spoke for the next half-hour. Fortunately, everyone in the immediate family was doing well. Most of Jacinto's six children were now married, some with children of their own. Jacinto had celebrated his seventieth birthday just a month earlier, and although he had seriously injured his foot the previous summer, he was now well enough to return to his farming work.

Jacinto's wife, Marta, was also doing well. The last time I had spoken with her was in 2007, when she desperately implored me to talk her eighteen-year-old son out of migrating to the United States as an undocumented worker. I guess it worked: he had decided to stay put.

Before saying goodbye, Eloisa insisted on giving me her cell phone number, as well as the cell phone numbers of all five of her siblings—"just in case you need to reach one of us directly," she said. And I gave her my number. I agreed to call again two days later, on a Sunday when her father would return from the coffee harvest.

• • •

On Sunday, I called back, and Eloisa told me that Marta insisted on talking with me first. Marta had me in stitches for nearly a half hour with her jokes. She hadn't forgotten any of the Zapotec nicknames her children had created for me a quarter century earlier: *bhni tuz* (bachelor man), *bugúpi* (armadillo, since I preferred to wear an armadillo shell basket when picking coffee or planting maize seed), *betu-zal* (a Zapotec version of Roberto

González, which, coincidentally, was the label villagers gave to a crusty Talean curmudgeon), *betu-guéru* (blonde Roberto). She told me that over the past few years many villagers had been asking about the whereabouts of *betu-látu*—yet another sobriquet that villagers had given me, since *látu* was Jacinto's family nickname. After more laughs and a warm goodbye, she passed the telephone to her husband.

As often happens with close friends, Jacinto and I picked up right where we had left off eight years earlier. Jacinto is not a sentimental man, but he is a compassionate one, and he immediately asked about the well-being of my parents, my siblings, and my wife. He sounded glad to hear that I had two healthy young children of my own; he was equally glad that I had plenty of work. "Work is the most important thing—that way you can provide for the family," he said, exactly as I had heard him say a thousand times before in the maize fields, the coffee plantations, and the lean-to shelter that was our home away from home—a full two-hour walk from Talea (see figure 21). I was thrilled to hear that, despite all of the attractions of wage labor and the allure of migration, both of Jacinto's sons had dedicated themselves to campesino life. His voice swelled with pride as he told me that his younger son, Fidel—now sixteen years old—was the proud co-owner of three oxen. He also possesses a cell phone that he occasionally uses to call and text his friends—even as he takes the oxen to pasture!

Reflecting on the rapid changes that have swept across the pueblo have made me realize that the men and women I met in Talea a quarter century ago are no longer the same people that I once knew. But then again, I am not the same person either. Time, technology, and circumstance have remade us all.

I apologized to Jacinto for having let so many years pass without contacting him or his family. His response was, "Thank you,

Figure 21. Field work, July 2007. Photo courtesy of Kike Arnal.

thank you for this call, we were concerned that *maybe something had happened to you*. But don't worry, we know that work keeps you busy." As he said these words, I thought about those parents in the pueblo with sons and daughters that intended to migrate to the United States but had gone missing. *Maybe something had happened to them*: maybe brutalized or violated as they made their way towards *el norte*; maybe unable to survive the heat of the sweltering Arizona desert or the deceptively swift currents of the Rio Grande; maybe jailed for a minor transgression committed in a strange land; maybe abducted by who knows who, who knows where, never to be heard from again.

There were melancholy moments in our conversation, particularly when I asked about his older brother (who had died suddenly four years ago) and one of his best friends (who had died even earlier, and not so suddenly). True to character, Jacinto was philosophical, not emotional: "We're all walking down the same road—but some finish the journey before others." For reasons I cannot explain I found these words to be extraordinarily comforting. I had missed Jacinto's voice, his wisdom, his sense of perspective.

As we talked, many memories rushed through my head, including the moment when Jacinto and Marta met my parents, who had insisted on traveling to Talea for a brief visit a few months before I had completed my work there. I suppose they were curious about the place where I had spent nearly two years of my life, the place to which I returned any time I had a chance. In their humble, earth floored adobe home, the family treated my parents to a hearty lunch of chicken soup, black beans, and fresh tortillas, and after eating and talking we prepared to say goodbye.

As we got up to leave, my father embraced Jacinto. In an uncharacteristically shaky voice, he said, *ahí le encargo a mi hijo*— "I leave my son in your hands." To my surprise, both men's eyes were welling up with tears. Then mine were too.

. . .

After nearly an hour on the phone, Jacinto and I bid each other a long farewell, and he promised to send my greetings to many villagers who had asked about me. In turn, I promised to keep in touch with him and his family.

And I have.

NOTES

CHAPTER ONE. CONNECTED

1. Associated Press 2013.

2. There is an ongoing global debate about whether or not internet access should be considered a human right. Essentially, the argument is that governments should ensure that citizens have universal access to the internet because it can be an important vehicle for providing economic opportunities for the world's poor. Proponents argue that, like water, electricity, and other utilities, the internet has become an essential part of the social infrastructure. Another argument is that the internet can potentially enable freedom of assembly in cyberspace and can therefore serve as a tool for mobilizing political protest.

3. Graeber 2004, 98–99.

4. Anthropologist Laura Nader (1990, 1) first made this observation thirty years ago in an ethnography about Talea's legal system.

5. Graeber 2004, 45.

6. This would not be the first time that an initiative led by Taleans would bring broader regional benefits. Villagers aggressively and successfully petitioned government officials in the 1950s to build a road linking the pueblo to Oaxaca City. By the late 1970s, the Mexican government proposed linking seven more Rincón villages (Juquila,

Reforma, Tanetze, Yaviche, Yagallo, Lachichina, and Yaeé) to Talea by extending the road, and the pueblo's elected officials invited their counterparts from those villages to create a cooperative bus service. Those officials declined and instead petitioned the government to create a separate road that would bypass Talea by branching off to one side, in a Y-shape. The villages succeeded, and their road was completed in 1984. For a description of these events, see Chávez López and Palerm Viqueira 2016, 255–59. The point here is that the construction of the road was greatly facilitated by the previous existence of a road linking Talea to towns in the adjacent Sierra Juárez region (including La Trinidad, Natividad, and Ixtlán de Juárez).

7. Nader 1964, 208.

8. There have been exceptions. For example, Laura Nader (1964, v) reported that weeks into her first visit in Talea, the resident Catholic priest and some townspeople accused her of being a Protestant missionary, and that this presented a problem since "Talea had had unpleasant contact with various missionaries two years previously." But in general the pueblo has been "a refuge town, a place that attracted Zapotecs who left their own villages for a variety of reasons, Mexican nationals escaping the series of revolutions that shook the country, or unemployed miners seeking a new means of subsistence" (212).

9. Just as importantly, subsistence farming provided families with high-quality produce that tasted better and was more satisfying and satiating than food imported from outside the region. See González 2001, 19–20. Since 2012, many coffee growers in northern Oaxaca have experienced low coffee yields due to *roya* or coffee rust, a fungus that attacks the leaves of the plant (Chaca 2016).

10. Turkle 2012.

11. Communication scholars have done significantly more research than anthropologists, in part because theirs is a larger discipline. For early examples, see Katz and Aakhus 2002, and Ling 2004, the former of which includes case studies from the Philippines, France, Israel, South Korea, Finland, Bulgaria, and the Netherlands.

12. Horst and Miller 2006, 6.

13. McIntosh 2010, 337.

14. Ito 2005, 2–3. See also Ito, Okabe, and Matsuda 2005.

15. Stammler 2013.

16. Stammler 2013, 229.

17. Stammler 2013, 240.

18. The herders complained because their neighbor was unable to receive calls. Therefore, they had to journey to his camp by foot in order to determine whether or not their grazing reindeer might have mingled with his herd.

19. Bell and Kuipers 2018.

20. Quoted in Gershon 2018. See also Tenhunen 2018.

21. Quoted in Gershon 2018.

22. For examples of ethnographies that focus on the internet, social media, and media more generally, see Boellstorff 2008; Burell 2012; Lange 2014; Miller and Slater 2001; Nardi 2010. Anthropological analyses include Kummels 2017; Magallanes-Blanco and Ramos Rodríguez 2016; Wortham 2013; and Zamorano Villarreal 2017. In recent years many books have outlined the methodological and theoretical possibilities of digital ethnography and anthropology. See, for example, Horst and Miller 2012; Pertierra 2018; Pink 2015; Underberg 2014.

23. Yannakakis 2008, xii–xiii.

24. Yannakakis 2008, 3.

25. Chance 1989, 114.

26. Wolf 1956, 1075.

27. Nader 1964, 214.

28. Yannakakis 2008, xii.

29. Graeber 2004, 12.

30. In Talea, the Secretariat of Finance and Public Credit collects taxes from small businesses; the Federal Electricity Commission provides electrical service; the Secretariat of Public Education, a national agency, employs teachers; and since the 1990s, the Attorney General of the Mexican Republic has maintained an office in the pueblo, staffed by a lawyer who was ostensibly there to investigate serious crimes in the Villa Alta district. Some government employees had little work to do in Talea. In the 1990s, I would occasionally see electricians from the Federal Electricity Commission or the lawyer from the federal

Attorney General's office idly spending long afternoons at a *comedor* (small restaurant) near their offices.

31. The state government gave municipalities the option of deciding whether or not to formally adopt *usos y costumbres*, and the vast majority (412 out of 570) chose to do so. In theory, *usos y costumbres* can "increase governing institutions' credibility and foster positive group identities," but in practice it seems that the Oaxaca state government initiated this effort as a desperate response to the political climate following the 1994 Zapatista uprising in neighboring Chiapas. See Aquino Centeno 2013; Eisenstadt 2006; Velásquez et al 1997.

32. Nader 1990, xxi.

33. Nader 1990, 8.

34. Nader 1990, 275.

35. Chance 1989.

36. Chance 1989; Chance 1986, 180.

37. Rénique and Poole 2008.

38. Meyer 2010, 14.

39. See, for example, Díaz 2001 and 2007, and Martínez Luna 1995 and 2010. Comunalidad gained international attention when Noam Chomsky discussed the concept at length in a 2004 interview. See Chomsky 2010.

40. See Díaz Gómez 2001, 2007; Martínez Luna 1995, 2010. Although Martínez Luna contrasts comunalidad with colonialism and capitalism, he also highlights the ways in which it differs from Marxism.

41. Another anthropologist with ties to Oaxaca, Benjamín Maldonado Alvarado (2002), builds upon this concept, and explicitly links comunalidad to notions of indigenous autonomy. Anthropologist Jeffrey Cohen has also analyzed a community-based ethos in the Zapotec valley community of Santa Ana del Valle. See Cohen 2000, especially chapters 4 and 5.

42. Baca-Feldman, Parra Hinojosa, and Huerta Velázquez 2017.

43. Esteva 2001, 129–30.

44. Graeber 2004, 35.

45. The term "addictive by design" comes from anthropologist Natasha Dow Schüll's (2012) analysis of machine gambling in Las Vegas. Schüll's work is well known among some in the tech industry—

including Nir Eyal, who advocates building "habit-forming products" to hook consumers. See Harris 2016.

CHAPTER TWO. INNOVATION

1. Flannery 1999; Smith 1998.

2. Long et al. 1989.

3. Rodríguez-Mega 2018.

4. González 2001, 3.

5. For a summary of the refugee hypothesis see Oudijk 2000. The idea of a utopian exodus is based upon a general discussion of the topic by Graeber (2004, 60–63).

6. Romero Frizzi 1996, 61.

7. This is a rough estimate based on extrapolations from Chance 1989, 62, 67–68.

8. Yannakakis 2008, 20.

9. Yannakakis 2008, 21.

10. See Chance 1989, 77 and Nader 1964, 208.

11. On shifting settlement patterns in the northern sierra, see Chance 1989, 69–70. Immediately prior to the Spanish Conquest, Mixe and Zapotec pueblos were periodically at war with each other. See Chance 1989, 125.

12. Yannakakis 2008, 21. See also Juan José Rendón's *Diversificación de las lenguas zapotecas* (1995), a foundational study of the diversity of Zapotec language.

13. See de Ávila Blomberg 2008 and Maffi 2005.

14. Boroditsky 2011.

15. The elders came from the pueblos of Tanetze, Yaee, Yagallo, Juquila, Yatoni, Yojobi, and the area that would later become Talea. Two Sierra Zapotec settlements, Capulálpam and Tepanzacoalco, also sent emissaries. See Nader 1964, 208.

16. Chance 1989, 16–17.

17. According to John Chance, the Talea document is one of a group of five that details accounts taken from lienzos after 1550. Although the documents are dated in the 1520s, they mention two Spaniards who did not arrive in region until the 1550s. Chance suggests that "the falsification

of dates on all these documents was probably done intentionally to enhance their 'authenticity'," but notes that is "very probable" that Talea was founded before 1548. See Chance 1989, 194, 79.

18. For examples of such scholarship, see Romero Frizzi and Vásquez Vásquez 2003, and Romero Frizzi and Oudijk 2003. I am grateful to Yanna Yannakakis for alerting me to this literature. She notes that "the trope of going to Mexico City to ask the viceroy to send friars to the sierra is common.... Rather than a violent imposition by the Spaniards, the trip to 'New Spain,' as they cast it, was an act of diplomacy initiated by the nobility of the sierra.... [According to the trope,] Christianity was something they actively sought, rather than submitted to" (Yanna Yannakakis, personal communication, July 31, 2019).

19. Romero Frizzi 1996, 143.

20. The population would not reach pre-Conquest levels again until the mid-twentieth century. See Chance 1989, 62–63.

21. *Cocolizti* is a Nahuatl word that was used to describe this epidemic disease. Recent analysis of DNA samples from bacteria dating to the 1540s suggests that salmonella killed many millions of Mesoamericans during that decade. See Callaway 2017.

22. González 2001, 102–6.

23. See for example Chance 1989, 23–29, 103–11.

24. González 2001, 44–45.

25. Chance 1989, 23–26.

26. Chance 1989, 1989, 94.

27. Chassen-López 2010, 188. The Bourbon Reforms of the late eighteenth century played a significant role in transforming the industry. Yanna Yannakakis (2008, 166) notes that "Echarrí's operation emerged in the context of Bourbon officials to revitalize mining.... The Crown slashed silver royalties and the price of mercury.... [The Bourbons also] instituted state-organized credit banks, and created privileged mining guilds, ... [and] awarded noble titles to successful miners."

28. Chance 1989, 96.

29. Yannakakis 2008, 167–68.

30. Chance 1989, 96.

31. Chance 1989, 139.

32. Yannakakis 2008, 167–68.

33. Wolf 1959, 148, 214.

34. Wolf 1956, 1076.

35. Yannakakis 2008, 4.

36. Yannakakis 2008, 11.

37. Yannakakis 2008, 107–14. Yannakakis rightly notes that Indian identity in colonial New Spain is a topic that deserves more attention. Apart from *indios ladinos*, and *indios bárbaros*, Spaniards used another term, *indios conquistadores*, to refer to those who had helped support the colonial enterprise, for example, by fighting against recalcitrant pueblos or serving as translators. In the Villa Alta district, a barrio of such people resided just outside the Villa Alta settlement, and consisted primarily of Tlaxcalans. See Yannakakis 2008, 192–219.

38. Chassen-López 2010, 206, 251; Pérez García 1956, 265.

39. Pérez García 1956, 162; McNamara 2007, 36, 144.

40. Hernández Trejo 2012, 101.

41. Garner 1985, 120; Pérez García 1956, 273–74.

42. Chance 1989, 52–53. If we take into account Laura Nader's estimate of a Talean population of one thousand at the turn of the twentieth century, then we can assume that Santa Getrudis was home to approximately the same number of people. See Nader 1964, 208.

43. Nader 1964, 213.

44. See Grañen Porrúa and Jiménez Santos 2016. The Vatican beatified the so-called "martyrs of Cajonos" in 2002.

45. Kellen Kee Mcintyre (1997) has noted that Olivera's painting *Los venerables mártires de Cajonos* was frequently cited by the modern Cajonos beatification committee (formed in Oaxaca in the 1980s) as evidence supporting the martyrs of Cajonos cult.

46. Pérez García 1956, 149–50.

47. González 2001, 200–201.

48. Berg 1968, 79–80, 289.

49. González 2001, 202.

50. Those who have taken a more cautious approach toward rapid social and technological change are not Luddites; nor are they opposed to innovation per se; they instead prefer to carefully experiment with technologies, tools, or crops to determine whether or how best to adopt them (González 2001).

51. Hannerz 1992, 212. See also Welz 2003.

52. Nader 1990, 55.

CHAPTER THREE. ENCHANTED

1. A professional engineer living in Oaxaca, who was born and raised in Talea, had donated the computer.

2. By the late 1990s, Talean youth were asking me about rappers including Tupac Shakur, Snoop Dogg, and Ice Cube.

3. Levi-Strauss 1955, 42.

4. Quoted in Nader and González 2012.

5. Weber was a social evolutionist who thought that human societies evolved from "primitive" forms to "civilized" ones. In fact, Weber's notion of disenchantment closely resembles that of late nineteenth-century anthropologist Edward Tylor, who hypothesized that "primitive" and "barbaric" societies tended to understand the world in terms of magic and religion, respectively. By contrast, they thought that "civilized" societies used science. Anthropologists had debunked social evolutionary schemes by the 1920s and 1930s. For example, in a widely read essay first published in 1928, Bronislaw Malinowski used ethnographic examples to critique the social evolutionists, arguing that in all societies—including our own—magic, religion, and science coexist.

6. Later I understood that the villagers were seeking common ground, so that I might feel at home in the village.

7. The *bhni glas* exist in other pueblos in the northern sierra, such as in the Cajonos Zapotec village of Yalalag. See de la Fuente 1948, 289–92.

8. Campesinos never described *bhni gui'a* as devils or demons, yet there are striking similarities to the notion of a Faustian bargain, or pact with the devil, found in many societies. Michael Taussig's classic ethnography *The Devil and Commodity Fetishism in South America* (1980) makes a compelling link between a Colombian version of this motif and capitalism.

9. The name of this being is derived from the Nahuatl word *matlacihuatl*, and, as you might expect, versions of the being are docu-

mented across different parts of Mesoamerica. See, for example, Sullivan 1987, 51 and Hunt 1977, 102.

10. See González 2001, 102–13.

11. Much has been written about Mexican "folk Catholicism" as a syncretic blend of European and Mesoamerican religious beliefs and practices. See Ricard (1933) 1966; Yannakakis 2008, 69–70 and 79–82.

12. Harmony is an ideology, not a reality, in Talea. See Nader 1990. Even during times of rapid change, villagers described the town as *un pueblo tranquilo*, literally a tranquil village.

13. Graeber 2004, 25–26.

14. Bandas arrived relatively recently in the northern sierra (only about a century ago), but it is difficult to overstate their political and social significance. More than fifty years ago, Laura Nader (1964, 240–41) noted that, in the Rincón, musical groups sometimes reflect factions within a village. Although the once intense rivalry between Talea's band and orchestra has dissipated—in fact today there are two bands, an orchestra, and several smaller groupings—musical organizations still often reflect local politics. To avoid controversy or the appearance of favoritism, I played with both the band and orchestra during much of my time in Talea. A social history of or *bandas municipales* in Oaxaca's indigenous communities is badly needed.

15. In this chapter I have chosen the term *enchantment* for several reasons, not least of which is its etymology: the term's root word is chant, from the Latin term *cantare*, which means to sing. In many societies, music is the primary means by which humans communicate with the supernatural.

16. Bennett 2001, 5.

17. E.E. Evans-Pritchard was among the first anthropologists to acknowledge how we sometimes get completely swept into other ways of experiencing the world: "I have often been asked whether, when I was among the Azande, I got to accept their ideas about witchcraft.... I suppose you can say I accepted them. I had no choice.... If one goes on arranging one's affairs, organizing one's life in harmony with the lives of one's hosts, whose companionship one seeks and without which one would sink into disorganized craziness, one must eventually give way." See Evans-Pritchard (1937) 1976, 244.

18. Paz (1950) 1989, 50–51. Jaime Martínez Luna, a Zapotec anthropologist from the Sierra Zapotec village of Guelatao, describes fiesta as one of the four pillars of *comunalidad* (literally "communality"), along with *asamblea, tequio,* and *gozona.* See Martínez Luna 2010.

19. Here I am alluding to Guy Debord's *Society of the Spectacle* ([1967] 2002), a searing (and entertaining) Marxist-Situationist critique of mass media, consumerism, and popular culture.

20. San Isidro Labrador is popular among campesinos throughout Latin America. He lived in the late eleventh and early twelfth centuries near Madrid, and the Vatican beatified him in 1619.

21. In this context, "Prepárense, cabrones" can be crudely translated as "Get ready, dudes!" In Mexico, the meaning of *cabrón*—like many slang words—ranges a great deal depending upon the circumstances. The term literally refers to a male goat.

22. Octavio Paz's ([1950] 1989) vivid description is worth quoting: "During those days [of fiesta] the silent Mexican whistles, cries out, sings, throws firecrackers, fires his pistol into the air. He unloads his soul. And his grito [soulful cry], like the fireworks that we love so dearly, rises to the heavens, bursts into a green, red, blue, and white explosion, and falls vertiginously, leaving a trail of golden sparks."

23. Timoteo Cruz Santos, a native of Oaxaca's Pacific coast region, composed the pieces in the 1970s. A *banda municipal* from the Mixe town of Totontepec, located in the northern sierra, recorded the arrangements. See *Sucedió en Oaxaca* 2017.

24. Several people told me that campesinos who do not take time off from their farming work to observe important fiestas may have bad fortune, such as a poor harvest or a runaway animal. See González 2001, 106.

25. See Ricard, (1933) 1966: 31; Brandes 2007.

26. See Barr 2018.

27. Campesino families (especially *gente humilde* or "humble people") often had more elaborate altars than *gente rica* or rich people. This is probably because they cultivated more food and had access to a greater variety of food crops than did merchants or professionals.

28. See de la Fuente 1949, 292.

29. Village citizens elected municipal policemen and other officials to one-year terms. *Policías* were unarmed except on rare occasions, when one of them might have carried a truncheon. Typically, the *policias* were very young men (eighteen to twenty-five years old) who were being initiated into the cargo system.

30. Over the past decade, the villagers of San Andrés Yaa have transformed the area around the Cruz Verde. There are now several permanent structures made of cement block, including a Catholic chapel and several dozen small shelters for housing pilgrims. Despite these improvements, most visitors continue to build improvised lean-tos, since there are not nearly enough rooms for everyone in the new buildings.

31. Chronicles written during the Spanish colonial period are a testimony to the persistence of such practices, particularly in the Cajonos Zapotec region (see Guillow (1889) 1994; Zilbermann 1966). Across the sierra the magical rites appear to have been similar. A group of villagers took turkeys, tortillas, candles, and a combination of other offerings (puppies, tamales, ears of corn, eggs, cigarettes) to a site in the forest marked by a stone altar. They slaughtered the animals and poured the blood poured over the altar and the earth, and petitioned the gods for abundant maize, sufficient rain, and good fortune (Beals 1945; de la Fuente 1949; Lipp 1992). Ralph Beals's account is particularly dramatic: he notes that on the slopes of Mount Zempoaltepetl, Mixe guides showed him "a stagnant pool of noxious-looking water in a depression below an overhanging rock … [and nearby was] a tiny shrine of slabs of rock…. Turkey feathers were scattered within the shrine and for some distance about. Horsehair, bits of wool, and the wrappings of many tamales lay within the shrine, while a log, much marked with blows from a machete, reposed in front … stained dark with blood." See Beals 1945, 85.

32. De la Fuente 1949, 266; Parsons 1936, 230.

33. As my fellow músicos and I encountered gente rica from Talea at the Cruz Verde, I could not help but think of the pilgrimage as a rite of passage. Pilgrims experienced separation, liminality, and eventually incorporation or transformation (Turner 1967; Van Gennep [1909] 1960).

34. Barabas 2000.

35. Graeber 2004, 36.

36. Graeber 2004, 26.

CHAPTER FOUR. NETWORKS

1. Here I borrow the idea of community cell phone networks as an intercultural dialogue between hackers and indigenous peoples from Loreto Bravo Muñoz 2017. For an anthropological analysis of hackers, see Coleman 2010 and 2012.

2. Quoted in Womack 1999, 303. The Zapatista army made global headlines on January 1, 1994 when it seized nearly forty municipalities in the southern Mexican state of Chiapas and declared them to be an autonomous region. The Zapatistas sought a broad social transformation that sought to protect the rights of indigenous peoples and women, radically democratize Mexican society, and counteract the destructive tendencies of neoliberal economic policies, among other things. During the time that I lived and worked in Talea in the 1990s, many young villagers were sympathetic to the ideas expressed by the Zapatista's leaders.

3. Gift economies can be defined as systems "not based on calculation, but on a refusal to calculate; they were rooted in an ethical system which consciously rejected most of what we would consider the basic principles of economics." (Graeber 2004, 21).

4. See Wolf 1957.

5. A rich description of Zapotec manufacturing in the mid-twentieth century can be found in Alba and Cristerna 1949.

6. For a thorough analysis of precontact Zapotec civilizations, see Marcus and Flannery 1996.

7. For an early assessment of the Papaloapan Commission's activities see Poleman 1964. The impacts of the economic development program were wide-reaching and complex. See and González 2001, 58; and Nader and González 2013.

8. Tequio is still a vitally important element of village life in Talea and across rural Oaxaca more generally. When I lived in Talea,

municipal authorities convened tequios ten to twelve times a year, often to clear away brush from streets and pathways in the countryside. Sometimes they organized tequios for larger public works projects such as the installation of a villagewide underground sewer system or the construction or repair of schools, health clinics, or other buildings used by residents.

9. Since villagers have now established a bus service, the airstrip is no longer used for planes. Youngsters, though, use it as a soccer field. See González 2001, 59.

10. See Nader 1964, 213.

11. The INI was renamed the Commission for the Development of Indigenous Peoples (CDI) several years ago. The government-sponsored radio stations were publicly funded, though editorial control and programming content were ostensibly overseen by indigenous directors. Some criticized these stations because they were economically dependent upon the federal government, which was widely distrusted. For a history of Mexico's INI-sponsored indigenous radio stations see Castells-Talens 2004.

12. See, for example, Bravo Muñoz 2017; Calleja and Solis 2004; Stephen 2013, 12–44.

13. For anthropological analyses of APPO, see Esteva 2008; Rénique and Poole 2008; Stephen 2013. APPO can be situated within a broader pan-American constellation of indigenous peoples' resistance to state repression and neoliberalism. See for example Meyer and Maldonado 2010.

14. Palabra Radio helped to create the Plataforma de Mujeres Radialistas de Oaxaca (Oaxaca Women's Radio Platform). See Plataforma de Mujeres Radialistas de Oaxaca 2014 for a collection of short articles by members of the network.

15. Bravo Muñoz 2017, 104.

16. Quoted in Pérez Salazar 2013.

17. The conference was convened under the auspices of the Coordinadora Latinoamericana de Cine y Comunicación de los Pueblos Indígenas, a pan-Latin American coalition of organizations dedicated to indigenous media. A detailed agenda of the conference is available

online at http://clacpi.org/observatorio/mexico-primer-encuentro
-estatal-de-comunicacion-indigena-en-oaxaca/.

18. See the Rhizomatica website for more information: https://
www.rhizomatica.org/who-we-are/.

19. Bloom 2017.

20. Huerta 2016, 10.

21. Bloom 2017.

22. See Bravo Muñoz 2017 and Bloom 2017.

23. For a technical explanation of how the Range Networks system
works, see Goodier 2010.

24. See Bloom 2017. A similar pattern occurred in the Sierra Zapoteca of Oaxaca (west of the Rincón), where government entities
granted mining concessions to the village of Capulálpam. See Aquino
Centeno 2017, 2019.

25. As a colleague and I discovered in a 2006 visit to Talea, the
political system has undergone dramatic changes over the past twenty-
five years (Nader and González 2013). A major change was the phasing
out of *principales*, or village elders, who served as an advisory council
to elected officials. Another significant transformation is the fact that
elected officials are now paid a salary by the state government, as
noted in chapter 1. In the past, village authorities were expected to
donate their time and therefore forego any compensation. For this reason, the hierarchy of political offices has long been known as the *sistema de cargos* (literally, "system of burdens"). Many anthropologists
have analyzed these systems in Mesoamerica. See for example Carrasco 1961 and Cancian 1965.

26. See Carrera Pineda 2017 for an account of the conflict in the
Cajonos communities. For a broader anthropological analysis of intervillage conflict in Oaxaca, see Dennis 1987.

27. Bloom 2017, 100. In some ways, this effort was reminiscent of an
earlier project that linked dozens of indigenous communities representing three different ethnolinguistic groups—Zapotec, Chatino,
and Mixtec. MICHIZA, a fair-trade coffee cooperative, was founded
in the 1980s with the support of a German NGO. For a detailed analysis of the cooperative, see Jaffee 2007.

28. Wolf 1956.

CHAPTER FIVE. BACKLASH

1. See Nader 1966; Nader and González 2013. Another reason for the relative decline in Talea's market has to do with the construction of a road linking the Rincón town of San Juan Yaee to other Rincón villages. Shortly after the road was completed, bus service was established and Yaee began hosting its own weekly market (Chávez and Palerm 2016, 258-259). Villagers have vied for commercial market rights for centuries (Chance 1989).

2. This description is based upon interviews with people who observed the event as well as numerous secondary sources including *Maya Sin Fronteras* 2014, Montes 2016, and Bloom 2015.

3. Martínez 2015 and Bloom 2015, 46–47.

4. *Maya Sin Fronteras* 2014 and *OaxacaTresPuntoCero* 2014.

5. *Reporte Indigo* 2017; *NVI Noticias* 2017.

6. *OaxacaTresPuntoCero* 2014.

7. Quoted in Montes 2016.

8. Montes 2016 and Wade 2015.

9. *NVI Noticias* 2017.

10. Magallanes-Blanco and Rodríguez-Medina 2016, 341.

11. Quoted in Montes 2016.

12. *Maya Sin Fronteras* 2014.

13. *OaxacaTresPuntoCero* 2014.

14. Martínez 2015 and Morbiato 2018.

15. Ricárdez 2014.

16. *Maya Sin Fronteras* 2014.

17. *NVI Noticias* 2017.

18. The election of Carlos Salinas de Gortari as Mexico's president in 1988, marred by widespread fraud, marked the beginning of the PRI's turn toward *laissez-faire* policies. See Grinspun and Cameron 2007.

19. See Robles 2013, *Así Somos* 2013, *OaxacaTresPuntoCero* 2014.

20. Santiago 2014, *Despertar de Oaxaca* 2014 and *Diario Oaxaca* 2014.

21. Guerrero 2016.

22. *Crónica de Oaxaca* 2018. It is worth noting that the PRI's power in the districts of Ixtlán and Villa Alta was drastically curtailed in the

2018 national elections. This was due in large part to the rise of Andrés Manuel López Obrador and the left-leaning MORENA party, which won a majority of the vote in Talea and many other indigenous communities in northern Oaxaca.

23. In the 1980s, Nahmad was unjustly jailed on trumped-up corruption charges. His imprisonment was clearly political retaliation for his activism. See Dalton 2002.

24. In an interview with Martha Rees, Nahmad noted that Carranza "and other indigenous leaders should have a voice in their own education. And I learned the hard way that this can be risky." In a footnote, he and Rees state that these men "went on to hold high posts in indigenous education, as well as political office." See Nahmad and Rees 2011, 10, 12n26.

25. Secretaría de Gobernación 2018.

26. Sánchez 2018.

27. Méndez 2015, Rodríguez García 2015.

28. *Oaxaca Entre Lineas* 2015.

29. UNOSJO et al. 2001.

30. Among other things, INI created the Indigenous Video Center in Oaxaca in the early 1990s, and the center's director participated in a meeting following the murder of a Zapotec activist in the northern Sierra. The center was widely perceived to be supportive of indigenous people's struggles for self-determination. It had close ties to XEGLO, an indigenous language radio station based in Guelatao. See Wortham 2013, 86.

31. See Nader and González 2012.

32. Nader and González 2012.

33. Until recent regulations were imposed, Mexican children viewed more than twelve thousand junk food advertisements a year, more than any other country. See *The Economist* 2013.

34. In 2010, Movistar outbid rival Telmex as an official sponsor of the Mexican national soccer team.

35. Myers 2016, 30.

36. Lay Arellano 2017, 12.

37. Quoted in *Reporte Indigo* 2017 and *NVI Noticias* 2017.

38. Malinchismo's best known theorists include Mexican philosopher Samuel Ramos and writer Octavio Paz. For an overview see Gerson 2004.

39. Townsend 2006.

40. Ramírez Cruz 2014.

41. Lay Arellano n.d., 11.

42. Huerta 2016.

43. Lay Arellano 2017, 12.

44. Peter Bloom, personal communication, April 27, 2018.

CHAPTER SIX. POSTS

1. BBC, 2013.

2. For a full analysis of this phenomenon, see Turkle 2011.

3. Several anthropologists have considered the ways in which memory affects the work that we do. See, for example, Mayer 1989.

4. The phrase "native's point of view" was first used by Bronislaw Malinowski in *Argonauts of the Western Pacific* (1922).

5. Boellstorff 2008, 4.

6. See Harris 2000. I am skeptical of the claim that danzas are primarily a form of cultural resistance. As noted wryly by Marshall Sahlins (2002, 23), anthropology has been plagued by "a hyper-inflation of significance" that involves "translating the apparently trivial into the fatefully political by a rhetoric that typically reads like a dictionary of trendy names and concepts, many of them French, a veritable La Ruse of postmodernism." Overusing terms like "resistance" and "counterhegemony" can have the effect of trivializing them.

7. Graeber 2004, 99.

8. For many reasons, particularly having to do with concerns about digital surveillance, I had avoided creating a Facebook account.

9. Though there are software programs that can automatically analyze social networks using Facebook data, I was more interested in using its "friends" feature to gather names selectively.

10. Zuckerberg 2018.

11. I am, of course, not the first anthropologist to suggest that what we do is akin to snooping. See, for example, Strathern 1979.

12. Edwards 2017, 185–92.

13. Edwards 2017, 192–98.

14. *Carnalitos* is an affectionate term that can be roughly translated as "little brothers and sisters."

15. Genetically modified coffee doesn't exist but what she probably means here is replacing *café arabe* with one of the hybrids or sun coffee.

16. Turkle 2012.

17. Paz (1950) 1989.

18. Villagers often found it odd that an American man as "tall" as me (five feet, seven inches) would be such a crummy basketball player. Although most Talean men were shorter than me, many of them were remarkably talented basketball players and spent a great deal of time honing their skills.

19. Some sierra villages have constructed full-size indoor basketball courts at a cost of hundreds of thousands of US dollars. There is a growing literature on Oaxaca basketball, mostly by journalists and photo and video documentarians. See, for example, Quinones and Mittelstaedt 2000; Rodríguez 2003. US-based photojournalist Jorge Santiago (2017), who is a native of the Sierra Zapotec village of Guelatao, has produced *Identity at Play*, a compelling photo series highlighting basketball in the northern sierra. Oaxacan youth basketball has received global media attention over the past decade due to the remarkable talent of a team of indigenous Triqui boys who won an international youth basketball tournament, the Barcelona Cup.

20. The most plausible explanation is that the sport was promoted in mountainous rural regions because basketball courts require very little physical space. There is now strong evidence that basketball was promoted in Puebla and Oaxaca by the Secretariat of Public Education during the presidency of Lázaro Cárdenas (1934–40) as part of a program to promote nationalist social hygiene—that is, to reinvigorate indigenous populations through sport: "Teachers promoted male team sports to counter alcoholism and foster productivist notions of bodily discipline. Villagers took to sports because they celebrated

peasant values of male physical prowess, competition, and solidarity" (Vaughan 1999, 293). I am grateful to Yanna Yannakakis for her help on this topic.

21. VideoRey, personal communication, July 30, 2018.

22. Somewhat different in terms of mission and scope is Oaxaca City-based Ojo de Agua Comunicación, which has been organized as a nonprofit *asociación civil* since the early 1990s. It was created in part to serve indigenous communities by training villagers to produce their own media. See also Kummels 2017.

23. What they are flaunting is Talea's history, its accomplishments, its homegrown talent, and much more.

24. Quoted in Grossman 2014.

25. Grossman 2014.

26. Quoted in *Forum* 2019.

27. Walker 2012.

CHAPTER SEVEN. AFTEREFFECTS

1. It seems likely that most villagers viewed ideologues as people who might upset the "harmony ideology" that has characterized village life for centuries. See Nader 1990.

2. See Alter 2016.

3. See Fuentes López 2017 and Soto Galindo 2018a.

4. Soto Galindo 2018a.

5. See Article 2, Section B, Clause 6 of the Constitution of Mexico (Constitute Project 2020). In addition, villagers also cited Article 50, Section II of the Federal Telecommunications Act, which states that the Secretariat of Communications and Transportation "will procure adequate provision of telecommunication services in all of the national territory.... [The Secretariat] will secure the availability of frequency bands in case a project related to social coverage [i.e., the social good] requires it, by negotiating with concession holders to who are not using assigned frequency bands, or by granting new frequency bands [for the social good]." (Ley Federal de Telecomunicaciones y Radiodifusión 2014).

6. Soto Galindo 2018b.

7. Salazar 2018.

8. Naturally, the exchange is much funnier in Mexican Spanish:

¡Tira esa chingadera, vale, tira esa chingadera!
¿Y tú que estás haciendo, vale?
¡Y tú tambien, con el telefonito en la mano!
Ese telefono no sirve, vale, no sirve!
Toda la juventud tiene telefono el la mano, anda buscando trabajo y picale y picale al telefono. Por eso la juventud no progresa vale, porque tienen telefono en la mano. Entiende, entiende, entiende, el telefono no da trabajo, no da trabajo ... Ahí está tu telefono ya ... Mañana te corro, te corro ... Ahí está tu maestro, a agarrar telefonito, que inteligente es ... ya mejor me voy! Me voy!

9. The statistics are frightening. According to the National Highway Traffic Safety Administration, approximately nine people are killed in the United States every day by "distracted driving." See NHTSA 2016.

10. Bloom 2017.

11. The last sentence is a popular saying across Latin America—literally, "little town, big hell."

12. See, for example, Boers, et al. 2019; Power, Taylor, and Horton 2017.

13. Villagers explained to me that in "the old days," a prosperous family with a marriageable daughter might insist that a prospective groom deliver thirty, forty, or even fifty turkeys in order to prove that he was a worthy husband.

14. Sennett and Cobb 1972.

15. Quoted in Baca-Feldman, Parra Hinojosa, and Huerta Velázquez 2017.

16. See Armstrong 2018.

17. See Nicolai 2018.

18. See Peinado, Palomo, and Galán 2018; Semple and Franco 2018.

19. Ahmed and Hakim 2018.

20. Ahmed and Hakim 2018.

21. See Nader 1990.

22. My account summarizes a detailed description documented by BBC reporter Marcos Martínez (2018).

23. For at least three decades rumors about abductors seeking to harvest children's internal organs have circulated across parts of Latin America, Asia, and Africa. In the case of Mexico, see for example Shadow and Rodríguez-Shadow 1991. Nancy Scheper-Hughes (2000) has written at length about the social and metaphorical realities underpinning global rumors of body snatching and child kidnapping.

24. Quoted in Martínez 2018.

25. Many more cases following a similar pattern have been reported across rural India, where WhatsApp is a tremendously popular form of communication. See Nazmi, Nenwani and Narhe 2018.

26. Citing the work of sociologist Antonio Fuentes Díaz, Leigh Binford and Nancy Churchill (2009: 301) note that lynchings tend to be concentrated in predominantly rural states such as Puebla, Oaxaca, Guerrero, and Chiapas. They suggest that lynchings have become especially pronounced during Mexico's neoliberal era—that is, since 1988. As a downsized state has failed to provide its rural citizens with reliable public security, towns and villages are left to fend for themselves. See also Gamallo 2015.

27. Nader and González 2012.

28. Nader and González 2012.

29. See Alter 2016; Harris 2016; Lewis 2017.

30. Srinivasan 2017, 3. See also Srinivasan 2019 for many examples of locally based high-tech innovation.

31. Quoted in Nader and González 2012.

GLOSSARY

AGENCIA Village community that is subordinate to a larger municipality.

AGUARDIENTE "Fire water"; potent, locally made rum.

ALCALDE MAYOR During the Spanish colonial period, the top administrator in a political district.

AMÉRICA MÓVIL Mexico's largest telecommunications company.

APPO (ASOCIACIÓN POPULAR DEL PUEBLO DE OAXACA) A 2006 alliance of Oaxacan teachers, students, workers, indigenous groups, rural and urban poor people, and activists.

ASAMBLEA "Assembly"; a village town hall meeting where citizens discuss matters affecting the community.

ASOCIACIÓN CIVIL Civil association, typically a nonprofit organization.

BANDA MUNICIPAL Musical group consisting of brass, woodwind, and percussion instruments, usually supported by a pueblo's municipal government.

BHNI GUI'A (ZAPOTEC) "Mountain men"; supernatural beings or spirits who inhabit and protect the forests of northern Oaxaca.

BHNI HUÉ (ZAPOTEC) "Wounded men"; cantors who sing in honor of deceased souls during the night and early morning of Todos Santos.

BRACEROS People who work as farm hands; often, the term refers to those who migrated to work in the United States during the 1940s and 1950s as guest laborers under the auspices of the Bracero Program.

CABILDO A village's governing council, typically elected to one-year terms by the citizens.

CACICAZGO During the Spanish colonial period (and before), an estate associated with a noble lineage.

CACIQUE During the Spanish colonial period (and before), a member of the elite class of landed native nobility.

CALENDAS Festival parades, which typically include a *calenda floral* (floral festival) during the day and a *calenda nocturna* (night festival) at night.

CALZONES White, loose-fitting cotton clothing typically worn by Mexican campesinos until the mid- to late-twentieth century.

CAMPESINO Farmer, particularly a small-scale subsistence farmer.

CANCHA DE BÁSQUETBOL Basketball court.

CANTOS Melodic prayers or religious chants, uttered in either Latin or Spanish.

CAUDILLO Political boss or strongman.

CELULAR Cellular phone.

CEMPAZÚCHITL Marigold flower associated with Día de los Muertos.

CERRADO Closed person; someone who is reluctant to accept new ideas.

CHAPULINES Roasted grasshoppers.

CHICHARRONES Fried pork rinds.

CHIFLA Loud, piercing whistle.

CHINANTECOS Ethnolinguistic group that has historically resided in northern Oaxaca.

CHINTEZLE (ZAPOTEC, FROM NAHUATL) Dried chili paste.

CHIRIMIYA Bamboo flute used for ceremonial events.

CIUDADANO Citizen of a village community.

COCOLITZI (NAHUATL) Pestilence; epidemic disease that killed millions of indigenous people during the Spanish colonial period.

COHETE Firecracker.

COHETERO Someone who makes firecrackers or fireworks displays.

COLADO *Tequio* (see below) in which participants create a concrete roof.

COMEDOR Small locally owned restaurant or eatery.

COMUNALIDAD Epistemological concept based on the principles of shared territory, communal labor, collective decision-making, community service, and convivial celebration.

COMUNERO Commoner; in Talea, a villager who owns land.

CÓNYUGE During the Spanish colonial period, a noble family or clan.

CORREGIDOR During the Spanish colonial period, an appointed deputy who collected tribute from indigenous communities.

CORRIDO In Mexico, a song that typically takes the form of a ballad, often set to a polka beat.

CRUZ VERDE "Green Cross"; sacred oak tree near San Andrés Yaa.

CUMBIA A genre of percussive Latin American dance music combining elements of African, European, and indigenous American influences.

CURANDERA Curer.

CURANDERISMO Folk medicine.

DANZA Elaborate, stylized dance typically depicting wars of conquest between Spaniards and Aztecs, Spaniards and Moors, and so on.

DANZANTE Someone who participates in a *danza*.

DERRAMA Head tax.

DÍA DE LOS MUERTOS Day of the Dead, a holiday celebrated on November 1 and 2.

DINERO ENCANTADO Enchanted money.

DISTRITO Literally, a district; a political jurisdiction.

DIZHA KIERU (ZAPOTEC) Our words.

DUENDES Mischievous dwarves who inhabit mountainous forests of northern Oaxaca.

DULCE NOMBRE DE JESÚS "Sweet Name of Jesus," a festival celebrated in Talea de Castro before and during the third Sunday of January.

ENCOMENDERO During the Spanish colonial period, someone who was granted the right to demand laborers from indigenous communities.

ENCOMIENDA During the Spanish colonial period, an arrangement that granted former conquistadors the right to demand laborers from indigenous communities.

FIESTA Festival that typically lasts from three to five days.

GENTE HUMILDE "Humble people"; poor people.

GENTE RICA Rich people.

GOZONA (FROM ZAPOTEC GOZÚN) Reciprocal exchange of gifts or labor.

GRITO Long, soulful cry.

HACIENDA Large agricultural estate or plantation.

HUARACHES Leather sandals often associated with campesinos.

HUIPIL Embroidered cotton blouse.

INDIOS BÁRBAROS "Savage Indians"; during the Spanish colonial period, indigenous people who resisted assimilating into Spanish society.

INDIOS CONQUISTADORES "Conquering Indians"; indigenous people who supported or aided Spanish conquistadors.

INDIOS LADINOS "Hispanicized Indians"; during the Spanish colonial period, indigenous people who spoke Spanish and/or wore European clothing.

INI (INSTITUTO NACIONAL INDIGENISTA) Federal government institute responsible for the integration of Mexico's indigenous peoples from 1938–2003.

JARABES Lively regional dance songs consisting of several melodies strung together.

LIENZO Illustrated tapestry depicting maps, genealogical lineages, and other historical materials.

LOTERÍA Board game similar to bingo.

MACEHUAL (ZAPOTEC, FROM NAHUATL) During the Spanish colonial period (and before), an indigenous commoner.

MATANZA Sacrificial slaughter of an animal.

MATLACIHUATL (ZAPOTEC, FROM NAHUATL) Supernatural enchantress.

MARMOTA Giant humanoid puppet that appears during fiestas in the Rincón.

MEZCAL Potent liquor distilled from the roasted heart of the blue agave (century plant).

MISCELÁNEA Convenience store.

MIXES Ethnolinguistic group that has historically resided in parts of northern and eastern Oaxaca state; also known by the Mixe term Ayuuk.

MIXTECOS Ethnolinguistic group that has historically resided in the western regions of Oaxaca and its central valley.

MOJADO/A Slang term for someone who swims from Mexico to the United States across the Rio Grande River, or crosses the border as an undocumented immigrant.

MOLE Rich sauce consisting of chiles, chocolate, spices, nuts, raisins, and many other ingredients, often served with poultry or used as a filling for tamales.

MORENA (MOVIMIENTO DE RENOVACIÓN NACIONAL) Center-left political party.

MOTOTAXI A small three-wheeled motor vehicle; auto rickshaw or tuk-tuk.

MOVISTAR Mexico's second largest telecom company.

NORTE, EL "The North"; the United States.

PAISANO/A Fellow countryman or woman; used to refer to a person from the same hometown.

PALACIO MUNICIPAL Municipal palace; center of village government.

PAN DE MUERTOS "Bread of the dead"; pastries associated with Todos Santos and Día de los Muertos.

PANELA Unrefined brown sugar.

PARENTELA Same as *cónyuge* (above).

POLACA Board game similar to bingo.

POLICIA MUNICIPAL Municipal police.

PRESIDENTE MUNICIPAL Municipal president or mayor.

PRI (PARTIDO REVOLUCIONARIO INSTITUCIONAL) Authoritarian political party that monopolized Mexican national politics from the 1920s to 2000.

PRIÍSTA A politician affiliated with the PRI, or a supporter of that political party.

PRINCIPAL Village elder.

PROGRESISTA Progressive person; someone who welcomes new ideas and "progress."

PROMESA Promise or commitment.

PUEBLOS UNIDOS DEL RINCÓN Cooperative alliance of seven Rincón villages (not including Talea).

QUERIDA/O Lover.

RADIO COMUNITARIA Community radio station.

RANCHERA Mexican country music song, often set to a polka beat.

REBOZO Shawl.

REPARTIMIENTO "Redistribution"; during the Spanish colonial period, a system of forced consumption of goods (*repartimiento de efectos*) or forced production of commodities (*repartimiento de labor*).

REPÚBLICA DE INDIOS "Indians' republic"; paternalistic legal and political system applied to indigenous societies during the Spanish colonial period.

RINCÓN Mountainous region of northern Oaxaca.

ROBACHICO Person who kidnaps children, either to sell them or to harvest their organs.

SAETA (SOCIEDAD DE AUTOTRANSPORTES ECOLÓGICAS DE TALEA) Cooperative bus providing daily transportation service between Talea and Oaxaca City.

SAN ISIDRO LABRADOR Patron saint of farmers and campesinos.

SAN MIGUEL ARCÁNGEL St. Michael the Archangel, the patron saint of Talea de Castro.

SCT (SECRETARÍA DE COMUNICACIÓN Y TRANSPORTES) Federal secretariat of communication and transportation.

SECCIONES Sections or quadrants of a village.

SEP (SECRETARÍA DE EDUCACIÓN PÚBLICA) Federal secretariat of public education.

SONES Lively regional dance songs characterized by alternating 3/4- and 6/8-time signatures.

TELCEL Mexico's largest wireless cell phone service provider.

TELEFONÍA COMUNITARIA Community operated telephone network.

TEQUIO Obligatory communal work that takes the form of mandatory public service, usually involving physical labor.

TIANGUIS Weekly regional market.

TIC (TELECOMUNICACIONES INDÍGENAS COMUNITARIAS) Nonprofit autonomous cell phone network that includes nearly twenty indigenous communities.

TÍTULOS PRIMORDIALES Genre of Spanish colonial writing that described the founding of Mesoamerican villages, land claims, and kinship groups.

TODOS SANTOS All Saints' Day, celebrated by Catholics on November 1.

TORITO "Small bull"; a portable fireworks structure hoisted onto a person's shoulders.

TORNEO DE BÁSQUET Basketball tournament.

USOS Y COSTUMBRES Long-established political and juridical norms practiced in indigenous communities.

VÍSPERA Eve; the night preceding the main day of a fiesta.

XEGLO Publicly funded indigenous language radio station based in the Zapotec village of Guelatao.

ZARAPE Wool blanket worn as a cloak.

ZÓCALO Central plaza of a town or city.

REFERENCES

Ahmed, Azam, and Danny Hakim. 2018. "Mexico's Hardball Politics Get Even Harder as PRI Fights to Hold on to Power." *New York Times*, June 24, 2018. https://www.nytimes.com/2018/06/24/world/americas/mexico-election-cambridge-analytica.html.

Alba, Carlos H., and Jesús Cristerna. 1949. "Las industrias Zapotecas." In *Los Zapotecos*, edited by Lucio Mendieta y Nuñez, 497–600. Mexico City: UNAM.

Alter, Adam. 2016. *Irresistible: The Rise of Addictive Technology and the Business of Getting Us Hooked.* New York: Random House.

Aquino Centeno, Salvador. 2013. "Interrogando la costumbre y la legislación indígena: Contribuciones y horizontes de la antropología jurídica en Oaxaca." *Nueva Antropología* 26, no. 8: 87–117.

———. 2017. "Territorios comunales indígenas y la minería: Las experiencias históricas de explotación y alternativas a la depredación del subsuelo." In *Pueblos indígenas y estado en México: La disputa por la justicia y los derechos*, edited by Santiago Bastos and María Teresa Sierra, 92–125. Mexico City: CIESAS.

———. 2019. "Metales pesados y otros fierros: Las tensiones históricas por las transformaciones territoriales y ambientales en la Sierra Zapoteca de Oaxaca." In *Despojo, conflictos socioambientales, y alternativas en México*, edited by Darcy Tetreault, Cindy McCulligh, and Carlos Lucio, 323–58. Mexico City: Universidad Autónoma de Zacatecas/ MA Porrúa.

Armstrong, Mia. 2018. "Mexico's Chapter in the Saga of Election Disinformation." *Slate*. August 2, 2018. https://slate.com/technology /2018/08/mexicos-presidential-election-was-rife-with-disinformation -from-inside-the-country.html.

Así Somos. 2013. "Llevar modelo telefónico de Talea a más pueblos indígenas, propone Benjamín Robles." Last modified September 13, 2013. http://www.revistasisomos.com/28028.

Associated Press. 2013. "Mexico Sees Its First Open-Source Village Cellphone Network." *USA Today*, September 16, 2013. https://www .usatoday.com/story/news/world/2013/09/16/mexico-sees-its-first -village-cellphone-network/2821643/.

Baca-Feldman, Carlos, Daniela Parra Hinojosa, and Erick Huerta Velázquez. 2017. "El espectro radioeléctrico como bien común: Una reflexión en torno a la comunalidad y las redes celulares comunitarias en Oaxaca, México." *Revista Latinoamericana de Ciencias de la Comunicación* 14, no. 26: 16–26.

Barabas, Alicia. 2000. *Utopías indias: Movimientos sociorreligiosos en México*. Mexico City: Editorial Grijalbo.

Barr, Sabrina. 2018. "Day of the Dead 2018: The Best Pictures from Mexico City's Día de Muertos Parade." *Independent*, October 28, 2018. https://www.independent.co.uk/life-style/day-of-the-dead -2018-mexico-city-dia-de-muertos-best-pictures-holiday-a8605526 .html.

BBC. 2013. "The Mexican Village That Got Itself Talking." BBC News, October 15, 2013. https://www.bbc.com/news/world-latin-america-24 450542.

Beals, Ralph. 1945. *The Ethnology of the Western Mixe*. Berkeley, CA: University of California Press.

Bell, Joshua A., and Joel C. Kuipers, eds. 2018. *Linguistic and Material Intimacies of Cell Phones*. London: Routledge.

Bennett, Jane. 2001. *The Enchantment of Modernity: Attachments, Crossings, and Ethics*. Princeton, NJ: Princeton University Press.

Berg, Richard. 1968. "The Impact of the Modern Economy on the Traditional Economy in Zoogocho, Oaxaca, Mexico." PhD diss., University of California at Los Angeles. ProQuest (AAT 6908092).

Binford, Leigh, and Nancy Churchill. 2009. "Lynching and States of Fear in Urban Mexico." *Anthropologica* 51, 301–12.

Bloom, Peter. 2015. "La Telefonía Celular Comunitaria como alternativa ante el sistema hegemónico de Telecomunicaciones en México. Un estudio de caso de las nuevas iniciativas en la Sierra Juárez de Oaxaca." Master's thesis, Universidad Autónoma Metropolitana-Xochimilco.

————. 2017. "La historia de la red comunitaria celular de Oaxaca." *La Red Autónoma* 2: 4–6. Accessed February 24, 2020. https://docs .wixstatic.com/ugd/68af39_c4ddd679bf4f4835b3d0cb349385aca2.pdf.

Boellstorff, Tom. 2008. *Second Life: An Anthropologist Explores the Virtually Human.* Princeton, NJ: Princeton University Press.

Boers, Elroy, Mohammad H. Afzali, Nicola Newton, Patricia Conrod. 2019. "Association of Screen Time and Depression in Adolescence." *JAMA Pediatrics*, July 15, 2019. https://jamanetwork.com/journals /jamapediatrics/fullarticle/2737909.

Boroditsky, Lera. 2011. "How Language Shapes Thought." *Scientific American*, February, 2011. Accessed September 10, 2019. https://www .scientificamerican.com/article/how-language-shapes-thought/.

Brandes, Stanley. 2007. *Skulls to the Living, Breads to the Dead: The Day of the Dead in Mexico and Beyond.* Hoboken, NJ: Wiley-Blackwell.

Bravo Muñoz, Loreto. 2017. "Soñando nuevas infraestructuras: Telefonía celular autónoma, la hija prodigio de la radio comunitaria en México." In *Radios, redes e Internet para la transformación social*, edited by Vicente Barragán and Ivan Terceros, 99–112. Quito: CIESPAL.

Burrell, Jenna. 2012. *Invisible Users: Youth in the Internet Cafes of Urban Ghana.* Cambridge, MA: MIT Press.

Callaway, Ewen. 2017. "Collapse of Aztec Society Linked to Catastrophic Salmonella Outbreak." *Nature* 542, no. 7642: February 16, 2017. https:// www.nature.com/news/collapse-of-aztec-society-linked-to-catas trophic-salmonella-outbreak-1.21485.

Calleja, Aleida, and Beatriz Solís. 2005. *Con permiso: La radio comunitaria en México*. Mexico City: Fundación Friedrich Ebert.

Cancian, Frank. 1965. *Economics and Prestige in a Maya Community*. Stanford, CA: Stanford University Press.

Carrasco, Pedro. 1961. "The Civil-Religious Hierarchy in Mesoamerican Communities: Pre-Spanish Background and Colonial Development." *American Anthropologist* 63: 483–97.

Carrera Pineda, Andrés. 2017. "Activos 364 conflictos agrarios en Oaxaca." *El Imparcial de Oaxaca*, December 29, 2017. http://imparcialoax aca.mx/los-municipios/104719/activos-364-conflictos-agrarios-en -oaxaca/.

Castells-Talens, Antoni. 2004. "The Negotiation of Indigenist Radio Policy in Mexico." PhD diss., University of Florida. ProQuest (AAT 3136930).

Chaca, Rosalia. 2016. "Roya acaba con café en Oaxaca." *El Universal*, August 1, 2016. http://www.eluniversal.com.mx/articulo/estados /2016/08/1/roya-acaba-con-cafe-en-oaxaca.

Chance, John K. 1986. "Colonial Ethnohistory of Oaxaca," in *Supplement to the Handbook of Middle American Indians*. Edited by Victoria R. Bricker. Vol. 4, edited by Ronald Spores, 165–89. Austin, TX: University of Texas Press.

——. 1989. *Conquest of the Sierra: Spaniards and Indians in Colonial Oaxaca*. Norman, OK: University of Oklahoma Press.

Chassen-López, Francie R. 2010. *From Liberal to Revolutionary Oaxaca: The View from the South, 1867–1911*. University Park, PA: Penn State Press.

Chávez López, Onésimo, and Jacinta Palerm Viqueira. 2016. "Los Pueblos Unidos del Rincón: Desarrollo y crisis de una organización multicomunitaria." *Relaciones* 147: 253–97.

Chomsky, Noam. 2010. "Resistance and Hope: The Future of *Comunalidad* in a Globalized World." Interview by Lois Meyer. In *New World of Indigenous Resistance*, edited by Lois Meyer and Benjamín Maldonado Alvarado, 41–62. San Francisco: City Lights Books.

Cohen, Jeffrey H. 2000. *Cooperation and Community: Economy and Society in Oaxaca*. Austin, TX: University of Texas Press.

Coleman, Gabriella. 2010. "The Anthropology of Hackers." *Atlantic*, September 21, 2010. https://www.theatlantic.com/technology/archive /2010/09/the-anthropology-of-hackers/63308/.

———. 2012. *Coding Freedom: The Ethics and Aesthetics of Hacking*. Princeton, NJ: Princeton University Press.

Constitute Project. 2020. *Mexico's Constitution of 1917 with Amendments through 2015*. Accessed February 26, 2020. https://www.constitute project.org/constitution/Mexico_2015.pdf?lang=en.

Coordinadora Latinoamericana de Cine y Comunicación de los Pueblos Indígenas. n.d. Clacpi.org. Last modified January 27, 2020. http://clacpi.org/observatorio/mexico-primer-encuentro-estatal-de -comunicacion-indigena-en-oaxaca/.

Crónica de Oaxaca. 2018. "En Ixtlán de Juárez ¡Ya ganamos! Adolfo García Morales." May 21, 2018. http://cronicadeoaxaca.com/en-ix tlan-de-juarez-ya-ganamos-adolfo-garcia-morales/.

Dalton, Margarita. 2002. "Encierro intelectual: Entrevista con Salomón Nahmad." *Desacatos* 9 (Spring-Summer 2002): 163–76.

de Ávila Blomberg, Alejandro. 2008. "La diversidad lingüística y el conocimiento etnobiológico." In *Conocimiento actual de la biodiversidad de Sarukhán Kermez, capital natural de México*, edited by J. Soberón, G. Halffter and J. Llorente-Bousquets, 497–556. Mexico City: CONABIO.

Debord, Guy. (1967) 2002. *Society of the Spectacle*. Translated by Ken Knabb. Detroit, MI: Black & Red.

de la Fuente, Julio. 1949. *Yalalag: Una villa zapoteca serrana*. Mexico City: Instituto Nacional Indigenista.

Dennis, Phillip. 1987. *Intervillage Conflict in Oaxaca*. New Brunswick, NJ: Rutgers University Press.

Despertar de Oaxaca. 2014. "Comuneros de Quiotepec enfrentan a los de Maninaltepec por terrenos." June 11, 2014. http://despertardeoaxaca .com/comuneros-de-quiotepec-enfrentan-a-los-de-maninaltepec-por -terrenos/.

Diario Oaxaca. 2014. "Emite Defensoría alerta temprana por conflicto entre San Miguel Maninaltepec y San Juan Quiotepec." September 6, 2014. http://www.diarioaxaca.com/capital/7-capital/72264

-emite-defensoria-alerta-temprana-por-conflicto-entre-san-miguel
-maninaltepec-y-san-juan-quiotepec.

Díaz Gómez, Floriberto. 2001. "Comunidad y comunalidad." *La Jornada Semanal.* March 11, 2001.

———. 2007. *Comunalidad: Energía viva del pensamiento Mixe.* Robles e Hernández, Sofía and Rafael Cardoso Jiménez, eds. Mexico City: UNAM.

Economist. 2013. "Cookie Monster Crumbles: Advertising to Children." November 23, 2013. https://www.economist.com/international/2013/11/23/cookie-monster-crumbles.

Edwards, David B. 2017. *Caravan of Martyrs: Sacrifice and Suicide Bombing in Afghanistan.* Oakland, CA: University of California Press.

Eisenstadt, Todd. 2007. "*Usos y Costumbres* and Postelectoral Conflicts in Oaxaca, Mexico, 1995–2004." *Latin American Research Review* 42, no. 1: 52–77.

Esteva, Gustavo. 2001. "The Meaning and Scope of the Struggle for Autonomy." *Latin American Perspectives* 28, no. 2: 120–48.

———. 2010. "The Oaxaca Commune and Mexico's Coming Insurrection." *Antipode* 42, no. 4: 978–93.

Evans-Pritchard, E. E. (1933) 1976. *Witchcraft, Oracles and Magic among the Azande* (abridged edition). Oxford: Clarendon Press.

Flannery, Kent. 1999. "Los orígenes de la agricultura en Oaxaca." *Cuadernos del Sur* 14: 5–14.

Forum. 2019. "Empathy as a Radical Act." KQED Radio. August 6, 2019. https://www.kqed.org/forum/2010101872598/empathy-as-a-radical-act.

Fuentes-López, Guadalupe. 2017. "Indígenas pagan 40 pesos al mes en sue red celular." SinEmbargo.mx, December 18, 2017. https://www.sinembargo.mx/18-12-2017/3364446.

Gamallo, Leandro A. 2015. "Los linchamientos en México en el siglo XXI." *Revista Mexicana de Sociología* 77, no. 2: 183–213.

Garner, Paul. 1985. "Federalism and Caudillismo in the Mexican Revolution: The Genesis of the Oaxaca Sovereignty Movement (1915–20)." *Journal of Latin American Studies* 17, no. 1: 111–33.

Gershon, Ilana. 2018. Interview by Sipra Tenhunen. *CaMP Anthropology* (blog), June 25, 2018. https://campanthropology.org/2018/06/25/sirpa -tenhunen-a-village-goes-mobile/.

Gerson, Jacqueline. 2004. "Malinchismo: Betraying One's Own." In *The Cultural Complex: Contemporary Jungian Perspectives on Psyche and Society*, edited by Thomas Singer and Samuel L. Kimbles, 35–45. New York: Routledge.

González, Alejandro. 2018. "Alistan red indígena satelital." *Reforma*, August 16, 2018. https://www.reforma.com/aplicacioneslibre/preacceso /articulo/default.aspx?id=1468104&v=2.

González, Roberto J. 2001. *Zapotec Science: Farming and Food in the Northern Sierra of Oaxaca*. Austin, TX: University of Texas Press.

———. 2016. "Zapotec Innovation in a Mexican Village: Creating an Autonomous Cell Phone Network." *Anthropology Today* 34, no. 4: 5–8.

Goodier, Rob. 2010. "Open-Source Cell Network Could Cut Costs." Engineering for Change. June 24, 2010. https://www.engineering forchange.org/news/open-source-cell-network-could-cut-costs/.

Graeber, David. 2004. *Fragments of an Anarchist Anthropology*. Chicago: Prickly Paradigm Press.

Grañen Porrúa, Maria Isabel, and Perla Jiménez Santos. 2016. "La Primera Misa en Oaxaca." *Fundación AHHO* (blog), January 6, 2016. http://fahho.mx/blog/2016/01/06/la-primera-misa-en-oaxaca/.

Grinspun, Ricardo, and Maxwell Cameron. 2007. "Mexico: The Wages of Trade." *NACLA Report on the Americas*, September 25, 2007. https:// nacla.org/article/mexico-wages-trade.

Grossman, Lev. 2014. "Inside Facebook's Plan to Wire the World." *Time*, December 15, 2014. http://time.com/facebook-world-plan/.

Guerrero, Jaime. 2016. "Autoridades indígenas de Oaxaca, acusan al diputado del PRI de desestabilización." *Página 3*, January 7, 2016. https://pagina3.mx/2016/01/autoridades-indigenas-de-oaxaca-acusan -a-diputado-del-pri-de-desestabilizacion/.

Guillow, Eulogio. (1889) 1994. "Idolatrías en Caxonos." In *Los Zapotecos de la Sierra Norte de Oaxaca*, edited by Manuel Ríos Morales, 167–84. Oaxaca: CIESAS.

Hannerz, Ulf. 1992. *Cultural Complexity: Studies in the Social Organization of Meaning.* New York: Columbia University Press.

Harris, Max. 2000. *Aztecs, Moors, and Christians: Festivals of Reconquest in Mexico.* Austin, TX: University of Texas Press.

Harris, Tristan. 2016. "How Technology Is Hijacking Your Mind— From a Magician and Google Design Ethicist." Medium.com, May 18, 2016. https://medium.com/thrive-global/how-technology-hijacks -peoples-minds-from-a-magician-and-google-s-design-ethicist-56d 62ef5edf3.

Hernández Trejo, Mario. 2012. "Diacronía de la organización territo- rial en la Chinantla Alta, Oaxaca." Bachelor's thesis, Universidad Autónoma Metropolitana-Iztapalapa. http://148.206.53.84/tesiuami /UAMI22089.pdf.

Horst, Heather, and Daniel Miller. 2006. *The Cell Phone: An Anthropology of Communication.* Oxford: Berg Publishers.

Horst, Heather, and Daniel Miller, eds. 2012. *Digital Anthropology.* Oxford: Berg Publishers.

Huerta, Erick. 2016. "La telefonía indígena comunitaria, comunicación, y la lucha por la autonomía." *Comunicares.* July 17, 2016. https://comunica res.org/2016/07/17/la-telefonia-indigena-comunicacion-comunicacion -y-lucha-por-la-autonomia/.

Hunt, Eva. 1977. *The Transformation of the Hummingbird.* Ithaca, NY: Cornell University Press.

Ito, Mizuko. 2005. "Personal, Portable, Pedestrian: Lessons from Japanese Mobile Phone Use." *Asia-Pacific Journal* 3, no. 5: 1–6.

Ito, Mizuko, Daisuke Okabe, and Misa Matsuda, eds. 2005. *Personal, Portable, Pedestrian: Mobile Phones in Japanese Life.* Cambridge, MA: The MIT Press.

Jaffee, Daniel. 2007. *Brewing Justice: Fair Trade Coffee, Sustainability, and Survival.* Berkeley, CA: University of California Press.

Kasser, Tim, and Susan Linn. 2016. "Growing Up under Corporate Capitalism." *Social Issues and Policy Review* 10, no. 1: 122–50.

Katz, James, and Mark Aakhus, eds. 2002. *Perpetual Contact: Mobile Com- munication, Private Talk, Public Performance.* Cambridge: Cambridge University Press.

Kummels, Ingrid. 2017. *Transborder Media Spaces: Ayuujk Videomaking between Mexico and the US.* Oxford: Berghahn Books.

Lange, Patricia. 2014. *Kids on YouTube: Technological Identities and Digital Literacy.* London: Routledge.

Lay Arellano, Israel Tonatiuh. 2017. "Redes comunitarias de telecomunicaciones: Los casos de Abasolo y Talea." *Revista Zócalo,* October 2017: 46–47. https://www.academia.edu/34846583/Redes_comunitarias _de_telecomunicaciones_los_casos_de_Abasolo_y_Talea.

Levi-Strauss, Claude. (1955) 1961. *Triste Tropiques.* Translated by John Russell. New York: Criterion Books.

Lewis, Paul. 2017. "'Our Minds Can Be Hijacked': The Tech Insiders Who Fear a Smartphones Dystopia." *Guardian,* October 6, 2017. https://www.theguardian.com/technology/2017/oct/05/smartphone -addiction-silicon-valley-dystopia.

Ley Federal de Telecomunicaciones y Radiodifusión. 2014. Accessed February 20, 2020. http://www.diputados.gob.mx/LeyesBiblio/pdf /LFTR_240120.pdf

Ling, Richard. 2004. *The Mobile Connection: The Cell Phone's Impact on Society.* Edinburgh: Elsevier.

Lipp, Frank. 1992. *The Mixe of Oaxaca.* Austin, TX: University of Texas Press.

Long, A., B.F. Benz, D.J. Donohue, A.J.T. Jull and L.J. Toolin. 1989. "First Direct AMS Dates on Early Maize from Tehuacán, Mexico." *Radiocarbon* 31, no. 3: 1035.

Maffi, Luisa. 2005. "Linguistic, Cultural, and Biological Diversity." *Annual Review of Anthropology* 34: 599–617.

Magallanes-Blanco, Claudia, and Juan José Ramos Rodríguez, eds. 2016. *Miradas propias: Pueblos indígenas, comunicación y medios en la sociedad global.* Quito: CIESPAL.

Magallanes-Blanco, Claudia, and Leandro Rodriguez-Medina. 2016. "Give Me a Mobile and I Will Raise a Community." In *Communication and Information Technologies Annual: Opportunities and Challenges of Inclusion in Latin America and the Caribbean,* Vol. 12. Edited by Laura Robinson, Jeremy Schulz, and Hopeton S. Dunn, 315–43. Bingley: Emerald Group Publishing.

Maldonado Alvarado, Benjamín. 2002. *Autonomía y comunalidad india: Enfoques y propuestas desde Oaxaca.* Oaxaca City: Secretaría de Asuntos Indígenas.

Malinowski, Bronislaw. 1922. *Argonauts of the Western Pacific.* London: Routledge & Kegan Paul, Ltd.

———. (1925) 1948. *Magic, Science, and Religion and Other Essays.* Garden City, NJ: Doubleday Anchor.

Marcus, Joyce, and Kent Flannery. 1996. *Zapotec Civilization: How Urban Society Evolved in Mexico's Oaxaca Valley.* London: Thames and Hudson.

Martínez, Ana. 2015. "Movistar conecta áreas rurales con franquicias." *El Financiero,* February 24, 2015. http://www.elfinanciero.com.mx /empresas/movistar-conecta-areas-rurales-con-franquicias.html.

Martínez, Marcos. 2018. "Burned to Death Because of a Rumour on WhatsApp." BBC News, November 12, 2018. https://www.bbc.com /news/world-latin-america-46145986.

Martínez Luna, Jaime. 1995. "¿Es la Comunidad Nuestra Identidad?" *Ojarasca,* vols. 42–43 (March-April): 34–38.

———. 2010. "The Fourth Principle." In *New World of Indigenous Resistance,* edited by Lois Meyer and Benjamín Maldonado, 85–100. San Francisco: City Lights Books.

Maya Sin Fronteras. 2014. "Oaxaca Talea: 'Pulgarcito' gana a telefónicas." June 9, 2014. http://www.mayasinfronteras.org/2014/06/oaxaca -talea-%E2%80%98pulgarcito%E2%80%99-gana-a-telefonicas/.

Mayer, Adrian C. 1989. "Anthropological Memories." *Man* 24, no. 2: 203–18.

McIntosh, Janet. 2010. "Mobile Phones and Mipoho's Prophecy: The Powers and Dangers of Flying Language." *American Ethnologist* 37, no. 2: 337–53.

McIntyre, Kellen Kee. 1997. "'The Venerable Martyrs of Cajonos': An 1890 Painted History of Zapotec Rebellion in 1700." PhD diss., University of New Mexico. ProQuest (AAT 9727500).

McNamara, Patrick. 2007. *Sons of the Sierra: Juarez, Díaz, and the People of Ixtlán, Oaxaca, 1855–1920.* Chapel Hill, NC: University of North Carolina Press.

Méndez, Ezequiel. 2015. "Denuncian que el priista Cándido Coheto compra conciencias y cobra favores a directores del Cobao." e-

Oaxaca, May 10, 2015. https://www.e-oaxaca.mx/2015/05/10/denuncian -que-el-priista-cándido-coheto-compra-conciencias-y-cobra-favores -a-a-directores-del-cobao/.

Meyer, Lois. 2010. "Introduction: A Hemispheric Conversation among Equals." In *New World of Indigenous Resistance,* edited by Lois Meyer and Benjamín Maldonado Alvarado, 7–40. San Francisco, CA: City Lights Books.

Meyer, Lois, and Benjamín Maldonado Alvarado, eds. 2010. *New World of Indigenous Resistance.* San Francisco: City Lights Books.

Miller, Daniel, and Don Slater. 2001. *The Internet: An Ethnographic Approach.* Oxford: Berg Publishers.

Montes, Paloma. 2016. "Talea de Castro, el pueblo que sobrevivió a dos monstruos de la telefonía celular." *El Ciudadano,* February 1, 2016. https://www.elciudadano.cl/general/talea-de-castro-el-pueblo-que -sobrevivio-a-dos-monstruos-de-la-telefonia-celular/01/02/.

Morbiato, Caterina. 2018. "Movistar tiene un plan para cerrar la brecha digital." Expansion.mx, August 24, 2018. https://expansion.mx/carrera /2018/08/24/movistar-tiene-un-plan-para-cerrar-la-brecha-digital.

Myers, Emily N. 2016. "Of Rhizomes and Radio: Networking Indige-nous Community Media in Oaxaca, Mexico." Master's thesis, Uni-versity of Oregon. ProQuest (AAT 10193233).

Nader, Laura. 1964. *Talea and Juquila: A Comparison of Zapotec Social Organization.* Berkeley, CA: University of California Press.

———. dir. 1966. *To Make the Balance.* Berkeley, CA: UC Berkeley Media Extension Center.

———. 1990. *Harmony Ideology: Justice and Control in a Zapotec Mountain Village.* Stanford, CA: Stanford University Press.

Nader, Laura, and Roberto J. González, dirs. 2012. *Losing Knowledge: 50 Years of Change.* Berkeley, CA: Berkeley Media LLC.

Nahmad, Salomón and Martha Rees. 2011. "Greasy Anthropology: Anthropologists, Indigenous Peoples, and the State." *Practicing Anthropology* 33, no 4: 4–12.

Nardi, Bonnie. 2010. *My Life as a Night Elf Priest: An Anthropological Account of World of Warcraft.* Ann Arbor, MI: University of Michigan Press.

NHTSA (National Highway Traffic Safety Administration). 2016. "Traf-fic Safety Facts Research Notes: Distracted Driving." Washington,

DC: U.S. Department of Transportation. Last modified April 2018. https://crashstats.nhtsa.dot.gov/Api/Public/ViewPublication/812517.

Nazmi, Shadab, Dhruv Nenwani, and Gagan Narhe. 2018. "Social Media Rumours in India: Counting the Dead." BBC News, November 13, 2018. https://www.bbc.co.uk/news/resources/idt-e5043092 -f7f0-42e9-9848-5274ac896e6d.

Nicolai, Aldo. 2018. "Circula boletín falso en WhatsApp sobre las acciones de gobierno de Morena." Verificado.mx, July 6, 2018. https://verificado.mx/boletin-falso-morena/.

NVI Noticias. 2017. "Ellos conectan las comunidades lejanas de Oaxaca." February 21, 2017. https://www.nvinoticias.com/nota/51885 /ellos-conectan-las-comunidades-lejanas-de-oaxaca.

Oaxaca Entre Lineas. 2015. "Por desvío de recursos, inhabilita Contraloría de Oaxaca a Cándido Coheto." June 6, 2015. https://oaxacaentre lineas.com/noticias/por-desvio-de-recursos-inhabilita-contraloria -de-oaxaca-a-candido-coheto-candidato-a-diputado-federal-del -pri/.

OaxacaTresPuntoCero. 2014. "Promueve diputado priísta suplantar Red Comunitaria de Talea por servicio de Movistar." May 21, 2014. http:// oaxacatrespuntocero.com/instalacion-de-antenas-telefonicas-en-la -sierra-norte.

Oudijk, Michel. 2000. *Historiography of the Bénizaá: The Postclassic and Early Colonial Periods (1000–1600 AD)*. Leiden: Research School of Asian, African, and Amerindian Studies, Leiden University.

Parsons, Elsie Clews. 1936. *Mitla: Town of the Souls*. Chicago: University of Chicago Press.

Paz, Octavio. (1950) 1989. *The Labyrinth of Solitude and Other Writings*. Translated by Lysander Kemp. New York: Grove Press.

Peinado, Fernando, Elvira Palomo, and Javier Galán. 2018. "The Distorted Online Networks of Mexico's Election Campaign." *El País*, March 22, 2018. https://elpais.com/elpais/2018/03/22/inenglish/152 1710735_571195.html.

Pertierra, Ana Cristina. 2018. *Media Anthropology for the Digital Age*. Cambridge: Polity.

Pérez García, Rosendo. 1956. *La Sierra Juárez*. Mexico City: Gráfica Cervantina.

Pérez Salazar, Juan. 2013. "El pueblo indígena que creó su propia red de telefonía móvil." BBC Mundo, October 15, 2013. http://www.bbc .com/mundo/noticias/2013/10/131013_mexico_talea_red_telefonica _celular_jcps.shtml.

Piazza, Rosalba. 2008. "Los 'mártires' de San Francisco Cajonos: Preguntas y respuestas ante los documentos de archivo." *Historia Mexicana* 58, no. 2: 657–752.

Pink, Sarah. 2015. *Digital Ethnography: Principles and Practice.* Thousand Oaks, CA: Sage Publications.

Plataforma de Mujeres Radialistas de Oaxaca. 2014. *Sentires y pensares: Voces y vivencias desde la radio comunitaria.* Oaxaca: Ojo de Agua Comunicación. https://issuu.com/palabraradio/docs/libro_plataforma _esmail.sjsu.

Poleman, Thomas. 1964. *The Papaloapan Commission: Agricultural Development in the Mexican Tropics.* Stanford, CA: Stanford University Press.

Power, Sally, Chris Taylor, and Kim Horton. 2017. "Sleepless in School? The Social Dimensions of Young People's Bedtime Rest and Routines." *Journal of Youth Studies* 8: 945–58.

Quinones, Sam, and Alan Mittelstaedt. 2000. "A League of Their Own." *LA Weekly*, February 2, 2000. https://www.laweekly.com /news/a-league-of-their-own-2131594.

Ramírez Cruz, Keyla Mesluemet. 2014. "Mujeres desmitificando la tecnología." In *Sentires y pensares: Voces y vivencias desde la radio comunitaria*, edited by Plataforma de Mujeres Radialistas de Oaxaca, 43–46. Oaxaca: Ojo de Agua Comunicación. https://issuu.com /palabraradio/docs/libro_plataforma_esmail.sjsu.

Rendón, Juan José. 1995. *Diversificación de las lenguas zapotecas.* Oaxaca City: Instituto Oaxaqueño de las Culturas/CIESAS.

Rénique, Gerardo, and Deborah Poole. 2008. "The Oaxaca Commune: Struggling for Autonomy and Dignity." *NACLA Report on the Americas* 41, no. 3: 24–30.

Reporte Indigo. 2017. "La red de telefonía móvil que cobra $40 al mes por su servicio." November 22, 2017. https://www.reporteindigo .com/reporte/la-red-telefonia-movil-indigena-cobra-40-al-mes -servicio/.

Rhizomatica. n. d. "Who We Are." Rhizomatica. Accessed Febraury 25, 2020. http://www.rhizomatica.org/who-we-are/.

Ricard, Robert. (1933) 1966. *The Spiritual Conquest of Mexico*. Translated by Lesley Byrd Simpson. Berkeley, CA: University of California Press.

Ricárdez, Maira. 2014. "Un fracaso telefonía celular de Talea de Castro." OroRadio.com, February 13, 2014. http://www.ororadio.com .mx/noticias/2014/02/un-fracaso-telefonia-celular-de-talea-de-castro -municipe/.

Robles, Benjamín. 2013. "Intervención del dia Jueves 12 de septiembre." Presentation before the Mexican Senate. September 12, 2013. http:// www.senado.gob.mx/64/intervenciones/567/2440.

Rodríguez, Olga, dir. 2003. *Oaxacan Hoops*. Berkeley, CA: University of California Berkeley Graduate School of Journalism MA Project.

Rodríguez García, Arturo. 2015. "Protagonistas de escándalos quieren ser diputados del PRI." Proceso, January 8, 2015. https://www .proceso.com.mx/392536/protagonistas-de-escandalos-quieren-ser -diputados-del-pri.

Rodríguez-Mega, Emiliano. 2018. "Small Farmers in Mexico Keep Corn's Genetic Diversity Alive." *Scientific American*, November 19, 2018. https://www.scientificamerican.com/article/small-farmers-in -mexico-keep-corns-genetic-diversity-alive/.

Romero Frizzi, María de los Ángeles. 1996. *El sol y la cruz: Los pueblos indios en Oaxaca colonial*. Mexico City: CIESAS-INI.

Romero Frizzi, María de los Ángeles, and Juana Vásquez Vásquez. 2003. "Memoria y escritura: La memoria de Juquila." In *Escritura zapoteca: 2,500 años de historia*, edited by Romero Frizzi and María de los Ángeles, 393–448. Mexico City: CIESAS/INAH/CONACULTA.

Romero Frizzi, María de los Ángeles, and Michel Oudijk. 2003. "Los títulos primordiales: Un género de tradición mesoamericana, del mundo prehispánico al siglo XXI." *Relaciones: Estudios de Historia y Sociedad* 24, no. 95: 19–48.

Romo, Patricia. 2013. "Movistar promoverá su franquicia rural." *El Economista*, May 15, 2013. https://www.eleconomista.com.mx/estados /Movistar-promovera-su-franquicia-rural-20130515-0079.html.

Sahlins, Marshall. 2002. *Waiting for Foucault, Still.* Chicago: Prickly Paradigm Press.

Salazar, Giovanna. 2018. "Red indígena de telecomuniciones en México ofrecerá internet y telefonía vía satélite." *Global Voices,* August 31, 2018. https://es.globalvoices.org/2018/08/31/red-indigena-de-telecomunica ciones-en-mexico-ofrecera-internet-y-telefonia-via-satelite/.

Sánchez, Felipe. 2018. "Nada para nadie." *El Imparcial de Oaxaca,* February 22, 2018. http://imparcialoaxaca.mx/opinion/127101/nada-para-nadie/.

Santiago, Jesús. 2014. "Adolfo García despoja de tierras a campesinos de Maninaltepec." e-oaxaca.mx, July 1, 2014. https://www.e-oaxaca .mx/2014/07/01/acusan-al-diputado-priista-adolfo-garcia-de-invadir -terrenos-en-maninaltepec/.

Santiago, Jorge. 2017. *Identity at Play* (documentary photo series). Accessed October 1, 2019. https://visura.co/jlsantiago/projects/identity -at-play-2.

Scheper-Hughes, Nancy. 2000. "The Global Traffic in Human Organs." *Current Anthropology* 41, no. 2: 191–224.

Schüll, Natasha D. 2012. *Addiction by Design: Machine Gambling in Las Vegas.* Princeton, NJ: Princeton University Press.

Secretaría de Gobernación. 2018. "Perfil del legislador—Cándido Coheto." Sistema de Informacíon Legislativa. Accessed February 25, 2020. http://sil.gobernacion.gob.mx/Librerias/pp_PerfilLegis lador.php?SID=&Referencia=931.

Semple, Kirk, and Marina Franco. 2018. "Bots and Trolls Elbow into Mexico's Crowded Electoral Field." *New York Times,* May 1, 2018. https:// www.nytimes.com/2018/05/01/world/americas/mexico-election -fake-news.html.

Sennett, Richard, and Jonathan Cobb. 1972. *The Hidden Injuries of Class.* New York: Alfred A. Knopf.

Shadow, Robert, and María Rodríguez-Shadow. 1991. "Los 'robachicos.'" *México Indígena* 22 (July): 41–46.

Soto Galindo, José. 2018a. "Telecomunicaciones Indígenas Comunitarias, en riesgo de asfixia." *El Economista,* January 18, 2018. https:// www.eleconomista.com.mx/opinion/Telecomunicaciones-Indigenas -Comunitarias-TIC-en-riesgo-de-asfixia-20180114-0009.html.

———. 2018b. "Otorgan amparo a las telecomunicaciones de comunidades indígenas." *El Economista*, April 8, 2018. https://www.eleconomista.com.mx/opinion/Otorgan-amparo-a-las-telecomunicaciones-de-comunidades-indigenas-20180408-0004.html.

Smith, Bruce. 1998. "The Initial Domestication of *Curcubita pepo* in the Americas 10,000 Years Ago." *Science* 276: 932–34.

Srinivasan, Ramesh. 2017. *Whose Global Village? Rethinking How Technology Shapes Our World*. New York: New York University Press.

———. 2019. *Beyond the Valley: How Innovators around the World are Overcoming Inequality and Creating the Technologies of Tomorrow*. Cambridge, MA: MIT Press.

Stammler, Florian. 2013. "Narratives of Adaptation and Innovation: Ways of Being Mobile and Mobile Technologies among Reindeer Nomads in the Russian Arctic." In *Nomadic and Indigenous Spaces: Productions and Cognitions*, edited by Judith Miggelbrink, Joachim Otto Habeck, Nuccio Mazzullo, and Peter Koch, 221–45. Farnham: Ashgate.

Stephen, Lynn. 2013. *We Are the Face of Oaxaca: Testimony and Social Movements*. Durham, NC: Duke University Press.

Strathern, Andrew. 1979. "Anthropology, 'Snooping,' and Commitment: A View from Papua New Guinea. In *The Politics of Anthropology: From Colonialism and Sexism toward a View from Below*, edited by Gerrit Huizer and Bruce Mannheim, 269–74. The Hague: De Gruyter Publishing.

Sucedió en Oaxaca. 2017. "Merecido homenaje al compositor Timoteo Cruz Santos." January 17, 2017. http://sucedioenoaxaca.com/2017/01/17/merecido-homenaje-al-compositor-timoteo-cruz-santos/.

Sullivan, Lawrence E. 1987. "Mesoamerican and South American Tricksters." In *The Encyclopedia of Religion*, edited by Mircea Eliade, 51–53. New York: Macmillan.

Taussig, Michael. 1980. *The Devil and Commodity Fetishism in South America*. Chapel Hill, NC: University of North Carolina Press.

Tenhunen, Sipra. 2018. *A Village Goes Mobile: Telephony, Mediation, and Social Change in Rural India*. Oxford: Oxford University Press.

Townsend, Camilla. 2006. *Malintzin's Choices: An Indian Woman in the Conquest of Mexico*. Albuquerque, NM: University of New Mexico Press.

Turkle, Sherry. 2011. *Alone Together: Why We Expect More from Technology and Less from Each Other.* New York: Basic Books.

———. 2012. "The Flight from Conversation." *New York Times,* April 21, 2012. https://www.nytimes.com/2012/04/22/opinion/sunday/the -flight-from-conversation.html.

Turner, Victor. 1967. *The Forest of Symbols: Aspects of Ndembu Ritual.* Ithaca, NY: Cornell University Press.

Underberg, Natalie. 2014. *Digital Ethnography: Anthropology, Narrative, and New Media.* Austin, TX: University of Texas Press.

Unión de Organizaciones de la Sierra Juárez de Oaxaca et al. 2018. "Advierten de posible agresión a videoasta" (letter to the editor). La Jornada, January 18, 2018. http://www.jornada.com.mx/2001/02/18 /correo.html.

Van Gennep, Arnold. (1909) 1960. *The Rites of Passage.* Translated by Solon Toothaker Kimball. Chicago: University of Chicago Press.

Vaughan, Mary Kay. 1999. "Cultural Approaches to Peasant Politics in the Mexican Revolution." *Hispanic American Historical Review* 79, no. 2: 269–305.

Velásquez, María Cristina. 1998. *El nombramiento: Antropología de los usos y costumbres para la renovación de los ayuntamientos de Oaxaca.* Oaxaca City: CIESAS-Instituto Estatal Electoral de Oaxaca.

VideoRey. 2018. Personal communication, July 30, 2018.

Wade, Lizzie. 2015. "Where Cellular Networks Don't Exist People Are Building Their Own." Wired.com. January 14, 2015. https://www .wired.com/2015/01/diy-cellular-phone-networks-mexico/.

Walker, Harry. 2012. "On Anarchist Anthropology." *Anthropology of This Century* 3 (April 2012). Accessed August 2, 2019. http://eprints.lse .ac.uk/41545/.

Welz, Gisela. 2003. "The Cultural Swirl: Anthropological Perspectives on Innovation." *Global Networks* 3, no. 3: 255–70.

Wolf, Eric. 1956. "Aspects of Group Relations in a Complex Society." *American Anthropologist* 58, no. 6: 1065–78.

———. 1957. "Closed Corporate Peasant Communities in Mesoamerica and Central Java." *Southwestern Journal of Anthropology* 13, no. 1: 1–18.

———. 1959. *Sons of the Shaking Earth.* Chicago: University of Chicago Press.

Womack, John. 1999. *Rebellion in Chiapas: An Historical Reader.* New York: The New Press.

Wortham, Erica. 2013. *Indigenous Media in Mexico: Culture, Community, and the State.* Durham: Duke University Press.

Yannakakis, Yanna. 2008. *The Art of Being In-between: Native Intermediaries, Indian Identity, and Local Rule in Colonial Oaxaca.* Durham, NC: Duke University Press.

Zamorano Villarreal, Gabriela. 2017. *Indigenous Media and Political Imaginaries in Contemporary Bolivia.* Lincoln, NE: University of Nebraska Press.

Zilberman, María Cristina. 1966. "Idolatrías de Oaxaca en el siglo XVIII." In *Proceedings of the Thirty-Sixth International Congress of Americanists,* 111–23. Seville: ECESA.

Zuckerberg, Mark. 2018. "We built Facebook to help people stay connected and bring us closer together with the people that matter to us." Facebook, January 11, 2018. https://www.facebook.com/zuck/posts/10104413015393571.

INDEX

Acatlán de Osirio, 185–87
activists, 3, 22, 85–86, 92, 223
adolescents, 80, 140, 179–80, 190
agriculture, 29, 31, 190, 194
alcaldes mayores, 38–39, 41–42
algorithms, 142, 167, 170
alliances, 26, 97, 104, 121, 129, 154, 173
All Saints' Day. *See* Todos Santos
All Souls' Day. *See* Todos Santos
altars, 73, 75, 77, 163, 210n27, 211n31
América Móvil, 2, 93, 118
Americans, 27, 131, 143, 189
ancestors, 9, 28–29, 31, 88
Antequera, 16, 40, 48. *See also* Oaxaca City
anthropologists, 2, 4, 18–19, 24, 34, 36, 131; and cell phones, 12–14, 202n11; and *comunalidad*, 23, 210n18; Día de los Muertos and, 72; and field work, 193, 195–96, 218n11; and innovation, 53; in Mexico, 42, 121, 139, 204n41; online research by, 137–39, 145,

166; peasant communities and, 87–88, 214n25; in the Rincón, 6, 16, 47, 53, 91
anthropology, 11–12, 49, 57, 193, 203n22, 217n6
APPO (Popular Association of the People of Oaxaca), 22, 92, 128, 213n13.
apps, 10, 13, 139, 167, 189
asambleas, 23, 100–1, 121, 178–79, 210n18. *See also* town hall meetings
autonomy, 18, 20, 133–34, 167, 171; as cultural legacy, 23; in economic systems, 21, 85, 120, 124; historical roots of, 30; and local communities, 22, 128; in indigenous societies, 23, 86, 133, 204n41; and politics, 8, 18–19, 85, 120, 124
Autotransportes SAETA, 131, 155, 173
Ayuuk. *See* Mixes
Aztecs, 21, 30, 72, 103, 139–41

249

Banda "Alma Taleana," 154, 165–66
Banda "Unión y Progreso," 63–64,
  66, 152, 154
bands, 63, 71, 79, 89, 91, 111, 154,
  209n14; of *bhni hué*, 76; as
  municipal organizations, 69, 158,
  163–64; on social media, 140, 154,
  158, 165–66. *See also* names of
  bands
basketball, 137, 156–57, 159–60,
  218n18–20; courts, 68, 70, 111,
  159–60, 181; tournaments, 62, 156,
  158–60
beans, 31, 71, 147–48, 157, 164, 200;
  cultivation of, 28, 180; native
  varieties of, 190; as staple food,
  5, 8, 50
bhni glas, 58–59, 208n7
bhni gui'a, 25, 59–60, 79, 208n8
bhni hué, 74–76, 163
Bijanos Zapotec, 32, 102
biodiversity, 29, 32, 34
Bloom, Peter, 101–2, 129–30, 178; as
  Rhizomatica's co-founder, 117;
  and Talea's cell phone network,
  95–99, 104–6, 134
Bracero Program, 25, 52
businesses, 4, 17, 96, 108, 111, 118,
  203n30; and Facebook, 154–55
bus service, 90, 102, 123, 213n9; to
  Oaxaca City, 155, 174; in Talea,
  131, 133, 173, 202n6, 213n30, 215n1.
  See also Autotransportes SAETA

cabildos, 19, 23; members of, 21; in
  Talea, 94, 100, 116, 129, 188;
  transformation of, 41–43
caciques, 21, 42, 122
Cajonos, 49, 102–3, 165; "martyrs
  of" 207n44–45
Cajonos Zapotec, 32, 50, 63, 78, 80,
  160, 173, 208n7; and intervillage

conflict, 214n26; and migration,
  81; religion among, 78, 211n31
campesinos, 58–59, 143, 174, 181,
  194–95, 198; and clothing, 165;
  creativity of, 29, 188; and farm
  work, 31, 37, 111, 175–76, 210n24;
  internet use by, 29, 138, 179; and
  phones, 9, 106–7; in Talea, 7–8,
  46, 56, 91, 93, 123, 165, 170, 210n27;
  on social media, 147, 149, 158;
  and the supernatural, 59, 65, 69,
  71–74, 78–79, 208n8, 210n20. *See
  also* farmers
capitalism, 7, 128, 191, 204n40, 208n8;
  and corporations, 19, 23, 57
Capulálpam de Méndez, 190,
  205n15, 214n24
Carranza, Candelario, 112, 119–24,
  216n24
Catholicism, 43, 44, 49, 209n11
cattle, 16, 37–38, 47, 80, 159, 198
celebrations, 10, 25; in San Andrés
  Yaa, 80, 82–83; and social media,
  139, 146; in Talea, 61–62, 65–66,
  72, 82–83, 194. *See also* fiestas
cell phones, 11–12, 91, 97, 136, 174,
  176–79; access to, 1, 61, 95;
  concerns about, 10–11, 27, 168,
  170, 174–90; as culturally
  embedded, 12–15, 61; and the
  internet, 98–99, 119, 127, 138; in
  Talea, 9–10, 93, 105–8, 113, 135, 170
cell phone networks, 10, 18, 26, 103,
  124, 136, 153–54; concerns about,
  170, 181–82; creation of, 22, 26, 85,
  91, 93, 96–102, 104–8; criticisms
  of, 113–14, 128–29; management
  of, 108–9; as open source, 86, 98;
  regulation of, 171–72; on social
  media, 158; in Talea, 2–4, 8–9, 17,
  23, 62, 95, 173–74
Chance, John, 16, 21, 41

Chiapas, 86, 150, 204n31, 212n2, 221n26

children, 45, 147–49, 152, 165, 179–82, 185, 196–98; of campesinos, 93, 123, 143, 147–49, 174, 180–81, 194; and cell phones, 14, 177, 182, 191; and immigration, 89–90; in Talea, 8, 56–57, 69, 70, 107, 129, 136–37; and Todos Santos, 76–77; and television advertising, 216n33

chilies, 28, 31, 60, 73, 147

Chinantecs, 21, 32, 39, 79, 81–82, 103, 113, 119–20

churches, 48, 78, 144, 164, 160, 211n30; construction of, 47; in Talea, 65–66, 68–69, 71, 74–76

cigarettes, 66, 68, 75–76, 79, 178, 211n31

cities, 6, 15, 17, 72; Taleans living in, 26, 88, 144, 152

citizens, 121–22, 131, 162, 170, 179, 215n2; and intervillage conflict, 120; of Rincón communities, 9; of Talea, 53, 100–1, 104, 119, 128–30, 170, 211n29; and *tequios*, 164, 177

cochineal, 16, 38–39, 41

coffee, 31, 75–76, 111, 137, 144, 147, 165, 176, 194; as a cash crop, 7–8, 25, 151; commercialization of, 154–55; in the Rincón, 45–46, 50–51, 57, 88, 180, 197

colonialism, 15–16, 21, 167, 191, 204n40, 207n37, 211n31; indigenous resistance to, 23; and labor practices, 21; and religion, 79; in the Rincón, 34–44

commodities, 16, 38, 45

commoners, 21, 30, 178

communication, 9, 12–13, 43, 94–95, 132, 172–73, 221n25; and cell phones, 86, 96; by means of social media, 152; in the Rincón,

170; with the supernatural, 65; in Talea, 88–90, 92–93, 95–96, 108, 148

communion, 26, 62, 65, 82

communities, 6, 16–17, 24–25, 86–88, 120–21, 124, 172; alliances between, 214n27; basketball in, 159, 160–61; cell phone service in, 18, 93–95, 97, 99–104, 120–21, 132–34; conflict between, 214n26; *danzas* in, 139; fiestas in, 161–62; and Movistar, 117; in Oaxaca, 5; in the Rincón, 5, 39–40, 42–43, 80–81; and the state, 16, 90

community radio, 26, 91–93, 95, 116

comunalidad, 23, 204n39, 204n40, 210n18

conflicts, 43, 44, 185; between villages, 103, 120, 160–61, 184–85, 214n26; within Talea, 3, 4

connectivity, 19, 61–62, 106, 127, 168, 189

construction, 172, 213n8; of airstrip, 52; of basketball court, 160; of road, 46, 51, 202n6, 215n1

control, 30, 167, 174, 183; over indigenous communities, 15, 36–37; over local politics, 19–20, 134; over Oaxaca Valley, 30

cooperative organizations, 5, 26, 103, 106, 108, 170, 214n27; for bus service, 122–23, 131, 134, 155, 202n6; for commercializing coffee, 154–55; for phone service, 124, 133, 171, 173, 188

corn. *See* maize

corruption, 24, 122, 129, 216n23

crops, 8, 28–29, 31, 37–38, 50, 60, 66, 174, 202n9, 207n50; as sentient beings, 25; for cash, 7, 25; from Old World, 37; for subsistence, 8, 31, 34, 180. *See also names of crops*

Cruz Verde, 63, 78–83, 211n30, 211n33
cultural brokers, 16, 43, 100, 104,
    128. *See also* intermediaries
culture, 17, 41, 55, 130, 146, 188; cell
    phones' relationship to, 11, 13;
    and indigenous societies, 36, 188,
    190; of Rincón Zapotec, 8, 24, 53
customs, 9, 20, 60, 78, 138, 191

danzas, 69, 137, 139–41, 158
deities, 43, 61, 60, 65, 72, 82, 211n31.
    See also supernatural beings
de la Fuente, Julio, 81, 208n7,
    210n28, 211n31
digital surveillance, 142, 167, 170,
    217n8
disinformation, 182–87

earth, as mother, 23, 59–60
education, 2, 8, 104, 122–23, 181,
    216n24. *See also* schools, teachers
elections, 120–21, 182–84, 215n18
electricity, 19, 51, 94, 99, 114, 119, 170,
    201, 203n30
engineers, 29, 57, 85, 90, 97, 125, 141,
    161
epidemic disease, 21, 25, 36, 206n21
ethnolinguistic groups, 5, 32, 82,
    214n27

Facebook, 142, 166–68, 188–89,
    217n8; and cell phones, 127,
    174–75; and cultural assump-
    tions, 145–46; cyberbullying on,
    179–80; and disinformation,
    182–85; as research tool, 138–39,
    144–45, 183–84; Taleans' use of,
    9, 26, 100, 122, 141, 143–58
families, 14, 17, 52, 65, 77, 93, 103, 118,
    130; of campesinos, 7–8, 123, 111,
    188, 194–98, 202n9, 210n27; use of
    phones by, 89, 107, 181; use of

social media by, 147–49; in
    Talea, 19, 21, 56, 58, 125, 180–81;
    and Todos Santos, 73–75
farmers, 7, 28–29, 46, 58, 65, 137;
    in Talea, 2, 46, 58, 65–66,
    180, 194
farming, 10, 25, 28, 62, 69, 137, 143,
    150, 158, 180–81, 210n24, 210n27; in
    Rincón, 31, 37; as subsistence, 7,
    103, 190, 194, 202n9; in Talea, 100,
    175, 197
federal government, 4, 91, 172, 183,
    213n11
Fernández, Abrám, 92, 95, 105, 182;
    and Kendra Rodríguez, 99–102,
    104, 128–29; and Talea GSM, 115,
    117–19
fiestas, 23, 89, 113, 152, 194, 210n22; in
    San Andrés Yaa, 78–83; on social
    media, 26, 146; in Talea, 61–66,
    68–77; on YouTube, 158–63
fireworks, 70–71, 158, 210n22
food, 8, 125, 183, 190, 194, 202n9,
    210n27; during colonial era,
    39–40; and fiestas, 63, 73, 75, 77,
    80–82; on social media, 143,
    152–54, 156, 163
forests, 59–60, 78, 80–83, 90, 94, 107,
    194, 211n31
freedom, 2, 19, 99, 201n2
friends, 89, 99, 147, 149, 156, 163,
    195–96; on Facebook, 142, 146,
    151–52, 179, 217n9; of Taleans,
    72, 198

gender, 101, 131, 151
gifts, 71, 75, 86, 164, 212n3
Gómez, Adalberto, 112–13, 117,
    119–21, 124
governance, 19, 21, 23, 134, 142, 170
government, role of, 2, 4, 170–71,
    201n6; agencies, 10, 133, 168, 171,

203n30. *See also* federal government; municipal authorities
Guelatao, 23, 91–92, 159, 210n18, 216n30

hackers, 3, 26, 85–86, 97–98, 134, 212n1
harmony, 83, 184, 209n12, 219n1
harvest, 66, 79, 82, 176, 194, 210n24
honor, for the dead, 72–73, 74–75, 163; for supernatural beings, 63, 66, 71–72, 79, 89, 152
houses, 69, 75, 79, 89, 105–6, 147, 150
Huerta, Erick, 102, 114; and Rhizomatica, 117, 133; and Talea's cell phone network, 95–97, 99; and TIC, 172–73
human rights, 3, 22, 85–86, 95, 201n2

ideologies, 20, 118, 150, 184, 209n12
immigration, 29, 81, 95, 144–45, 147, 198; to the United States, 25, 52, 55, 62, 72, 76, 80
indigenous communities, 43, 97, 99, 104, 216n22; alliances between, 120–21, 129, 214n27; *bandas* in, 209n14; basketball in, 159; conflict between, 103, 120, 160, 184; during colonial era, 38–44, 139; and government, 90, 99, 120, 133; and intermediaries, 16; fiestas in, 162; and NGOs, 94; political structure of, 100
indigenous media, 15, 26, 94, 213n17. *See also* community radio
indigenous peoples, 21, 24, 39, 42, 83, 124, 133; in Oaxaca, 85–86, 92, 171–72
ingenuity, 37, 47, 53

INI (National Indigenist Institute), 91, 121, 124, 213n11, 216n30
innovation, 13, 24, 28–29, 32, 53–54, 188, 207n50; and biodiversity, 32–34; in Talea, 51, 134, 191
intermediaries, 15–18, 42–43, 104, 119
internet, 13, 106, 143, 163, 168, 183, 189, 203n22; for cell phone communication, 98, 114, 173; children's use of, 27, 181; and indigenous media, 15; as locally oriented, 189; Taleans' use of, 138–39, 141, 160, 170
internet access, 119, 135, 144, 173, 181; as a human right, 3, 86, 201n2; in Talea, 90, 99, 126–27, 138
Ixtlán de Juárez, 46, 202n6, 215n22

jarabes, 66–67, 71, 91
jokes, 70, 76, 143, 155, 178, 197
journalists, 18, 108, 130, 171, 218n1
Juquila, 33, 35, 40, 57, 201n6, 205n15

labor, 21, 84, 92, 198; and cell phone network, 102; for road construction, 90; Spanish exploitation of, 38–40, 42; *tequio* as, 23, 176
land, 23, 30, 65, 147, 149–50, 199; during colonial period, 35; conflicts over, 103, 120; for farming, 7; ownership of, 24; in Talea, 25, 47, 50, 149–50
landlines, 14, 106, 170, 195–96
languages, 12, 24, 53, 91, 102–3, 108, 205n12; and cognition, 34; in northern Oaxaca, 5, 32
Latin America, 117–18, 130, 136, 210n20, 213n17, 220n11
Los Angeles, 8, 62, 72, 106, 144, 145, 160; migration to, 56, 88–89
lynchings, 186–87, 221n26

machetes, 37, 76, 78, 111, 211n31
magic, 3, 58, 61, 208n5, 211n31
maize, 2, 5, 7–8, 28, 31, 39, 50–51, 57, 73, 137, 164, 166, 194, 211n31; genetic diversity of, 29; as offering, 71, 79–80; planting season for, 65, 69, 80; as sentient being, 37, 60; for subsistence, 7–8, 34, 180, 90
maize fields, 60, 76, 107, 194, 198
markets, 2, 24, 46–47, 69, 132, 170; in Talea, 46–47, 51, 88, 110–11, 113, 215n1
Martínez Luna, Jaime, 23, 204n40, 210n18
mass hysteria, 27, 185
matlacihuatl, 25, 59
media, 10, 15, 108, 116–17, 124, 131, 136, 182; alternative forms of, 22, 26, 91, 94, 133; concerns about, 190–92; ethnographies of, 203n22, 219n22; Taleans' appropriation of, 142, 166–67
merchants, 16, 40, 51, 80–81, 170, 180, 210n27; and cell phones, 9, 92–93; children of, 126; in Talea, 46, 88, 110, 125
Mesoamerica, 36–37, 72, 139, 209n9, 214n25
Mexico, 52, 96, 110, 130–31, 149, 152, 154, 187; biological diversity in, 34; bureaucracy in, 171; Catholicism in, 209n11; central valleys of, 30; government of, 58, 112, 120, 122, 124, 167, 201n6; Gulf of, 31; constitution of, 172; democratization of, 212n2; development projects in, 51; and Día de los Muertos, 72; elections in, 183; political parties in, 16, 115; during Porfiriato, 45; presidents of, 67, 182; telecom

companies in, 93, 118; use of cell phones in, 27
Mexico City, 8, 17, 35, 49, 106, 163; and Dia de los Muertos, 72; NGOs based in, 26; Talean migrants in, 62–63, 88, 93, 129, 144–45, 147, 162–63
mezcal, 66, 68, 75–76, 89, 111, 178
middlemen. *See* intermediaries
migration, 13, 29, 31, 58, 88. *See also* immigration
milpas. *See* maize fields
miners, 40, 50, 160, 202n8, 206n27; in Oaxaca, 44; at Santa Gertrudis, 40, 46, 87
Mixes, 5, 21, 23, 32, 39, 79, 81–82, 92, 103, 108, 171, 205n11, 210n23, 211n31
Mixtecs, 30, 103, 108, 171, 185, 214n27
mole, 73, 162
money, 38, 50–51, 58–59, 94, 111, 119, 181–82, 186
MORENA (Movimiento de Renovación Nacional), 115, 128, 183, 216n22
mototaxis, 9, 108, 155, 176, 184
Movistar, 112–14, 116–20, 123–27, 133–34, 182
municipal authorities: police, 75, 178, 184, 185–86; president, 112–13, 120, 124, 188; secretary, 55, 58, 93, 107, 129, 149; in Talea, 21, 34, 68, 93, 100, 114, 165. *See also* cabildos
municipalities, role of, 19, 103, 121, 204n31, 213n8
municipal palace, 51, 69–71, 83, 101, 144, 165; construction of, 47; in Talea, 51, 104, 111–12, 119, 159, 165
music: varieties of, 52, 209n15; at fiestas, 63–64, 66–67, 69, 74, 79,

89, 112; in Talean videos, 140, 164–65. *See also* bands

Nader, Laura, 6, 16, 20, 91, 201n4, 202n8, 209n14
New Spain, 38, 49, 130, 206n18, 207n37. *See also* colonialism
Nexitzo Zapotec, 32, 41, 58, 102, 121. *See also* Rincón Zapotec
NGOs (nongovernmental organizations), 7, 85, 94–95, 97, 133, 214n27; in Mexico, 26, 117, 172
nobility, 15–16, 21, 30, 41–42, 206n18, 224
nonprofit organizations, 26, 95–96, 170, 219n22
Northern Sierra, 5, 80, 91, 120, 161, 205n11, 208n7; *bandas* from, 209n14, 210n23, 216n30; basketball in, 218n19; history of, 29–32, 36, 38–45, 49–51, 53; music of, 66, 91, 120, 161
nostalgia, 26, 65, 123, 148, 151, 163–64

Oaxaca, 8, 15, 53, 57, 59, 114, 118, 138, 185; *bandas* in, 69; basketball in, 159–60; and cell phone networks, 5, 97, 104, 108; and coffee, 46, 202n9; colonial history of, 15–16, 32–35, 38; community-based media in, 10, 213n14; and cultural diversity, 7, 103; and fiestas, 161; gender roles in, 131; government of, 19, 21, 45; indigenous autonomy in, 21, 171, 178, 204n31; indigenous communities in, 120, 162, 191, 209; intervillage conflict in, 103, 160; lynchings in, 187; mines in, 44–45; and native intermediaries, 17; political movements

in, 22, 92, 128, 129; during pre-Hispanic period, 24, 28–31; and PRI political party, 121–22; pueblos in, 3, 20; radio stations in, 91–93; topography of, 102
Oaxaca City, 16–17, 22, 44, 48, 105–6, 128, 141, 161, 166, 190–91; bus service to, 90, 102, 123, 125, 131, 155, 174; as commercial center, 8; markets in, 110; road to, 10, 25, 46, 50, 57, 170, 201n6; schools in, 126; Taleans in, 8, 63, 93, 144. *See also* Antequera
Oaxaca Valley, 5, 21, 24, 28–31, 35, 44, 57, 88, 135, 204n41
Olivera, Urbano, 48–50
outsiders, 29, 45, 103, 159, 163; Taleans' acceptance of, 6, 9, 16, 85; villagers' relationships with, 90, 155

phones, 14, 87, 90, 98, 116, 169, 174–75, 189, 193–98, 200; campesinos' use of, 176; concerns about, 181–83; as distraction, 174, 175–77; in Talea, 90, 105, 107–8, 119, 127, 136, 168. *See* cell phones; landlines; smartphones
photos, 6, 10, 105, 186; of deceased, 75; on social media, 26, 143–44, 147–50, 152–55, 158, 179
pilgrimages, 78–82, 83, 211n30, 211n33
platforms, 14, 139, 145–46, 150, 167, 184
political parties, 18, 101, 121, 128, 183. *See also* MORENA; PRI
politicians, 45, 112–13, 120, 123–24, 128, 132–34, 170, 188

politics, 1, 76, 112, 118, 129, 131, 178,
184, 209n14
power, 4, 16, 39, 42–43, 51, 81, 128,
167
PRI (Institutional Revolutionary
Party), 16, 18, 112, 115, 119, 121–24,
128–29, 184
priests, 49, 69, 76, 78, 80, 202n8
privacy, 14, 109, 144, 174, 187
protests, 22, 40–41, 92, 201n2
Puebla, 28, 185–86, 218n20,
221n26

radios, 10, 26, 91, 115–16, 170
radio stations, 22, 55, 91–92, 95, 100,
216n30
reciprocal exchange, 12, 86,
164, 167
religion, 26, 61, 63, 146, 208n5
Rhizomatica, 96, 98–99, 103, 106,
108, 114, 117, 133
Rincón, 8, 56–57, 59–63, 102–3,
159–60, 187–89; development
programs in, 16; history of,
24–25, 27–29, 32, 34–36, 41, 46–47,
50–51; intervillage differences
in, 6; location of, 5; people of, 19,
34–35, 37, 41, 80, 103, 111, 142;
musical groups in, 209n14; and
native intermediaries, 15–18;
villages in, 25, 35, 41, 50, 57,
129, 201n6
Rincón Zapotec, 18, 37, 44,
53, 189. *See also* Nexitzo
Zapotec
rituals, 49, 54, 79, 80–81; in Talea,
25, 60–62, 163
road from Talea to Oaxaca City,
10, 25, 50–52, 57, 90, 125, 170,
201n6, 215n1
Rodríguez, Kendra, 92, 95, 130–31,
150–51; and Abrám Fernández,

99–102, 104–5, 128–29; and Talea
GSM, 115, 117–19
rumors, 113, 115, 184, 187, 221n23

saints, 25, 65, 71–74, 77, 82, 89, 144
San Andrés Yaa, 63, 78, 80–81,
211n30
San Isidro Labrador, 63, 65–66, 69,
71–72, 82, 210n20
San Miguel Arcángel, 63, 72,
144, 152
Santa Gertrudis, 39–40, 42,
44–47, 87
schools, 63, 69, 93, 121, 123, 213n8; in
Oaxaca, 122, 126, 159; Taleans in,
93, 149–50, 179
SCT (Secretariat of Communications and Transportation),
92–93, 104, 172–73, 219n5
self-determination, 21, 23,
216n30
Serrano Zapotec, 32, 102, 191
settlements, 8, 30–32, 35, 37, 53, 81,
103, 144, 205n11
Sierra Zapotec, 23, 29, 92, 121,
159, 161, 190, 205n15, 210n18,
218n19
smartphones, 15, 181–82, 185–86;
social consequences of, 14,
27, 185–86; Taleans' use of,
9, 26
social classes, 70, 82–83, 180–81;
hierarchies of, 14, 21, 30
social media, 14, 61–62, 92, 127,
180–81, 187, 203n22; concerns
about, 174–78, 180–81, 185–87;
and propaganda, 183; Taleans'
use of, 9–11, 26, 138–39, 141, 143,
151–66
social movements, 22, 91–92, 95, 128.
See also APPO
sones, 66, 69, 71, 91

souls, 25, 37, 59, 61, 66, 73–74, 76–77. *See also* supernatural beings

Spaniards, 69, 205n17, 206n18, 207n37; as conquistadors, 32, 35, 37–39, 130, 167; exploitation of indigenous people by, 36, 38, 42; as missionaries, 35, 48, 139, 169; in Villa Alta district, 15, 35–36; as Talea's founders, 24–25

Spanish Conquest, 15, 24, 32, 53, 88, 169, 191, 205n11; and disease, 36; and *malinchismo*, 130–31; and Talea's founding, 34–35. *See also* colonialism

squash, 28, 31, 34, 73

state government, 19, 22, 122, 124, 204n31, 214n25

sugar, 37, 162, 175–76, 194

supernatural beings, 25–26; in Talea, 53, 59–62, 65, 72–74, 82, 84

Tabaa, 40, 103, 160–61, 184

Talea de Castro, 6–8, 18–21; *asambleas* in, 100–1, 178–79; *bandas* in, 63–64, 152, 154, 165–66; bus service to, 131, 133, 173, 202n6, 213n30, 215n1; and cell phone networks, 2–4, 8–9, 17, 23, 62, 95, 173–74; cell phone use in, 9–10, 93, 105–8, 113, 135, 170; campesinos in, 7–8, 46, 56, 91, 93, 123, 165, 170, 210n27; children in, 8, 56–57, 69, 70, 107, 129, 136–37; families in, 19, 21, 56, 58, 125, 180–81; fiestas in, 61–66, 68–77; founding of, 31, 34–35, 53, 206n17; history of, 8, 34–35, 44–46, 55–61, 85–89, 219n23; innovation in, 51, 134, 191; location of, 5–6; as market center, 46–47, 51, 88,

110–11, 113, 215n1; merchants in, 46, 88, 110, 125; and Movistar, 123–27, 133–34, 182; as a "new town", 25, 34–35; roads in, 10, 25, 50–52, 57, 90, 201n6, 215n1; the supernatural in, 53, 59–62, 65, 72–74, 82, 84; *tequios* in, 90, 102, 164, 212n8; weddings in, 145, 163–64, 194

Talea GSM, 107, 120; creation of, 104–7, 134; criticism of, 115, 118, 124; decline of, 127–28, 130, 132–34; limitations of, 114–17; and Movistar, 118–19, 127–28. *See also* cell phone networks

Taleans, 7, 35, 47, 103, 113, 119, 122, 124, 196; and autonomy, 19; and cell phone network, 4, 8, 17, 85–88, 90–91, 100–2, 104, 108–9; and harmony, 4, 83; as innovators, 25–26, 51, 87–88; pragmatism of, 131–32, 134–35; and the supernatural , 58–59, 61–63, 65, 72, 77; use of cell phones by, 9, 27, 93, 105–7, 178; use of social media by, 127, 137–38, 142–44, 149, 154–55, 165–67, 181

tamales, 75–76, 79, 152–53, 211n31

Tanetze de Zaragoza, 6, 202n6, 205n15

teachers, 6, 22, 92, 108, 175, 203n30, 218n20

technologies, 5, 15, 27, 31, 61–62, 127, 146, 166, 198; adoption of, 88; experiments with, 29; and indigenous societies, 190; social consequences of, 1, 3, 10–12, 14, 170, 174, 182, 187–89; in Talea, 9, 51, 53, 85, 134, 141–42, 207n50

teenagers, 56, 58, 69, 126, 156, 174–75, 180–81, 190
telecommunications companies, 1–2, 93, 113–14, 118–19, 126, 132. See also América Móvil; Movistar
telecommunications laws, 93, 99, 113, 171–72
telephone antennas, 94, 104–6, 113, 116, 119, 132, 173
television, 58, 117, 125, 137, 179, 186; advertisements on, 216n33; satellite dishes for, 52, 75, 87
tequio, 23, 90, 164, 210n18, 212n8
text messaging, 9, 11–12, 27, 106, 127, 136, 174–75, 195, 212
tianguis. See markets
TIC (Telecomunicaciones Indígenas Comunitarias), 108, 124, 127, 132–33, 171–73
Tijuana, 88, 144, 153
Todos Santos, 72–77, 82. See also Día de los Muertos
tools, 9, 16, 29, 31, 37, 50, 111, 207n50; cell phones as, 12, 124, 188; digital technologies as, 142, 166, 201n2
toritos. See fireworks
tortillas, 147–48, 150, 165, 176, 200, 211n31; as bride price, 164, 180; as staple food, 125
town hall meetings, 27, 100–1, 115, 119, 178–79. See also asambleas
traditional practices, knowledge of, 52, 58, 125, 187–88
trees, spirits of, 25, 63, 78, 81
tuk-tuks. See mototaxi
turkeys, 39, 73, 164, 180, 211n31, 220n13

United States, 52, 58, 89, 125, 131, 143, 146; cell phone use in, 27, 170–71, 178; and Día de los Muertos, 72; migration to, 7, 9, 25, 52, 63, 76, 80, 197, 199; phone calls to, 106; political campaigns in, 27, 183–84; Taleans in, 55, 62, 63, 111, 139, 144

video games, 9, 58, 136, 177–78, 189
VideoRey, 161–62, 164, 219n21
videos, 14, 105, 136, 144, 174; on social media, 26, 139–41, 154, 158–64, 166, 176
Villa Alta, 15, 38–39, 41, 203n30, 207n37, 215n22
virtual village, 108, 138–41, 158, 161, 163, 165–66
virtual worlds, 127, 136–38, 181

wages, 21, 39–40, 106, 163, 184, 198
WhatsApp, 9, 27, 127, 138, 142, 182–85, 187–88, 221n25
women: and cell phones, 14, 107; and Palabra Radio, 92–93; and social media, 150–53, 164; at town hall meetings, 100–2; and Zapatistas, 212n2
workers, 22, 39–41, 50, 52, 151, 197

Xaca, 147–49
XEGLO (radio station), 91, 216n30

Yaee, 40, 46, 57, 162, 205n15, 215n1
Yalalag, 81, 165, 208n7
Yannakakis, Yanna, 15, 17, 30, 32, 43, 206n18
Yatoni, 35, 157, 205n15

YouTube, 9, 26, 139–40, 154, 168, 187;
channels on, 142, 161–62; Talean
fiestas on, 158–64; videos posted
to, 108, 139–40, 165–66; viewers
of, 164

Zapatistas, 86, 128, 150, 204n31,
212n2
Zapotec people, 29, 32, 34, 169,
191; ancestors of, 28–30; in

Bijanos region, 32, 102; in
Cajonos region, 32, 50, 63, 78,
80, 160, 173; and *comunalidad*, 23;
history of, 21, 30–44; as
innovators, 28–32; migration
patterns of, 24; in Rincón
region, 18, 37, 44, 53, 189; in
Sierra region, 23, 29, 92, 121,
159, 161, 190; in Oaxaca Valley,
30–31, 88

Founded in 1893,
UNIVERSITY OF CALIFORNIA PRESS
publishes bold, progressive books and journals
on topics in the arts, humanities, social sciences,
and natural sciences—with a focus on social
justice issues—that inspire thought and action
among readers worldwide.

The UC PRESS FOUNDATION
raises funds to uphold the press's vital role
as an independent, nonprofit publisher, and
receives philanthropic support from a wide
range of individuals and institutions—and from
committed readers like you. To learn more, visit
ucpress.edu/supportus.